Sources of
THE MAKING OF THE WEST

PEOPLES AND CULTURES

Volume II: Since 1560

KATHARINE J. LUALDI
Colby College

BEDFORD/ST. MARTIN'S   Boston ◆ New York

History Editor: Katherine E. Kurzman
Developmental Editor: Molly Kalkstein
Production Editor: Thomas P. Crehan
Production Supervisor: Catherine Hetmansky
Marketing Manager: Jenna Bookin Barry
Copyeditor: Barbara Sutton
Text Design and Composition: DeNee Reiton Skipper
Cover Design: Donna Lee Dennison
Printing and Binding: Malloy Lithography Inc.

President: Charles H. Christensen
Editorial Director: Joan E. Feinberg
Director of Editing, Design, and Production: Marcia Cohen
Director of Marketing: Karen Melton
Managing Editor: Elizabeth M. Schaaf

Library of Congress Control Number: 00–106452

Manufactured in the United States of America.

5   4   3   2   1
f   e   d   c   b

For information, write: Bedford/St. Martin's, 75 Arlington Street, Boston, MA 02116 (617-399-4000)

ISBN:0-312-18384-4

Sources of
THE MAKING OF THE WEST

PEOPLES AND CULTURES

Volume II: Since 1560

Preface

COMPILED SPECIFICALLY TO ACCOMPANY *The Making of the West: Peoples and Cultures, Sources of THE MAKING OF THE WEST* is intended to help instructors bring the history of Western civilization to life for students. The collection is organized chapter by chapter to parallel *The Making of the West* and thereby enrich the major issues, ideas, and events discussed therein with the thoughts and experiences of people living at the time. In this way, the documents offer instructors varied opportunities to ignite a dialogue in the classroom between the past and present.

Together, these primary source documents provide a colorful array of voices for such a dialogue within the thematic and chronological framework provided by *The Making of the West*. For example, while the textbook outlines the basic details concerning the European slave trade, students can see it for themselves in the document reader through the eyes of Olaudah Equiano, an African slave who survived to tell his story (Volume II, Chapter 18, Document 1). Facts and chronology thus come alive with the emotions, opinions, and observations of people living at the time, revealing that the study of history is not fixed but is an ongoing process of evaluation and interpretation. *Sources of THE MAKING OF THE WEST* provides the raw materials for this process.

The criteria governing the selection of documents reflect historians' changing understanding of Western civilization. Although traditional political sources are included in the collection, these views are broadened by less conventional documents illuminating not only social and cultural life but also Europe's increasing interconnectedness with the world beyond its borders. Women's voices were also granted a special place in the selection process because of their crucial and often underappreciated role in shaping the course of Western history from both within and outside the corridors of power. In Volume II, Chapter 20, for instance, students can hear the collective voice of the National Assembly as it launched the French Revolution (Document 2) alongside that of a female political activist, Olympe de Gouges (Document 3), and Toussaint L'Ouverture, a revolutionary leader in the French colony of St. Domingue (Document 4). Here as elsewhere in the collection, I chose documents that work well together to elucidate important events and opinions of a specific historical era. The documents were also selected based on their accessibility and appeal to students. For this reason, I have carefully edited each document to speak to specific themes without impairing its overall sense and tone.

To assist students with their journey into the past, I have provided a summary for every chapter that situates the documents within the broader historical context and addresses their relationship to one another. An explanatory headnote accompanies each document to provide fundamental background information on the author and the source while highlighting its significance. Discussion questions are also included to help students examine the key points and issues in greater depth. Finally, each chapter concludes with a few comparative questions intended to encourage students to see both the harmony and discordance among the documents. Although these editorial features intentionally strengthen the coherency of each chapter as a unit, they also allow instructors to choose documents and questions that best suit their specific teaching goals and methods.

Acknowledgments

I owe many people thanks for helping to bring this project to fruition. First among them are the authors of *The Making of the West*, Lynn Hunt, Thomas Martin, Barbara Rosenwein, R. Po-chia Hsia, and Bonnie Smith, who provided invaluable suggestions, advice, and insight. I would also like to thank Larissa Juliet Taylor, Julia O'Brien, Megan Armstrong, and David K. Smith for their help and encouragement, as well as my development editor, Molly Kalkstein, for her careful eye and enthusiasm. Those at Bedford/St. Martin's also helped make this book possible.

I also owe a debt of gratitude to the staff of the University of Maine library system who patiently endured my seemingly endless requests for books and articles. Without them, compiling this collection would not have been possible.

Lastly, I would like to thank my husband, John, for his sense of humor and understanding as I lost myself in books and Post-it notes.

Introduction

THE LONG HISTORY OF WESTERN CIVILIZATION encompasses a broad range of places and cultures. Textbooks provide an essential chronological and thematic framework for understanding the formation of the West as a cultural and geographical entity. Yet the process of historical inquiry extends beyond textbook narratives into the thoughts, words, and experiences of people living at the time. Documents expose this world so that you can observe, analyze, and interpret the past as it unfolds before you. History is thus not a static collection of facts and dates. Rather, it is an ongoing attempt to make sense of the past and its relationship to the present through the lens of historical documents.

Sources of THE MAKING OF THE WEST provides this lens for you, with engaging firsthand accounts representing a wide range of sources—from Egyptian chronicles, to English feminist tracts, to Prussian political memoirs. When combined, the documents reflect historians' growing appreciation of the need to examine Western civilization from different conceptual angles (political, social, cultural, economic) and geographic viewpoints. The composite picture that emerges as a result reveals a variety of historical experiences shaping each era from both within and outside Europe's borders. Furthermore, the documents demonstrate that the most historically significant of these experiences are not always those of people in formal positions of power. Women, minorities, and everyday folk likewise influenced the course of Western history.

The sources in this reader were selected with an eye to their ability not only to capture the multifaceted dimensions of the past but also to ignite your intellectual curiosity. Each document is a unique product of human endeavor and as such is often colored by the author's personal concerns, biases, and objectives. Among the most exciting challenges facing you is to sift through such nuances for what they reveal about the source and its links to the broader historical context.

Understanding how each document is connected to its author and to larger historical issues is key to the study of history. To this end, as you read each document, you should keep a series of questions at the front of your mind, just like a reporter investigating a breaking news story: Who wrote the document, when, for whom, why, and where? Each of these questions represents a crucial piece of the puzzle of the past and is an essential means of charting change and continuity over time.

A Nazi propaganda pamphlet written in 1930 (Volume Two, Chapter 27, Document 1) offers an instructive example. The author of the pamphlet, Joseph Goebbels, was the propaganda chief of Adolf Hitler, the leader of the Nazi party.

Both men were bounded by similar political goals and beliefs, including virulent anti-Semitism. At the time Goebbels wrote the document, Germany was mired in economic recession. Capitalizing on the downhearted mood of the day with promises of a better life, he successfully used pamphlets such as this one to broaden the Nazis' popular support on the eve of Hitler's rise to power. All of these factors—Goebbels's position within the Nazi party, what he was writing, for whom, when, and why—shaped the document's content, and thus should inform your interpretation of what it suggests about the Nazis and Germany in this period. By contrast, the recollections of Jews who were the victims of this propaganda (Volume Two, Chapter 27, Document 3) offer a far different view of the Nazis and the human impact of their regime. This difference can be attributed not only to the nature of the sources themselves but also to the opposing perspectives they represent.

Mining documents for their multiple layers of meaning thus requires a careful balancing act between fact and interpretation, and between the content of the document and the larger historical backdrop. To aid you with this process, *Sources of* THE MAKING OF THE WEST is designed to be used alongside THE MAKING OF THE WEST. Each chapter in the collection contains four documents illustrative of the central ideas, issues, and events discussed in the corresponding textbook chapter. In addition, *Sources of* THE MAKING OF THE WEST includes a variety of useful editorial features that supplement the basic information found in the textbook. A summary linking the documents to the historical period in which they were written prefaces each chapter. Every document has an introductory headnote that provides essential information about the author and the source and why the document is historically significant. Finally, several questions conclude each document and chapter to help you probe beneath the surface to understand what each document says and means, and to see the similarities and differences among them.

The documents included in *Sources of* THE MAKING OF THE WEST invite you to become active participants in discovering how history was actually lived over time by an array of different people in an array of different places. In this way, the documents offer snapshots of the past that, when viewed and interpreted together within the broader historical context, will help you paint a colorful and interconnected picture of the development of Western values, traditions, and institutions.

Contents

Sources of
THE MAKING OF THE WEST

PEOPLES AND CULTURES

Volume II: Since 1560

16

Wars over Beliefs
1560–1648

SUMMARY   For kings, nobles, and ordinary folk alike, the late sixteenth through mid-seventeenth centuries were a time of turmoil and change, as the following documents illustrate. Religious wars galvanized much of Europe in this period, fueled by both ecclesiastical and lay leaders' attempts to maintain the commonly held idea that political and social stability depended on religious conformity. With the escalation of violence, however, some people argued successfully that peace would come only if state interests took precedence over religious ones. Europeans' views of the Earth and the heavens also expanded because of the rise of new scientific methods and overseas exploration. At the same time, the lure of traditional beliefs remained strong within communities struggling to make sense of the upheavals occurring around them.

1
Henry IV
Edict of Nantes
1598

Henry IV's promulgation of the Edict of Nantes in 1598 marked the end of the French Wars of Religion by recognizing French Protestants as a legally protected religious minority. Drawing largely on earlier edicts of pacification, the Edict of Nantes was comprised of ninety-two general articles, fifty-six secret articles, and two royal warrants. The two series of articles represented the edict proper and were registered by the highest courts of law in the realm (parlements). The following excerpts from the general articles reveal the triumph of political concerns over religious conformity on the one hand, and the limitations of religious tolerance in early modern France on the other.

Henry, By the Grace of God, King of *France,* and *Navarre,* To all Present, and to Come, greeteth. Among the infinite Mercies that God hath pleased to bestow upon us, that most Signal and Remarkable is, his having given us Power and Strength not to yield to the dreadful Troubles, Confusions, and Disorders, which were found at our coming to this Kingdom, divided into so many Parties and Factions, that the most Legitimate was almost the least, enabling us with Constancy in such manner to oppose the Storm, as in the end to surmount it, reducing this Estate to Peace and Rest. . . . For the general difference among our good Subjects, and the particular evils of the soundest parts of the State, we judged might be easily cured, after the Principal cause (the continuation of the Civil Wars) was taken away, in which we have, by the blessing of God, well and happily succeeded, all Hostility and Wars through the Kingdom being now ceased, and we hope he will also prosper us in our other affairs, which remain to be composed, and that by this means we shall arrive at the establishment of a good Peace, with tranquility and rest. . . . Amongst our said affairs . . . one of the principal hath been, the many complaints we received from divers of our Provinces and Catholick Cities, for that the exercise of the Catholick Religion was not universally re-established, as is provided by Edicts or Statutes heretofore made for the Pacification of the Troubles arising from Religion; as also the Supplications and Remonstrances which have been made to us by our Subjects of the reformed Religion, as well upon the execution of what hath been granted by the said former Laws, as that they desire to have some addition for the exercise of their Religion, the liberty of their Consciences and the security of their Persons and Fortunes; presuming to have just reasons for desiring some inlargement of Articles, as not being without great apprehensions, because their Ruine hath been the principal pretext and original foundation of the late Wars, Troubles, and Commotions. Now not to burden us with too much business at once, as also that the fury of War was not compatible with the establishment of Laws, how good soever they might be, we have hitherto deferred from time to time giving remedy herein. But now that it hath pleased God to give us a beginning of enjoying some Rest, we think we cannot imploy our self better, than to apply to that which may tend to the glory and service of his holy name, and to provide that he may be adored and prayed unto by all our Subjects: and if it hath not yet pleased him to permit it to be in one and the same form of Religion, that it may at the least be with one and the same intention, and with such rules that may prevent amongst them all troubles and tumults. . . . For this cause, we have upon the whole judged it necessary to give to all our said Subjects one general Law, Clear, Pure, and Absolute, by which they shall be regulated in all differences which have heretofore risen among them, or may hereafter rise, wherewith the one and other may be contented, being framed according as the time requires: and having had no other regard in this deliberation than solely the Zeal we have to the service of God, praying that he would henceforward render to all our subjects a durable and Established peace. . . . We

---

English text of "The Edict" as in Edmund Everard, *The Great Pressures and Grievances of the Protestants in France,* London, 1681. Appendix 4 in Roland Mousnier, *The Assassination of Henry IV,* trans. Joan Spencer (London: Faber and Faber, 1973), 316–47.

have by this Edict or Statute perpetuall and irrevocable said, declared, and ordained, saying, declaring, and ordaining;

That the memory of all things passed on the one part and the other, since the beginning of the month of *March,* 1585. untill our coming to the Crown, and also during the other precedent troubles, and the occasion of the same, shall remain extinguished and suppressed, as things that had never been. . . .

We prohibit to all our Subjects of what State and Condition soever they be, to renew the memory thereof, to attaque, resent, injure, or provoke one the other by reproaches for what is past, under any pretext or cause whatsoever, by disputing, contesting, quarrelling, reviling, or offending by factious words; but to contain themselves, and live peaceably together as Brethren, Friends, and fellow-Citizens, upon penalty for acting to the contrary, to be punished for breakers of Peace, and disturbers of the publick quiet.

We ordain, that the Catholick Religion shall be restored and re-established in all places, and quarters of this Kingdom and Countrey under our obedience, and where the exercise of the same hath been intermitted, to be there again, peaceably and freely exercised without any trouble or impediment. . . .

And not to leave any occasion of trouble and difference among our Subjects, we have permitted and do permit to those of the Reformed Religion, to live and dwell in all the Cities and places of this our Kingdom and Countreys under our obedience, without being inquired after, vexed, molested, or compelled to do any thing in Religion, contrary to their Conscience. . . .

We permit also to those of the said Religion to hold, and continue the Exercise of the same in all the Cities and Places under our obedience, where it hath by them been Established and made publick by many and divers times, in the Year 1586, and in 1597, until the end of the Month of *August.* . . .

In like manner the said Exercise may be Established, and re-established in all the Cities and Places where it hath been established, or ought to be by the Statute of Pacification, made in the Year 1577. . . .

As also not to exercise the said Religion in our Court, nor in our Territories and Countries beyond the Mountains, nor in our City of *Paris,* nor within five Leagues of the said City. . . .

We prohibit all Preachers, Readers, and others who speak in public, to use any words, discourse, or propositions tending to excite the People to Sedition; and we enjoin them to contain and comport themselves modestly, and to say nothing which shall not be for the instruction and edification of the Auditors, and maintaining the peace and tranquillity established by us in our said Kingdom. . . .

They shall also be obliged to keep and observe the Festivals of the Catholick Church, and shall not on the same dayes work, sell, or keep open shop, nor likewise the Artisans shall not work out of their shops, in their chambers or houses privately on the said Festivals, and other dayes forbidden, of any trade, the noise whereof may be heard without by those that pass by, or by the Neighbours. . . .

We ordain, that there shall not be made any difference or distinction upon the account of the said Religion, in receiving Scholars to be instructed in the Universities, Colledges, or Schools, nor of the sick or poor into Hospitals, sick houses or publick Almshouses. . . .

We Will and Ordain, that all those of the Reformed Religion, and others who have followed their party, of what State, Quality or Condition soever they be, shall be obliged and constrained by all due and reasonable wayes, and under the penalties contained in the said Edict or Statute relating thereunto, to pay tythes to the Curates, and other Ecclesiasticks, and to all others to whom they shall appertain. . . .

To the end to re-unite so much the better the minds and good will of our Subjects, as is our intention, and to take away all complaints for the future; We declare all those who make or shall make profession of the said Reformed Religion, to be capable of holding and exercising all Estates, Dignities, Offices, and publick charges whatsoever. . . .

We declare all Sentences, Judgments, Procedures, Seisures, Sales, and Decrees made and given against those of the Reformed Religion, as well living as dead, from the death of the deceased King *Henry* the Second our most honoured Lord and Father in Law, upon the occasion of the said Religion, Tumults and Troubles since happning, as also the execution of the same Judgments and Decrees, from henceforward cancelled, revoked, and annulled. . . .

Those also of the said Religion shall depart and desist henceforward from all Practices, Negotiations, and Intelligences, as well within as without our Kingdom; and the said Assemblies and Councels established within the Provinces, shall readily separate, and also all the Leagues and Associations made or to be made under what pretext soever, to the prejudice of our present Edict, shall be cancelled and annulled, . . . prohibiting most expresly to all our Subjects to make henceforwards any Assesments or Leavy's of Money, Fortifications, Enrolments of men, Congregations and Assemblies of other than such as are permitted by our present Edict, and without Arms. . . .

We give in command to the People of our said Courts of Parliaments, Chambers of our Courts, and Courts of our Aids, Bayliffs, Chief-Justices, Provosts and other our Justices and Officers to whom it appertains, and to their Leivetenants, that they cause to be read, published, and Registred this present Edict and Ordinance in their Courts and Jurisdictions, and the same keep punctually, and the contents of the same to cause to be injoyned and used fully and peaceably to all those to whom it shall belong, ceasing and making to cease all troubles and obstructions to the contrary, for such is our pleasure: and in witness hereof we have signed these presents with our own hand; and to the end to make it a thing firm and stable for ever, we have caused to put and indorse our Seal to the same. Given at *Nantes* in the Month of *April* in the year of Grace 1598. and of our Reign the ninth
Signed

HENRY

Discussion Questions

1. What are the edict's principal objectives?
2. In what ways does the edict balance the demands of both French Catholics and Protestants?
3. What limits does the edict place on Protestants' religious rights?
4. Did Henry IV regard this edict as a permanent solution to the religious divisions in the realm?

2

Galileo

Letter to the Grand Duchess Christina
1615

Italian-born and educated, Galileo Galilei (1564–1642) was among the most illustrious proponents of the new science in the seventeenth century. Early in his studies, he embraced Copernicus's theory that the sun, not the Earth, was at the center of the universe. Having improved on the newly invented telescope in 1609, he was able to substantiate the heliocentric view through his observations of the moon and other planets. Because Galileo's work challenged traditional scientific views, it sparked considerable controversy. In the letter excerpted here, written in 1615 to the Grand Duchess Christina of Tuscany, an important Catholic patron of learning, Galileo defends the validity of his findings while striving to separate matters of religious faith from the study of natural phenomena.

Galileo Galilei

to

The Most Serene
Grand Duchess Mother:

Some years ago, as Your Serene Highness well knows, I discovered in the heavens many things that had not been seen before our own age. The novelty of these things, as well as some consequences which followed from them in contradiction to the physical notions commonly held among academic philosophers, stirred up against me no small number of professors—as if I had placed these things in the sky with my own hands in order to upset nature and overturn the sciences. . . .

Well, the passage of time has revealed to everyone the truths that I previously set forth. . . . But some, besides allegiance to their original error, possess I know not what fanciful interest in remaining hostile not so much toward the things in question as toward their discoverer. No longer being able to deny them, these men now take refuge in obstinate silence, but being more than ever exasperated by that which has pacified and quieted other men, they divert their thoughts to other fancies and seek new ways to damage me. . . .

Persisting in their original resolve to destroy me and everything mine by any means they can think of, these men are aware of my views in astronomy and philosophy. They know that as to the arrangement of the parts of the universe, I hold the sun to be situated motionless in the center of the revolution of the celestial orbs while the earth rotates on its axis and revolves about the sun. . . .

Now as to the false aspersions which they so unjustly seek to cast upon me, I have thought it necessary to justify myself in the eyes of all men, whose judgment

Stillman Drake, trans., *Discoveries and Opinions of Galileo* (New York: Doubleday, 1957), 175–86.

in matters of religion and of reputation I must hold in great esteem. I shall therefore discourse of the particulars which these men produce to make this opinion detested and to have it condemned not merely as false but as heretical. To this end they make a shield of their hypocritical zeal for religion. They go about invoking the Bible, which they would have minister to their deceitful purposes. Contrary to the sense of the Bible and the intention of the holy Fathers, if I am not mistaken, they would extend such authorities until even in purely physical matters— where faith is not involved—they would have us altogether abandon reason and the evidence of our senses in favor of some biblical passage, though under the surface meaning of its words this passage may contain a different sense. . . .

The reason produced for condemning the opinion that the earth moves and the sun stands still is that in many places in the Bible one may read that the sun moves and the earth stands still. Since the Bible cannot err, it follows as a necessary consequence that anyone takes an erroneous and heretical position who maintains that the sun is inherently motionless and the earth movable.

With regard to this argument, I think in the first place that it is very pious to say and prudent to affirm that the holy Bible can never speak untruth—whenever its true meaning is understood. But I believe nobody will deny that it is often very abstruse, and may say things which are quite different from what its bare words signify. Hence in expounding the Bible if one were always to confine oneself to the unadorned grammatical meaning, one might fall into error. Not only contradictions and propositions far from true might thus be made to appear in the Bible, but even grave heresies and follies. Thus it would be necessary to assign to God feet, hands, and eyes, as well as corporeal and human affections, such as anger, repentance, hatred, and sometimes even the forgetting of things past and ignorance of those to come. These propositions uttered by the Holy Ghost were set down in that manner by the sacred scribes in order to accommodate them to the capacities of the common people, who are rude and unlearned. For the sake of those who deserve to be separated from the herd, it is necessary that wise expositors should produce the true senses of such passages, together with the special reasons for which they were set down in these words. This doctrine is so widespread and so definite with all theologians that it would be superfluous to adduce evidence for it.

Hence I think that I may reasonably conclude that whenever the Bible has occasion to speak of any physical conclusion (especially those which are very abstruse and hard to understand), the rule has been observed of avoiding confusion in the minds of the common people which would render them contumacious toward the higher mysteries. Now the Bible, merely to condescend to popular capacity, has not hesitated to obscure some very important pronouncements, attributing to God himself some qualities extremely remote from (and even contrary to) His essence. Who, then, would positively declare that this principle has been set aside, and the Bible has confined itself rigorously to the bare and restricted sense of its words, when speaking but casually of the earth, of water, of the sun, or of any other created thing? Especially in view of the fact that these things in no way concern the primary purpose of the sacred writings, which is the service of God and the salvation of souls—matters infinitely beyond the comprehension of the common people.

This being granted, I think that in discussions of physical problems we ought to begin not from the authority of scriptural passages, but from sense-experiences and necessary demonstrations; for the holy Bible and the phenomena of nature proceed alike from the divine Word, the former as the dictate of the Holy Ghost and the latter as the observant executrix of God's commands. It is necessary for the Bible, in order to be accommodated to the understanding of every man, to speak many things which appear to differ from the absolute truth so far as the bare meaning of the words is concerned. But Nature, on the other hand, is inexorable and immutable; she never transgresses the laws imposed upon her, or cares a whit whether her abstruse reasons and methods of operations are understandable to men. For that reason it appears that nothing physical which sense-experience sets before our eyes, or which necessary demonstrations prove to us, ought to be called in question (much less condemned) upon the testimony of biblical passages which may have some different meaning beneath their words. For the Bible is not chained in every expression to conditions as strict as those which govern all physical effects; nor is God any less excellently revealed in Nature's actions than in the sacred statements of the Bible. . . .

From this I do not mean to infer that we need not have an extraordinary esteem for the passages of holy Scripture. On the contrary, having arrived at any certainties in physics, we ought to utilize these as the most appropriate aids in the true exposition of the Bible and in the investigation of those meanings which are necessarily contained therein, for these must be concordant with demonstrated truths. I should judge that the authority of the Bible was designed to persuade men of those articles and propositions which, surpassing all human reasoning, could not be made credible by science, or by any other means than through the very mouth of the Holy Spirit.

Yet even in those propositions which are not matters of faith, this authority ought to be preferred over that of all human writings which are supported only by bare assertions or probable arguments, and not set forth in a demonstrative way. This I hold to be necessary and proper to the same extent that divine wisdom surpasses all human judgment and conjecture.

But I do not feel obliged to believe that that same God who has endowed us with senses, reason, and intellect has intended to forgo their use and by some other means to give us knowledge which we can attain by them. He would not require us to deny sense and reason in physical matters which are set before our eyes and minds by direct experience or necessary demonstrations. This must be especially true in those sciences of which but the faintest trace (and that consisting of conclusions) is to be found in the Bible. Of astronomy, for instance, so little is found that none of the planets except Venus are so much as mentioned, and this only once or twice under the name of "Lucifer." If the sacred scribes had had any intention of teaching people certain arrangements and motions of the heavenly bodies, or had they wished us to derive such knowledge from the Bible, then in my opinion they would not have spoken of these matters so sparingly in comparison with the infinite number of admirable conclusions which are demonstrated in that science. . . .

From these things it follows as a necessary consequence that, since the Holy Ghost did not intend to teach us whether heaven moves or stands still, whether its shape is spherical or like a discus or extended in a plane, nor whether the earth is located at its center or off to one side, then so much the less was it intended to settle for us any other conclusion of the same kind. And the motion or rest of the earth and the sun is so closely linked with the things just named, that without a determination of the one, neither side can be taken in the other matters. Now if the Holy Spirit has purposely neglected to teach us propositions of this sort as irrelevant to the highest goal (that is, to our salvation), how can anyone affirm that it is obligatory to take sides on them, and that one belief is required by faith, while the other side is erroneous? Can an opinion be heretical and yet have no concern with the salvation of souls? Can the Holy Ghost be asserted not to have intended teaching us something that does concern our salvation? I would say here something that was heard from an ecclesiastic of the most eminent degree: "That the intention of the Holy Ghost is to teach us how one goes to heaven, not how heaven goes." . . .

From this it is seen that the interpretation which we impose upon passages of Scripture would be false whenever it disagreed with demonstrated truths. And therefore we should seek the incontrovertible sense of the Bible with the assistance of demonstrated truth, and not in any way try to force the hand of Nature or deny experiences and rigorous proofs in accordance with the mere sound of words that may appeal to our frailty. . . .

To that end they would forbid him the use of reason, divine gift of Providence, and would abuse the just authority of holy Scripture—which, in the general opinion of theologians, can never oppose manifest experiences and necessary demonstrations when rightly understood and applied. If I am correct, it will stand them in no stead to go running to the Bible to cover up their inability to understand (let alone resolve) their opponents' arguments.

Discussion Questions

1. What is Galileo's goal in writing this letter to the Grand Duchess?
2. What is the basis of the attacks by Galileo's critics?
3. According to Galileo, what role should the Bible play in scientific inquiry?
4. Historians have credited Galileo for helping to popularize the principles and methods of the new science. How does this document lend support to this view?

3

David Pieterzen DeVries
Voyages from Holland to America
1655

In the seventeenth century, the Dutch Republic entered its golden age as the center of a thriving maritime economy. Like other European states at the time, Holland expanded its commercial markets and established permanent colonies in the newly explored regions of North America. The Dutch thus contributed to Europeans' growing knowledge of the topography, peoples, and cultures of the New World. In this excerpt, a French-born Dutch merchant and colonist, David DeVries (1593–1655), describes a violent conflict in 1643 between Dutch settlers and Native Americans in the area around modern New York City. The conflict was sparked by the Native Americans' refusal to relinquish their land. DeVries's account provides a vivid testimony of the clash between the two societies.

The 24th of February, sitting at the table with the governor, he began to state his intentions, that he had a mind to *wipe the mouths* of the Indians; that he had been dining at the house of Jan Claesz. Damen, where Maryn Adriaensz. and Jan Claesz. Damen, together with Jacob Planck, had presented a petition to him to begin this work. I answered him that there was no sufficient reason to undertake it. . . . But it appeared that my speaking was of no avail. He had, with his co-murderers, determined to commit the murder, deeming it a Roman deed, and to do it without warning the inhabitants in the open lands, that each one might take care of himself against the retaliation of the Indians, for he could not kill all the Indians. When I had expressed all these things in full, sitting at the table, and the meal was over, he told me he wished me to go to the large hall, which he had been lately adding to his house. Coming to it, there stood all his soldiers ready to cross the river to Pavonia to commit the murder. Then spoke I again to Governor William Kieft: "Stop this work; you wish to break the mouths of the Indians, but you will also murder our own nation, for there are none of the farmers who are aware of it. My own dwelling, my people, cattle, corn, and tobacco will be lost." He answered me, assuring me that there would be no danger; that some soldiers should go to my house to protect it. But that was not done. So was this business begun between the 25th and 26th of February in the year 1643. I remained that night at the governor's, sitting up. I went and sat in the kitchen, when, about midnight, I heard a great shrieking, and I ran to the ramparts of the fort, and looked over to Pavonia. Saw nothing but firing, and heard the shrieks of the Indians murdered in their sleep. I returned again to the house by the fire. Having sat there awhile, there came an Indian with his squaw, whom I knew well, and who lived about an hour's walk from my house, and told me that they two had fled in a small skiff; that they had betaken themselves to Pavonia; that the Indians from Fort Orange had surprised them; and that they had come to conceal themselves in the fort. I told them that they must go away immediately; that there was no occasion for them to come to the fort to conceal themselves; that they who had killed their people at Pavonia were not Indians, but the Swannekens, as they call the Dutch, had done it. They then asked me how they should get out of the fort. I took them to the door, and there was no sentry there, and so they betook themselves to the woods. When it was day, the soldiers returned to the fort, having

David Pieterzen DeVries, *Voyages from Holland to America*, A.D. *1632 to 1644*, trans. Henry C. Murphy (New York: Billin and Brothers, 1853), 167–71.

massacred or murdered eighty Indians, and considering they had done a deed of
Roman valour, in murdering so many in their sleep; where infants were torn from
their mother's breasts, and hacked to pieces in the presence of the parents, and
the pieces thrown into the fire and in the water, and other sucklings were bound
to small boards, and then cut, stuck, and pierced, and miserably massacred in a
manner to move a heart of stone. Some were thrown into the river, and when the
fathers and mothers endeavored to save them, the soldiers would not let them
come on land, but made both parents and children drown,—children from five
to six years of age, and also some old and decrepit persons. Many fled from this
scene, and concealed themselves in the neighbouring sedge, and when it was
morning, came out to beg a piece of bread, and to be permitted to warm themselves; but they were murdered in cold blood and tossed into the water. Some
came by our lands in the country with their hands, some with their legs cut off,
and some holding their entrails in their arms, and others had such horrible cuts
and gashes, that worse than they were could never happen. . . . This is indeed a
disgrace to our nation, who have so generous a governor in our Fatherland as the
Prince of Orange, who has always endeavoured in his wars to spill as little blood
as possible. As soon as the Indians understood that the Swannekens had so treated
them, all the men whom they could surprise on the farm-lands, they killed; but
we have never heard that they have ever permitted women or children to be killed.
They burned all the houses, farms, barns, grain, haystacks, and destroyed everything they could get hold of. So there was an open destructive war begun. They
also burnt my farm, cattle, corn, barn, tobacco-house, and all the tobacco. My
people saved themselves in the house where I lived, which was made with embra-
sures, through which they defended themselves. Whilst my people were in this
state of alarm, the Indian whom I had aided to escape from the fort came there,
and told the other Indians that I was a good chief, that I had helped him out of
the fort, and that the killing of the Indians took place contrary to my wish. Then
they all cried out together to my people that they would not shoot them; that if
they had not destroyed my cattle they would not do it; that they would not burn
my house; that they would let my little brewery stand, though they had melted
the copper-kettle, in order to make darts for their arrows; but hearing now that it
(the massacre) had been done contrary to my wish, they all went away, and left
my house unbesieged. When now the Indians had destroyed so many farms and
men in revenge for their people, I went to Governor William Kieft, and asked
him if it was not as I had said it would be, that he would only effect the spilling of
Christian blood.

DISCUSSION QUESTIONS

1. What are DeVries's attitudes toward the Native Americans, and how do they differ from those of the governor and the soldiers who carried out his orders?
2. Why does DeVries describe the massacre as a disgrace to his nation?
3. What does this account reveal about the Dutch settlers' way of life?

4
Trial Record of Johannes Junius
The Witch-Persecution at Bamberg
1628

Even as the new science gained support, most Europeans continued to believe in the supernatural, especially at this time of religious wars, economic decline, and social strife. This belief found violent expression in a wave of witchcraft persecutions across Europe between 1560 and 1640. The following selections from the minutes of the witchcraft trial of Johannes Junius and a letter he wrote to his daughter in 1628 attest to the predominant notion that witches were agents of the devil. The trial took place in Bamberg in the Holy Roman Empire during the Thirty Years' War. In content and form, Junius's trial is representative of others from the region with one striking exception, his gender. Accused witches were far more typically women.

. . . On Wednesday, June 28, 1628, was examined without torture Johannes Junius, Burgomaster at Bamberg, on the charge of witchcraft: how and in what fashion he had fallen into that vice. Is fifty-five years old, and was born at Niederwaysich in the Wetterau. Says he is wholly innocent, knows nothing of the crime, has never in his life renounced God; says that he is wronged before God and the world, would like to hear of a single human being who has seen him at such gatherings [as the witch-sabbaths].

Confrontation of Dr. Georg Adam Haan. Tells him to his face he will stake his life on it [*er wolle daraf leben und sterben*], that he saw him, Junius, a year and a half ago at a witch-gathering in the electoral council-room, where they ate and drank. Accused denies the same wholly.

Confronted with Hopffens Elsse. Tells him likewise that he was on Hauptsmoor at a witch-dance; but first the holy wafer was desecrated. Junius denies. Hereupon he was told that his accomplices had confessed against him and was given time for thought.

On Friday, June 30, 1628, the aforesaid Junius was again without torture exhorted to confess, but again confessed nothing, whereupon, . . . since he would confess nothing, he was put to the torture, and first the

Thumb-screws were applied. Says he has never denied God his Saviour nor suffered himself to be otherwise baptized;[1] will again stake his life on it; feels no pain in the thumb-screws.

---

[1] "Otherwise baptized" is the usual phrase for the rite, a parody of baptism, by which the Devil was believed to initiate his followers. [trans.]

Translations and Reprints from the Original Sources of European History (Philadelphia: University of Pennsylvania, 1912), vol. III, no. 4 pp. 23–28.

Leg-screws. Will confess absolutely nothing; knows nothing about it. He has never renounced God; will never do such a thing; has never been guilty of this vice; feels likewise no pain.

Is stripped and examined; on his right side is found a bluish mark, like a clover leaf, is thrice pricked therein, but feels no pain and no blood flows out.

Strappado. He has never renounced God; God will not forsake him; if he were such a wretch he would not let himself be so tortured; God must show some token of his innocence. He knows nothing about witchcraft. . . .

On July 5, the above named Junius is without torture, but with urgent persuasions, exhorted to confess, and at last begins and confesses:

When in the year 1624 his law-suit at Rothweil cost him some six hundred florins, he had gone out, in the month of August, into his orchard at Friedrichsbronnen; and, as he sat there in thought, there had come to him a woman like a grass-maid, who had asked him why he sat there so sorrowful; he had answered that he was not despondent, but she had led him by seductive speeches to yield him to her will. . . . And thereafter this wench had changed into the form of a goat, which bleated and said, "Now you see with whom you have had to do. You must be mine or I will forthwith break your neck." Thereupon he had been frightened, and trembled all over for fear. Than the transformed spirit had seized him by the throat and demanded that he should renounce God Almighty, whereupon Junius said, "God forbid," and thereupon the spirit vanquished through the power of these words. Yet it came straightway back, brought more people with it, and persistently demanded of him that he renounce God in Heaven and all the heavenly host, by which terrible threatening he was obliged to speak this formula: "I renounce God in Heaven and his host, and will henceforward recognize the Devil as my God."

After the renunciation he was so far persuaded by those present and by the evil spirit that he suffered himself to be otherwise baptized in the evil spirit's name. The Morhauptin had given him a ducat as dower-gold, which afterward became only a potsherd.

He was then named Krix. His paramour he had to call Vixen. Those present had congratulated him in Beelzebub's name and said that they were now all alike. At this baptism of his there were among others the aforesaid Christiana Morhauptin, the young Geiserlin, Paul Glaser, [and others]. After this they had dispersed.

At this time his paramour had promised to provide him with money, and from time to time to take him to other witch-gatherings. . . . Whenever he wished to ride forth [to the witch-sabbath] a black dog had come before his bed, which said to him that he must go with him, whereupon he had seated himself upon the dog and the dog had raised himself in the Devil's name and so had fared forth.

About two years ago he was taken to the electoral council-room, at the left hand as one goes in. Above at a table were seated the Chancellor, the Burgomaster Neydekher, Dr. George Haan, [and many others]. Since his eyes were not good, he could not recognize more persons.

More time for consideration was now given him. On July 7, the aforesaid Junius was again examined, to know what further had occurred to him to confess. He confesses that about two months ago, on the day after an execution was held, he was at a witch-dance at the Black Cross, where Beelzebub had shown himself to them all and said expressly to their faces that they must all be burned together on this spot, and had ridiculed and taunted those present. . . .

Of crimes. His paramour had immediately after his seduction demanded that he should make away with his younger son Hans Georg, and had given him for this purpose a gray powder; this, however, being too hard for him, he had made away with his horse, a brown, instead.

His paramour had also often spurred him on to kill his daughter, . . . and because he would not do this he had been maltreated with blows by the evil spirit.

Once at the suggestion of his paramour he had taken the holy wafer out of his mouth and given it to her. . . .

A week before his arrest as he was going to St. Martin's church the Devil met him on the way, in the form of a goat, and told him that he would soon be imprisoned, but that he should not trouble himself—he would soon set him free. Besides this, by his soul's salvation, he knew nothing further; but what he had spoken was the pure truth; on that he would stake his life. On August 6, 1628, there was read to the aforesaid Junius this his confession, which he then wholly ratified and confirmed, and was willing to stake his life upon it. And afterward he voluntarily confirmed the same before the court.

[So ended the trial of Junius, and he was accordingly burned at the stake. But it so happens that there is also preserved in Bamberg a letter, in quivering hand, secretly written by him to his daughter while in the midst of his trial (July 24, 1628):]

Many hundred thousand good-nights, dearly beloved daughter Veronica. Innocent have I come into prison, innocent have I been tortured, innocent must I die. For whoever comes into the witch prison must become a witch or be tortured until he invents something out of his head and—God pity him—bethinks him of something. I will tell you how it has gone with me. When I was the first time put to the torture, Dr. Braun, Dr. Kötzendörffer, and two strange doctors were there. Then Dr. Braun asks me, "Kinsman, how come you here?" I answer, "Through falsehood, through misfortune." "Hear, you," he says, "you are a witch; will you confess it voluntarily? If not, we'll bring in witnesses and the executioner for you." I said "I am no witch, I have a pure conscience in the matter; if there are a thousand witnesses, I am not anxious, but I'll gladly hear the witnesses." Now the chancellor's son was set before me . . . and afterward Hoppfen Elss. She had seen me dance on Haupts-moor. . . . I answered: "I have never renounced God, and will never do it—God graciously keep me from it. I'll rather bear whatever I must." And then came also—God in highest Heaven have mercy—the executioner, and put the thumb-screws on me, both hands bound together, so that the blood ran out at the nails and everywhere, so that for four weeks I could not use my hands, as you can see from the writing. . . . Thereafter they first stripped me, bound my hands behind me, and drew me up in the torture.[2] Then I thought heaven and earth were at an end; eight times did they draw me up and let me fall again, so that I suffered terrible agony. . . .

And this happened on Friday, June 30, and with God's help I had to bear the torture. . . . When at last the executioner led me back into the prison, he said to me: "Sir, I beg you, for God's sake confess something, whether it be true or not. Invent something, for you cannot endure the torture which you will be put to; and, even if you bear it all, yet you will not escape, not even if you were an earl, but one torture will follow after another until you say you are a witch. Not before that," he said, "will they let you go, as you may see by all their trials, for one is just like another." . . .

And so I begged, since I was in wretched plight, to be given one day for thought and a priest. The priest was refused me, but the time for thought was given. Now, my dear child, see in what hazard I stood and still stand. I must say that I am a witch, though I am not,— must now renounce God, though I have never done it before. Day and night I was deeply troubled, but at last there came to me a new idea. I would not be anxious, but, since I had been given no priest with whom I could take counsel, I would myself think of something and say it. It were surely better that I just say it with mouth and words, even though I had not really done it; and afterwards I would confess it to the priest, and let those answer for it who compel me to do it. . . . And so I made my confession, as follows; but it was all a lie. . . .

Dear child, keep this letter secret so that people do not find it, else I shall be tortured most piteously and the jailers will be beheaded. So strictly is it forbidden. . . . Dear child, pay this man a dollar. . . . I have taken several days to write this; my hands are both lame. I am in a sad plight. . . .

Good night, for your father Johannes Junius will never see you more. July 24, 1628.

DISCUSSION QUESTIONS

1. According to the trial minutes, why was Junius targeted for persecution? What does this reveal about contemporary beliefs in witches and their powers?
2. How does Junius's own account of his trial conflict with that of the trial minutes?
3. What does this document suggest about the religious anxieties of the times?

COMPARATIVE QUESTIONS

1. Scholars argue that amidst the conflicts of this period, many European leaders and thinkers increasingly gave precedence to secular concerns over religious ones. How do the Edict of Nantes and Galileo's letter support this argument?
2. Despite this gradual trend towards secularization, what do Galileo's letter and the witchcraft trial minutes reveal about the continued importance of religion in shaping Europeans' understanding of the everyday world?
3. What do the third and fourth documents suggest about the role of violence in European society and culture?

---

[2] This torture of the strappado, which was that in most common use by the courts, consisted of a rope, attached to the hands of the prisoner (bound behind his back) and carried over a pulley at the ceiling. By this he was drawn up and left hanging. To increase the pain, weights were attached to his feet or he was suddenly jerked up and let drop.

State Building and the Search for Order
1648–1690

S U M M A R Y   The wars over religion not only left bitter memories in late-seventeenth-century Europe, but also ruined economies and weakened governments. In response, many people sought to impose order on the turbulent world in a variety of ways. As the first two documents reveal, politically, the quest for order fueled the development of two rival systems of state building: absolutism and constitutionalism, with France and England, respectively, taking the lead. Despite their differences, rulers in both systems centralized their power and expanded their bureaucracies, casting an increasingly wide net over their subjects' lives. The third document indicates that not everyone submitted willingly to the expansion of state power, but such resistance was typically fruitless. Even so, as the final document suggests, the emergence of a new literary genre, the novel, in this period points to other, less overt forces at work, counteracting the search for order.

1
Louis de Rouvroy, Duke of Saint-Simon
Memoirs
1694–1723

A nobleman and godson of Louis XIV, Louis de Rouvroy, Duke of Saint-Simon (1675–1755), was raised at the royal palace of Versailles. He began recording his life and impressions of the court at the age of nineteen and continued for almost three decades. The result was his multivolume Memoirs, *which paint an intimate portrait of the Sun King and the workings of the absolutist state. Saint-Simon was not an entirely objective observer, however. Having never achieved great success within the court, he often viewed it through the lens of his own resentment. This excerpt provides insight into both the reasons behind Louis XIV's move to Versailles and his method of rule there.*

Let me touch now upon some other incidents in his career, and upon some points in his character.

He early showed a disinclination for Paris. The troubles that had taken place there during the minority made him regard the place as dangerous; he wished, too, to render himself venerable by hiding himself from the eyes of the multitude; all these considerations fixed him at St. Germains soon after the death of the Queen, his mother. It was to that place he began to attract the world by fêtes and gallantries, and by making it felt that he wished to be often seen.

His love for Madame de la Vallière, which was at first kept secret, occasioned frequent excursions to Versailles, then a little card castle, which had been built by Louis XIII.—annoyed, and his suite still more so, at being frequently obliged to sleep in a wretched inn there, after he had been out hunting in the forest of Saint Leger. That monarch rarely slept at Versailles more than one night, and then from necessity; the King, his son, slept there, so that he might be more in private with his mistress; pleasures unknown to the hero and just man, worthy son of Saint Louis, who built the little château.

These excursions of Louis XIV. by degrees gave birth to those immense buildings he erected at Versailles; and their convenience for a numerous court, so different from the apartments at St. Germains, led him to take up his abode there entirely shortly after the death of the Queen. He built an infinite number of apartments, which were asked for by those who wished to pay their court to him; whereas at St. Germains nearly everybody was obliged to lodge in the town, and the few who found accommodation at the château were strangely inconvenienced.

The frequent fêtes, the private promenades at Versailles, the journeys, were means on which the King seized in order to distinguish or mortify the courtiers, and thus render them more assiduous in pleasing him. He felt that of real favours he had not enough to bestow; in order to keep up the spirit of devotion, he therefore unceasingly invented all sorts of ideal ones, little preferences and petty distinctions, which answered his purpose as well.

He was exceedingly jealous of the attention paid him. Not only did he notice the presence of the most distinguished courtiers, but those of inferior degree also. He looked to the right and to the left, not only upon rising but upon going to bed, at his meals, in passing through his apartments, or his gardens of Versailles, where alone the courtiers were allowed to follow him; he saw and noticed everybody; not one escaped him, not even those who hoped to remain unnoticed. He marked well all absentees from the court, found out the reason of their absence, and never lost an opportunity of acting towards them as the occasion might seem to justify. With some of the courtiers (the most distinguished), it was a demerit

Bayle St. John, trans., *The Memoirs of the Duke of Saint Simon,* vol. II (Philadelphia: Gebbie and Co., 1890), 363–69.

not to make the court their ordinary abode; with others 'twas a fault to come but rarely; for those who never or scarcely ever came it was certain disgrace. When their names were in any way mentioned, "I do not know them," the King would reply haughtily. Those who presented themselves but seldom were thus characterised: "They are people I never see;" these decrees were irrevocable. He could not bear people who liked Paris.

Louis XIV. took great pains to be well informed of all that passed everywhere; in the public places, in the private houses, in society and familiar intercourse. His spies and tell-tales were infinite. He had them of all species; many who were ignorant that their information reached him; others who knew it; others who wrote to him direct, sending their letters through channels he indicated; and all these letters were seen by him alone, and always before everything else; others who sometimes spoke to him secretly in his cabinet, entering by the back stairs. These unknown means ruined an infinite number of people of all classes who never could discover the cause; often ruined them very unjustly; for the King, once prejudiced, never altered his opinion, or so rarely, that nothing was more rare. He had, too, another fault, very dangerous for others and often for himself, since it deprived him of good subjects. He had an excellent memory; in this way, that if he saw a man who, twenty years before, perhaps, had in some manner offended him, he did not forget the man, though he might forget the offence. This was enough, however, to exclude the person from all favour. The representations of a minister, of a general, of his confessor even, could not move the King. He would not yield.

The most cruel means by which the King was informed of what was passing— for many years before anybody knew it—was that of opening letters. The promptitude and dexterity with which they were opened passes understanding. He saw extracts from all the letters in which there were passages that the chiefs of the post-office, and then the minister who governed it, thought ought to go before him; entire letters, too, were sent to him, when their contents seemed to justify the sending. Thus the chiefs of the post, nay, the principal clerks were in a position to suppose what they pleased and against whom they pleased. A word of contempt against the King or the government, a joke, a detached phrase, was enough. It is incredible how many people, justly or unjustly, were more or less ruined, always without resource, without trial, and without knowing why. The secret was impenetrable; for nothing ever cost the King less than profound silence and dissimulation. . . .

He liked splendour, magnificence, and profusion in everything: you pleased him if you shone through the brilliancy of your houses, your clothes, your table, your equipages. Thus a taste for extravagance and luxury was disseminated through all classes of society; causing infinite harm, and leading to general confusion of rank and to ruin.

DISCUSSION QUESTIONS

1. How did Louis XIV use court etiquette as a form of power?
2. Why did nobles reside at Versailles? What benefits did they gain?
3. What is Saint-Simon's attitude toward Louis XIV's style of governing?
4. In what ways did court life embody the principles of absolutism?

2
British Parliament
The English Bill of Rights
1689

Louis XIV had many admirers in Europe, including King James II of England. Unlike Louis, however, James faced a major challenge to his power: Parliament. The king and Parliament had been at odds for decades concerning the nature of royal authority, and James's absolutist policies proved too much for Parliament to bear. As a result, in 1688 they ousted the king and offered the throne to Prince William of Orange and his wife, Mary, the eldest of James's adult daughters. In exchange, William and Mary agreed to accept the Bill of Rights, which legally defined the role of Parliament as the monarchy's partner in government. The bill not only marked the victory of constitutionalism over absolutism in England, but it also formed the cornerstone of the idea that government should ensure certain rights by law to protect its citizens from the dangers of arbitrary power.

Whereas the said late King James II having abdicated the government, and the throne being thereby vacant, his Highness the prince of Orange (whom it hath pleased Almighty God to make the glorious instrument of delivering this kingdom from popery and arbitrary power) did (by the advice of the lords spiritual and temporal, and diverse principal persons of the Commons) cause letters to be written to the lords spiritual and temporal, being Protestants, and other letters to the several counties, cities, universities, boroughs, and Cinque Ports, for the choosing of such persons to represent them, as were of right to be sent to parliament, to meet and sit at Westminster upon the two and twentieth day of January, in this year 1689, in order to such an establishment as that their religion, laws, and liberties might not again be in danger of being subverted; upon which letters elections have been accordingly made.

And thereupon the said lords spiritual and temporal and Commons, pursuant to their respective letters and elections, being now assembled in a full and free representation of this nation, taking into their most serious consideration the best means for attaining the ends aforesaid, do in the first place (as their ancestors in like case have usually done), for the vindication and assertion of their ancient rights and liberties, declare:

1. That the pretended power of suspending laws, or the execution of laws, by regal authority, without consent of parliament is illegal.

2. That the pretended power of dispensing with the laws, or the execution of law by regal authority, as it hath been assumed and exercises of late, is illegal.

3. That the commission for erecting the late court of commissioners for ecclesiastical causes, and all other commissions and courts of like nature, are illegal and pernicious.

Great Britain, *The Statutes*, rev. ed. (London: Eyre and Spottiswoode, 1871), vol. II, 10–12.

4. That levying money for or to the use of the crown by pretense of prerogative, without grant of parliament, for longer time or in other manner than the same is or shall be granted, is illegal.

5. That it is the right of the subjects to petition the king, and all commitments and prosecutions for such petitioning are illegal.

6. That the raising or keeping a standing army within the kingdom in time of peace, unless it be with consent of parliament, is against law.

7. That the subjects which are Protestants may have arms for their defense suitable to their conditions, and as allowed by law.

8. That election of members of parliament ought to be free.

9. That the freedom of speech, and debates or proceedings in parliament, ought not to be impeached or questioned in any court or place out of parliament.

10. That excessive bail ought not to be required, nor excessive fines imposed, nor cruel and unusual punishments inflicted.

11. That jurors ought to be duly impaneled and returned, and jurors which pass upon men in trials for high treason ought to be freeholders.

12. That all grants and promises of fines and forfeitures of particular persons before conviction are illegal and void.

13. And that for redress of all grievances, and for the amending, strengthening, and preserving of the laws, parliament ought to be held frequently.

And they do claim, demand, and insist upon all and singular the premises, as their undoubted rights and liberties: and that no declarations, judgments, doings, or proceedings, to the prejudice of the people in any of the said premises, ought in any wise to be drawn hereafter into consequence or example.

To which demand of their rights they are particularly encouraged by the declaration of his Highness the prince of Orange, as being the only means for obtaining a full redress and remedy therein.

Having therefore an entire confidence that his said Highness the prince of Orange will perfect the deliverance so far advanced by him, and will still preserve them from the violation of their rights, which they have here asserted, and from all other attempt upon their religion, rights, and liberties:

The said lords spiritual and temporal, and commons, assembled at Westminster, do resolve that William and Mary, prince and princess of Orange, be, and be declared, king and queen of England, France, and Ireland, the dominions thereunto belonging, to hold the crown and royal dignity of the said kingdoms and dominions to them the said prince and princess during their lives. . . .

Upon which their said Majesties did accept the crown and royal dignity of the kingdoms of England, France, and Ireland, and the dominions thereunto belonging, according to the resolution and desire of the said lords and commons contained in the said declaration.

DISCUSSION QUESTIONS
1. In what ways does the bill limit the powers of the crown?
2. What role does the bill grant Parliament in government?
3. How does the Bill of Rights give weight to the attitude of some members of Parliament at the time that they had "made" the king and queen, William and Mary?

3

Ludwig Fabritius
The Revolt of Stenka Razin
1670

Despite its geographical and cultural isolation from the rest of Europe, Russia followed France's lead down the path of absolutism. In the process, Czar Alexei (r. 1645–1676) legally combined millions of slaves and free peasants into a single serf class bound to the land and their aristocratic masters. Not everyone passively accepted this fate, however. In 1667, a Cossak named Stenka Razin led a revolt against serfdom that gained considerable support among people whose social and economic status was threatened by the czar's policies, including soldiers from peasant stock. Razin's ultimate defeat at the hands of the czar elucidates the close ties between the Russian government's enhanced power and the enforcement of serfdom. A Dutch soldier, Ludwig Fabritius, who lived in Russia from 1660 to 1677 while employed as a military expert in the Russian army, wrote the following account of one stage of the revolt.

Then Stenka with his company started off upstream, rowing as far as Tsaritsyn, whence it took him only one day's journey to Panshin, a small town situated on the Don. Here he began straightaway quietly gathering the common people around him, giving them money, and promises of great riches if they would be loyal to him and help to exterminate the treacherous boyars.[1]

This lasted the whole winter, until by about spring he had assembled 4,000 to 5,000 men. With these he came to Tsaritsyn and demanded the immediate surrender of the fortress; the rabble soon achieved their purpose, and although the governor tried to take refuge in a tower, he soon had to give himself up as he was deserted by one and all. Stenka immediately had the wretched governor hanged; and all the goods they found belonging to the Tsar and his officers as well as to the merchants were confiscated and distributed among the rabble.

Stenka now began once more to make preparations. Since the plains are not cultivated, the people have to bring their corn from Nizhniy-Novgorod and Kazan down the Volga in big boats known as *nasady*, and everything destined for Astrakhan has first to pass Tsaritsyn. Stenka Razin duly noted this, and occupied the whole of the Volga, so that nothing could get through to Astrakhan. Here he captured a few hundred merchants with their valuable goods, taking possession of all kinds of fine linen, silks, striped silk material, sables, soft leather, ducats, talers, and many thousands of rubles in Russian money and merchandise of every description. . . .

In the meantime four regiments of *streltsy*[2] were dispatched from Moscow to subdue these brigands. They arrived with their big boats and as they were not used to the water, were easily beaten. Here Stenka Razin gained possession of a

---

[1] **boyars:** Noblemen.

[2] **streltsy:** Sharpshooters.

Anthony Glenn Cross, ed. *Russia under Western Eyes, 1517–1825* (London: Elek Books, 1971), 120–23.

large amount of ammunition and artillery-pieces and everything else he required. While the above-mentioned *streltsy* were sent from Moscow, about 5,000 men were ordered up from Astrakhan by water and by land to capture Stenka Razin. As soon as he had finished with the former, he took up a good position, and, being in possession of reliable information regarding our forces, he left Tsaritsyn and came to meet us half way at Chernyy Yar, confronting us before we had suspected his presence or received any information about him. We stopped at Chernyy Yar for a few days and sent out scouts by water and by land, but were unable to obtain any definite information. On 10 July [*sic:* June] a council of war was held at which it was decided to advance and seek out Stenka. The next morning, at 8 o'clock, our look-outs on the water came hurriedly and raised the alarm as the Cossacks were following at their heels. We got out of our boats and took up battle positions. General Knyaz Semen Ivanovich Lvov went through the ranks and reminded all the men to do their duty and to remember the oath they had taken to His Majesty the Tsar, to fight like honest soldiers against these irresponsible rebels, whereupon they all unanimously shouted: "Yes, we will give our lives for His Majesty the Tsar, and will fight to the last drop of our blood."

In the meantime Stenka prepared for battle and deployed on a wide front; to all those who had no rifle he gave a long pole, burnt a little at one end, and with a rag or small hook attached. They presented a strange sight on the plain from afar, and the common soldiers imagined that, since there were so many flags and standards, there must be a host of people. They [the common soldiers] held a consultation and at once decided that this was the chance for which they had been waiting so long, and with all their flags and drums they ran over to the enemy. They began kissing and embracing one another and swore with life and limb to stand together and to exterminate the treacherous boyars, to throw off the yoke of slavery, and to become free men.

The general looked at the officers and the officers at the general, and no one knew what to do; one said this, and another that, until finally it was decided that they and the general should get into the boats and withdraw to Astrakhan. But the rascally *streltsy* of Chernyy Yar stood on the walls and towers, turning their weapons on us and opened fire; some of them ran out of the fortress and cut us off from the boats, so that we had no means of escape. In the meantime those curs of ours who had gone over to the Cossacks came up from behind. We numbered about eighty men, officers, noblemen, and clerks. Murder at once began. Then, however, Stenka Razin ordered that no more officers were to be killed, saying that there must be a few good men among them who should be pardoned, whilst those others who had not lived in amity with their men should be condemned to well-deserved punishment by the Ataman and his *Krug*. A *Krug* is a meeting convened by the order of the Ataman, at which the Cossacks stand in a circle with the standard in the centre; the Ataman then takes his place beside his best officers, to whom he divulges his wishes, ordering them to make these known to the common brothers and to hear their opinion on the matter]. . . .

A *Krug* was accordingly called and Stenka asked through his chiefs how the general and his officers had treated the soldiers under their command. Thereupon the unscrupulous curs, *streltsy* as well as soldiers, unanimously called out that there was not one of them who deserved to remain alive, and they all asked that their father Stepan Timofeyevich Razin should order them to be cut down. This was granted with the exception of General Knyaz Semen Ivanovich Lvov, whose life was specially spared by Stenka himself. The officers were now brought in order of rank out of the tower, into which they had been thrown bound hand and foot the previous day, their ropes were cut and they were led outside the gate. When all the bloodthirsty curs had lined up, each was eager to deal his former superior the first blow, one with the sword, another with the lance, another with the scimitar, and others again with martels, so that as soon as an officer was pushed into the ring, the curs immediately killed him with their many wounds; indeed, some were cut to pieces and straightaway thrown into the Volga. My step-father, Paul Rudolf Beem, and Lt. Col. Wundrum and many other officers, senior and junior, were cut down before my eyes.

My own time had not yet come: this I could tell by the wonderful way in which God rescued me, for as I — half-dead — now awaited the final blow, my [former] orderly, a young soldier, came and took me by my bound arms and tried to take me down the hill. As I was already half-dead, I did not move and did not know what to do, but he came back and took me by the arms and led me, bound as I was, through the throng of curs, down the hill into the boat and immediately cut my arms free, saying that I should rest in peace here and that he would be responsible for me and do his best to save my life . . . Then my guardian angel told me not to leave the boat, and left me. He returned in the evening and brought me a piece of bread which I enjoyed since I had had nothing to eat for two days.

The following day all our possessions were looted and gathered together under the main flag, so that both our bloodthirsty curs and the Cossacks got their share.

Discussion Questions

1. What motivated Razin and his followers to take action?
2. Why were Razin and his forces able to defeat the czar's soldiers?
3. What does this account suggest about the role of the military in the growth of the Russian government's authority?
4. With whom do you think Fabritius's sympathies lie, and why?

4

Madame de Lafayette
The Princess of Clèves
1678

Like the Duke of Saint-Simon, French author Marie-Madeline de La Vergne (b. 1634), Countess of Lafayette, was well acquainted with the court of Louis XIV. She also had close ties to intellectual circles in Paris, where she cultivated her formidable writing talents. In 1678, she published anonymously The Princess of Clèves, *which was an overnight literary sensation. The following letters help us to under-*

stand why. Set during the reign of Henry II, the book centers on the character of Mademoiselle de Chartres, who, upon captivating the court with her wit and beauty, weds the Prince of Clèves. Their union proves an unhappy one, and the princess falls in love with another man, Nemours. She never succumbs to her desire, however, even after her husband's death. The book's portrayal of her emotional struggle scandalized many readers by challenging conventional notions of marriage and proper aristocratic behavior. At the same time, the book abandoned the idealized and lengthy style of the romantic genre, giving birth to a new literary form, the novel.

Madame de Lafayette to Joseph Marie de Lescheraine

13 April 1678

A little book which appeared fifteen years ago and that people attributed to me makes them want to credit me with *The Princess of Clèves*. But I assure you that I had nothing to do with it and that M. de La Rochefoucauld, to whom the book has also been attributed, had as little to do with it as I did. He declared this under oath so many times that he cannot be doubted, especially about something that could be admitted without shame. As for me, I am flattered that people suspect me of being the author, and I believe that I would acknowledge the book as mine if I could be sure that the author would never show up and ask for it back. I find it a very pleasant work, well written without being perfectly polished, so full of admirably subtle details that it has to be read more than once. And most of all, I find in it a perfect representation of the world of the court and of the way one lives there. The book does not seem like a romance, and there is nothing overdone in it. Assuredly it is not a romance but rather a book of memoirs, and I have been told that such was its title, but they changed it.

So there, Monsieur, is my opinion of *Madame de Clèves*. I would ask yours as well. People are so divided over this book that they could come to blows. Some condemn what others admire in it. So, no matter what you say, don't be afraid of being the only one to say it.

Roger de Bussy-Rabutin to Marie de Sévigné

26 June 1678

But I forgot to tell you that I have finally given *The Princess of Clèves* an impartial reading, not at all prejudiced by the good and bad things people have written. I found the first part admirable; the second didn't seem as good. In the first volume, except a few words that are repeated too often—just a small number—everything is pleasing, everything is natural, nothing is stilted. In the second part, Madame de Clèves's confession is preposterous, and could only be told in a true

John D. Lyons, ed. and trans., *Marie-Madeleine de Lafayette*, The Princess of Clèves (New York: Norton, 1994), 121–22.

history; but when one is making a story up it is absurd to depict the heroine as having a sentiment that is so out of the ordinary. The author, by doing so, was thinking of ways to be different from the old romances and was not paying attention to common sense. A wife rarely tells her husband that a man is in love with her and *never* tells her husband that she is in love with another man, and especially not by throwing herself at his feet, a gesture that can make him think she has committed the ultimate offense. Besides, it is implausible that passionate love and virtue should remain for a long time equal in strength. In court society if a woman hasn't completely rejected a suitor in two or three weeks, or at most a month, she is only trying to make herself appear more desirable. And if, against all the odds and in spite of custom, the conflict between love and virtue should last until her husband's death, she would be delighted to harmonize virtue and love by marrying a man of his [Nemours's] quality, the handsomest gallant of his day. The first incident in the gardens at Coulommiers is not plausible and smacks of romance. It is very a calculated arrangement that when the Princess confesses to her husband that she loves another man, M. de Nemours, at just the right moment, is behind the fence listening to them; I don't even see why he had to know her confession, and in any event it should have been arranged so that he learned about [it] in some other way. It's like a romance, as well, when people talk to themselves. Besides the fact that it is not customary for people to talk to themselves, it isn't possible to know what someone says to herself unless she writes her own story: and even then she would say only what she thought. The letter to the Vidame is also like the letters in a romance, obscure, too long, and not at all natural. Just the same, in this second volume everything is just as well narrated, and the turns of phrase are just as beautiful as in the first volume.

Roger de Rabutin, comte de Bussy

DISCUSSION QUESTIONS

1. In seventeenth-century France, it was not deemed proper for noblewomen to publish their writings. In the first letter, how does Madame de Lafayette confront this prejudice and use it to her advantage?

2. Why is Roger de Bussy-Rabutin critical of *The Princess of Clèves?*

3. What do his criticisms suggest about the development of the novel as a new type of literature?

Comparative Questions

1. What do both Saint-Simon and Roger Bussy-Rabutin reveal about court culture during the reign of Louis XIV?

2. Based on the first three documents, how would you describe the relationship between the individual and the state in England, France, and Russia? What similarities and differences do you see?

3. What do these similarities and differences suggest about the basis of authority in constitutional and absolutist governments?

The Atlantic System and Its Consequences

1690–1740

S U M M A R Y   The growth of European domestic economies and overseas colonization in the eighteenth century infused Europe with money, new products, and a new sense of optimism about the future. Yet, as the first document illustrates, the good times came at a horrible price for the millions of African slaves who formed the economic backbone of the colonial system. Changes were afoot on the political front, too, with the stabilization of the European state system. Consequently, states such as Russia shone more brightly over the political landscape while others lost their luster. The second document brings Russia's new prominence to life in its leader's own words. The third and fourth documents reveal that intellectual circles were also ablaze with change as scholars and writers cast political, social, and religious issues in a new, critical light. Even women's traditional place in society was for the first time systematically called into question.

1

Olaudah Equiano
The Interesting Narrative of the Life of Olaudah Equiano Written by Himself
1789

The autobiography of Olaudah Equiano (c. 1745–1797) puts a human face on the eighteenth-century Atlantic slave trade and its tragic consequences. Born in what is now Nigeria, Equiano was captured by local raiders and sold into slavery in his early teens. He gained his freedom in 1766 and soon thereafter became a vocal supporter of the English abolitionist movement. Having learned English as a young man, he published his autobiography in 1789, a best-seller in its day, with numerous editions published in Britain and America. In the following excerpt, Equiano recounts his experience on the slave ship that took him away from his homeland, his freedom, and his very identity. Millions of others shared this same fate.

The first object which saluted my eyes when I arrived on the coast was the sea, and a slave ship which was then riding at anchor and waiting for its cargo. These filled me with astonishment, which was soon converted into terror when I was carried on board. I was immediately handled and tossed up to see if I were sound by some of the crew, and I was now persuaded that I had gotten into a world of bad spirits and that they were going to kill me. Their complexions too differing so much from ours, their long hair and the language they spoke (which was very different from any I had ever heard) united to confirm me in this belief. Indeed such were the horrors of my views and fears at the moment that, if ten thousand worlds had been my own, I would have freely parted with them all to have exchanged my condition with that of the meanest slave in my own country. When I looked round the ship too and saw a large furnace or copper boiling and a multitude of black people of every description chained together, every one of their countenances expressing dejection and sorrow, I no longer doubted of my fate; and quite overpowered with horror and anguish, I fell motionless on the deck and fainted. When I recovered a little I found some black people about me, who I believed were some of those who had brought me on board and had been receiving their pay; they talked to me in order to cheer me, but all in vain. I asked them if we were not to be eaten by those white men with horrible looks, red faces, and loose hair. They told me I was not, and one of the crew brought me a small portion of spirituous liquor in a wine glass, but being afraid of him I would not take it out of his hand. One of the blacks therefore took it from him and gave it to me, and I took a little down my palate, which instead of reviving me, as they thought it would, threw me into the greatest consternation at the strange feeling it produced, having never tasted such any liquor before. Soon after this the blacks who brought me on board went off, and left me abandoned to despair.

I now saw myself deprived of all chance of returning to my native country or even the least glimpse of hope of gaining the shore, which I now considered as friendly; and I even wished for my former slavery in preference to my present situation, which was filled with horrors of every kind, still heightened by my ignorance of what I was to undergo. I was not long suffered to indulge my grief; I was soon put down under the decks, and there I received such a salutation in my nostrils as I had never experienced in my life: so that with the loathsomeness of the stench and crying together, I became so sick and low that I was not able to eat, nor had I the least desire to taste anything. I now wished for the last friend, death, to relieve me; but soon, to my grief, two of the white men offered me eatables, and on my refusing to eat, one of them held me fast by the hands and laid me across I

Abridged and Edited by Paul Edwards, *Equiano's Travels: His Autobiography* (London: Heinemann, 1967), 25–32.

think the windlass, and tied my feet while the other flogged me severely. I had never experienced anything of this kind before, and although, not being used to the water, I naturally feared that element the first time I saw it, yet nevertheless could I have got over the nettings I would have jumped over the side, but I could not; and besides, the crew used to watch us very closely who were not chained down to the decks, lest we should leap into the water: and I have seen some of these poor African prisoners most severely cut for attempting to do so, and hourly whipped for not eating. This indeed was often the case with myself. In a little time after, amongst the poor chained men I found some of my own nation, which in a small degree gave ease to my mind. I inquired of these what was to be done with us; they gave me to understand we were to be carried to these white people's country to work for them. I then was a little revived, and thought if it were no worse than working, my situation was not so desperate: but still I feared I should be put to death, the white people looked and acted, as I thought, in so savage a manner; for I had never seen among my people such instances of brutal cruelty, and this not only shewn towards us blacks but also to some of the whites themselves. One white man in particular I saw, when we were permitted to be on deck, flogged so unmercifully with a large rope near the foremast that he died in consequence of it; and they tossed him over the side as they would have done a brute. This made me fear these people the more, and I expected nothing less than to be treated in the same manner. . . . At last, when the ship we were in had got in all her cargo, they made ready with many fearful noises, and we were all put under deck so that we could not see how they managed the vessel. But this disappointment was the last of my sorrow. The stench of the hold while we were on the coast was so intolerably loathsome that it was dangerous to remain there for any time, and some of us had been permitted to stay on the deck for the fresh air; but now that the whole ship's cargo were confined together it became absolutely pestilential. The closeness of the place and the heat of the climate, added to the number in the ship, which was so crowded that each had scarcely room to turn himself, almost suffocated us. This produced copious perspirations, so that the air soon became unfit for respiration from a variety of loathsome smells, and brought on a sickness among the slaves, of which many died, thus falling victims to the improvident avarice, as I may call it, of their purchasers. This wretched situation was again aggravated by the galling of the chains, now become insupportable, and the filth of the necessary tubs, into which the children often fell and were almost suffocated. The shrieks of the women and the groans of the dying rendered the whole a scene of horror almost inconceivable. Happily perhaps for myself I was soon reduced so low here that it was thought necessary to keep me almost always on deck, and from my extreme youth I was not put in fetters. In this situation I expected every hour to share the fate of my companions, some of whom were almost daily brought upon deck at the point of death, which I began to hope would soon put an end to my miseries. . . . At last we came in sight of the island of Barbados, at which the whites on board gave a great shout and made many signs of joy to us. We did not know what to think of this, but as the vessel drew nearer we plainly saw the harbour and other ships of different kinds and sizes, and we soon anchored amongst them off Bridgetown. Many merchants and planters now came on board, though it was in the evening. They put us in separate parcels and examined us attentively. They also made us jump, and pointed to the land, signifying we were to go there. . . . We were not many days in the merchant's custody before we were sold after their usual manner, which is this: On a signal given, (as the beat of a drum) the buyers rush at once into the yard where the slaves are confined, and make choice of that parcel they like best. The noise and clamour with which this is attended and the eagerness visible in the countenances of the buyers serve not a little to increase the apprehensions of the terrified Africans, who may well be supposed to consider them as the ministers of that destruction to which they think themselves devoted. In this manner, without scruple, are relations and friends separated, most of them never to see each other again. I remember in the vessel in which I was brought over, in the men's apartment there were several brothers who, in the sale, were sold in different lots; and it was very moving on this occasion to see and hear their cries at parting. O, ye nominal Christians! might not an African ask you, Learned you this from your God who says unto you, Do unto all men as you would men should do unto you?

DISCUSSION QUESTIONS

1. What are Equiano's impressions of the white men on the ship and their treatment of the slaves?
2. How does this treatment reflect the slave traders' primary concerns?
3. What message do you think Equiano sought to convey to his readers?
4. Based on this message, to whom do you think his book especially appealed?

2

Tsar Peter I
Letter to his Son, Alexei
October 11, 1715,

and Alexei's Response
October 31, 1715

In the eighteenth century, European states turned much of their attention to the political and military scene burgeoning within Europe, vying to keep one step ahead of their rivals. Tsar Peter I of Russia was especially successful at this game. During his rule from 1689 to 1725, he transformed Russia into a great European power with all the trappings of a Western absolutist state, including a strong army and centralized bureaucracy. Peter wrote the following letter to Alexei, who was then his only son and heir, during the Great Northern War against Sweden, which Peter ultimately won to Russia's great advantage. The letter elucidates the tsar's relentless drive toward greatness on the European stage. Alexei's response reveals not only the striking differences in personality between the two men, but also the tension that marked their tumultuous relationship.

[Peter to Alexis, October 11, 1715:]

Declaration to my son:

Everyone knows how, before the beginning of this war, our people were hemmed in by the Swedes, who not only stole the essential ports of our fatherland . . . but cut us off from communication with the whole world. And also later, in the beginning of this war (which enterprise was and is directed by God alone), oh, what great persecution we had to endure from those eternal enemies of ours because of our incompetence in the art of war, and with what sorrow and endurance we went to this school and, with the help of the above-mentioned guide, achieved a creditable degree [of effectiveness]. We were thus found worthy of looking on this enemy now trembling before us, trembling, perhaps, even more than we did before him. All this has been accomplished with the help of God through my modest labors and through those of other equally zealous and faithful sons of Russia.

However, when, considering this great blessing given by God to our fatherland, I think of my successor, a grief perhaps as strong as my joy gnaws me, when I see you, my heir, unfit for the management of state affairs (for it is not the fault of God, who has not deprived you of mind or health; for although not of a very strong constitution, you are not very weak either). But above all, you have no wish to hear anything about military affairs, which opened to us the way from darkness to light, so that we who were unknown before are now honored. I do not teach you to be inclined to wage war without a just cause, but to love this art and to endow and learn it by all means, for it is one of the two activities necessary for government: order and defense.

I have no wish to give you many examples, but I will mention only the Greeks, who are of the same religion as we. Did they not perish because they laid their arms aside, and were they not vanquished because of their peaceableness? Desirous of tranquil living, they always gave way to their enemy, who changed their tranquillity into endless servitude to tyrants. Perhaps you think that it can all be left to the generals; but this is really not so, for everyone looks up to his chief, to comply with his desires, which is an obvious fact. Thus, in the days of my brother's reign [Theodore, 1676–82], everyone liked clothes and horses above all things, and now they like arms. They may not be really interested in one or the other; but in what the chief is interested all take an interest, and to what he is indifferent, all are indifferent. And if they turn away so lightly from the frivolous pastimes, which are only a pleasure to man, how much more easily will they abandon so burdensome a game as war!

Furthermore, you do not learn anything because you have no desire to learn it, and you have no knowledge of military affairs. Lacking all knowledge, how can you direct these affairs? How can you reward the diligent and punish the negli-

A Source Book for Russian History From Early Times to 1917 (New Haven and London: Yale University Press, 1972), vol. II, 338–39.

gent when you yourself do not understand their work? You will be forced to look into people's mouths like a young bird. Do you pretend to be unfit for military work because of weak health? But that is no reason. I ask of you not work, but good will, which no malady can destroy. Ask anyone who remembers my brother whom I spoke of but now, who was, beyond comparison, sicklier than you and could not ride spirited horses, but he had a great liking for them and was always looking at them and kept them before his eyes. . . . So you see, not everything is done by great labor, but also by a strong desire. You say to yourself, perhaps, that many rulers do not themselves go to war, and yet campaigns are still carried on. This is true when, although not going themselves, they have a desire for it, as had the late French king [Louis XIV], who went to war himself but little, and who yet had a great taste for it and showed such magnificent deeds in war that his wars were called the theater and school for the whole world. But he had a taste not only for war, but also for other affairs and for manufactures, through all of which he procured glory for his state more than anybody else.

Now that I have gone into all this, I return again to my original point, thinking of you. I am a man, and subject to death. To whom shall I leave all this sowing, done with God's help, and that harvest which has already grown? To one who, like the idle slave in the Gospel, buried his talent in the ground (which means that he threw away everything that God had given him)? I also keep thinking of your wicked and stubborn disposition; for how many times I used to scold you for that, and not only scold but beat you, and also how many years I have now gone without speaking to you, and all without success! . . .

I have pondered this with much grief, and, seeing that I can in no wise dispose you toward good, I have deemed it appropriate to write to you this last admonition, and to wait a short time for you to mend your ways, and that *not hypocritically* [Peter's emphasis]. If you do not, know that I shall totally disinherit you like a gangrenous member; and do not imagine that, because you are my only son, I write this only to frighten you; I will do it indeed (with God's consent), because I have never spared my own life for my fatherland and people, nor do I now; therefore how can I spare you, unworthy one? Better a good stranger than an unworthy kinsman.

Peter

October 11, 1715

Saint Petersburg

[Alexis to Peter, October 31, 1715:]

Most gracious sovereign and father:

I have read [the letter] that was given me on your behalf on October 27, 1715, after the funeral of my wife. I have nothing to say about it, except that if you wish to disinherit me of the Russian crown because of my worthlessness, let it be as you will. Most humbly I ask you for this very thing, Sire, for I consider myself unqualified and unfit for this task, being most deficient in memory (without which it is impossible to accomplish anything). All my mental and physical capacities are weakened by various illnesses, and I have become unfit to rule such a people, which task requires a man less rotten than I. Therefore, I do not make a claim, nor will I make claim in the future, to the inheritance of the Russian throne after you—God give you health for many years—even if I did not have a brother (but now, thank God, I have one [note: Prince Peter, born to Peter and Catherine on October 29, 1715], God give him health); let God be my witness [in this matter], and to show that I testify truthfully I write this with my own hand.

I entrust my children to your will and ask only for maintenance for myself to the end of my life. This is submitted to your decision and merciful will.

Your most humble slave and son Alexis
Saint Petersburg
October 31, 1715

DISCUSSION QUESTIONS

1. Why does Peter regard the "art of war" as so important to government, and what did he gain by practicing it?
2. Why is Peter so critical of his son?
3. Whom does Peter single out as a political role model, and why is this significant?
4. What do these letters reveal about the tsar's personality?

3

Montesquieu
Persian Letters: Letter 37
1721

As Europe's economy expanded, so did its intellectual horizons with the birth of the Enlightenment in the 1690s. Charles-Louis de Secondat, Baron of Montesquieu (1689–1755), was an especially important literary figure on this front. In 1721 he published Persian Letters, *in which he uses fictional characters to explore an array of topics with the critical, reasoning spirit characteristic of the period. Letter 37 points to one of his and other Enlightenment writers' main targets: Louis XIV and his absolutist state. Along with its criticism of the king's vanity, ostentation, and life at court, the letter implicitly passes even more serious judgment on the aging ruler in noting his esteem for "oriental policies." Montesquieu condemns these same policies elsewhere in the letters as inhumane and unjust.*

Usbek to Ibben, at Smyrna

The King of France is old.[1] We have no examples in our histories of such a long reign as his. It is said that he possesses in a very high degree the faculty of making himself obeyed: he governs with equal ability his family, his court, and his king-

---

[1] Louis XIV. was then seventy-five years old, and had reigned for seventy. [All notes are Davidson's.]

Montesquieu, *Persian Letters*, vol. I, trans. John Davidson (London: Privately printed, 1892), 85–86.

dom: he has often been heard to say, that, of all existing governments, that of the Turks, or that of our august Sultan, pleased him best: such is his high opinion of Oriental statecraft.[2]

I have studied his character, and I have found certain contradictions which I cannot reconcile. For example, he has a minister who is only eighteen years old,[3] and a mistress who is fourscore;[4] he loves his religion, and yet he cannot abide those who assert that it ought to be strictly observed;[5] although he flies from the noise of cities, and is inclined to be reticent, from morning till night he is engaged in getting himself talked about; he is fond of trophies and victories, but he has as great a dread of seeing a good general at the head of his own troops, as at the head of an army of his enemies. It has never I believe happened to anyone but himself, to be burdened with more wealth than even a prince could hope for, and yet at the same time steeped in such poverty as a private person could ill brook.

He delights to reward those who serve him; but he pays as liberally the assiduous indolence of his courtiers, as the labours in the field of his captains; often the man who undresses him, or who hands him his serviette at table, is preferred before him who has taken cities and gained battles; he does not believe that the greatness of a monarch is compatible with restriction in the distribution of favours; and, without examining into the merit of a man, he will heap benefits upon him, believing that his selection makes the recipient worthy; accordingly, he has been known to bestow a small pension upon a man who had run off two leagues from the enemy, and a good government on another who had gone four.

Above all, he is magnificent in his buildings; there are more statues in his palace gardens[6] than there are citizens in a large town. His bodyguard is as strong as that of the prince before whom all the thrones of the earth tremble;[7] his armies are as numerous, his resources as great, and his finances as inexhaustible.

Paris, the 7th of the moon of Maharram, 1713.

DISCUSSION QUESTIONS

1. What contradictions does Usbek see in Louis's character, and what do they reveal about his method of rule?

---

[2] When Louis XIV. was in his sixteenth year, some courtiers discussed in his presence the absolute power of the Sultans, who dispose as they like of the goods and the lives of their subjects. "That is something like being a king," said the young monarch. Marshal d'Estrées, alarmed at the tendency revealed in that remark, rejoined, "But, sire, several of these emperors have been strangled even in my time."

[3] Barbezieux, son of Louvois, Louis's youngest minister, held office at twenty-three, not eighteen; and he was dead in 1713.

[4] Madame de Maintenon.

[5] The Jansenists.

[6] At Versailles.

[7] The Shah of Persia.

2. In what ways does this letter reflect Montesquieu's general interest in the foundation of good government?

3. Based on this letter, why do you think that scholars regard Montesquieu as a herald of the Enlightenment?

4
Mary Astell
Reflections upon Marriage
1706

Like Montesquieu, English author Mary Astell (1666–1731) helped to usher in the Enlightenment by surveying society with a critical eye. First published anonymously in 1700, Reflections upon Marriage *is one of her best-known books; it shows her keen interest in the institution of marriage, education, and relations between the sexes. Only the third edition (1706) divulged her gender, but still not her name. As the following excerpt reveals, Astell held a dim view of women's inequality in general and of their submissive role in marriage in particular. She argues that one should abhor the use of arbitrary power within the state, and so, too, within the family. Among the book's principal goals was to present spinsterhood as a viable alternative to marriage. Perhaps not surprisingly, Astell herself never married.*

These Reflections being made in the Country, where the Book that occasion'd them came but late to Hand, the *Reader* is desir'd to excuse their Unseasonableness as well as other Faults; and to believe that they have no other Design than to Correct some Abuses, which are not the less because Power and Prescription seem to Authorize them. If any are so needlessly curious as to enquire from what Hand they come, they may please to know, that it is not good Manners to ask, since the Title-Page does not tell them: We are all of us sufficiently Vain, and without doubt the Celebrated Name of *Author*, which most are so fond of, had not been avoided but for very good Reasons: To name but one; *Who will care to pull upon themselves an Hornet's nest?* 'Tis a very great Fault to regard rather who it is that Speaks, than what is Spoken; and either to submit to Authority, when we should only yield to Reason; or if Reason press too hard, to think to ward it off by Personal Objections and Reflections. Bold Truths may pass while the Speaker is Incognito, but are not endur'd when he is known; few Minds being strong enough to bear what Contradicts their Principles and Practices without Recriminating when they can. And tho' to tell the Truth be the most Friendly Office, yet whosoever is so hardy as to venture at it, shall be counted an Enemy for so doing.

Bridget Hill, ed., *The First English Feminist:* Reflections upon Marriage *and Other Writings by Mary Astell* (New York: St. Martin's Press, 1986), 69–76.

Thus far the old Advertisement, when the Reflections first appear'd, A.D.1700.

But the *Reflector*, who hopes *Reflector* is not bad English, now Governor is happily of the feminine Gender, had as good or better have said nothing; For People by being forbid, are only excited to a more curious Enquiry. A certain Ingenuous Gentleman (as she is inform'd) had the Good-Nature to own these Reflections, so far as to affirm that he had the Original M.S. in his Closet, a Proof she is not able to produce;[1] and so to make himself responsible for all their Faults, for which she returns him all due Acknowledgment. However, the Generality being of Opinion, that a Man would have had more Prudence and Manners than to have Publish'd such unseasonable Truths, or to have betray'd the *Arcana Imperii* of his Sex, she humbly confesses, that the Contrivance and Execution of this Design, which is unfortunately accus'd of being so destructive to the government, of the Men I mean, is entirely her own. She neither advis'd with Friends, nor turn'd over Antient or Modern Authors, nor prudently submitted to the Correction of such as are, or such as *think* they are good Judges, but with an *English* Spirit and Genius, set out upon the Forlorn Hope, meaning no hurt to any body, nor designing any thing but the Publick Good, and to retrieve, if possible, the Native Liberty, the Rights and Privileges of the Subject.

Far be it from her to stir up Sedition of any sort, none can abhor it more; and she heartily wishes that our Masters wou'd pay their Civil and Ecclesiastical Governors the same Submission, which they themselves extract from their Domestic Subjects. Nor can she imagine how she any way undermines the Masculine Empire, or blows the Trumpet of Rebellion to the Moiety of Mankind. Is it by exhorting Women, not to expect to have their own Will in any thing, but to be entirely Submissive, when once they have made choice of a Lord and Master, tho' he happen not to be so Wise, so Kind, or even so Just a Governor as was expected? She did not indeed advise them to think his Folly Wisdom, nor his Brutality that Love and Worship he promised in his Matrimonial Oath, for this required a Flight of Wit and Sense much above her poor Ability, and proper only to Masculine Understandings. However she did not in any manner prompt them to Resist, or to Abdicate the Perjur'd Spouse, tho' the Laws of GOD and the Land make special Provision for it, in a case wherein, as is to be fear'd, few Men can truly plead Not Guilty.

Tis true, thro' Want of Learning, and of that Superior Genius which Men as Men lay claim to, she was ignorant of the *Natural Inferiority* of our Sex, which our Masters lay down as a Self-Evident and Fundamental Truth.[2] She saw nothing in the Reason of Things, to make this either a Principle or a Conclusion, but much to the contrary; it being Sedition at least, if not Treason to assert it in this Reign. For if by the Natural Superiority of their Sex, they mean that every Man is

---

[1] Alas, Mary Astell never revealed the identity of this 'Ingenuous Gentleman'. [All notes are Hill's.]

[2] Possibly a reference to William Nichols, D.D., *The Duty of Inferiours Towards their Superiours in Five Practical Discourses*, 1701, in which he argued that man possesses "a higher state of natural perfection and dignity, and thereupon puts in a just claim of superiority, which everything which is of more worth has a right to, over that which has less" (pp. 87–88).

by Nature superior to every Woman, which is the obvious meaning, and that which must be stuck to if they would speak Sense, it wou'd be a Sin in *any* Woman to have Dominion over *any* Man, and the greatest Queen ought not to command but to obey her Footman, because no Municipal Laws can supersede or change the Law of Nature; so that if the dominion of the Men be such, the *Salique Law*, as unjust as *English Men* have ever thought it, ought to take place over all the Earth, and the most glorious Reigns in the *English, Danish, Castilian*, and other Annals, were wicked Violations of the Law of Nature!

If they mean that *some* Men are superior to *some* Women, this is no great Discovery; had they turn'd the Tables they might have seen that *some* Women are Superior to *some* Men. Or had they been pleased to remember their Oaths of Allegiance and Supremacy, they might have known that *One* Woman is superior to *All* the Men in these Nations, or else they have sworn to very little purpose. And it must not be suppos'd, that their Reason and Religion wou'd suffer them to take Oaths, contrary to the Law of Nature and Reason of things.

By all which it appears, that our Reflector's Ignorance is very pitiable, it may be her Misfortune but not her Crime, especially since she is willing to be better inform'd, and hopes she shall never be so obstinate as to shut her Eyes against the Light of Truth, which is not to be charg'd with Novelty, how late soever we may be bless'd with the Discovery. Nor can Error, be it as Antient as it may, ever plead Prescription against Truth. And since the only way to remove all Doubts, to answer all Objections, and to give the Mind entire Satisfaction, is not by *Affirming*, but by *Proving*, so that every one may see with their *own* Eyes, and Judge according to the best of their *own* Understandings, She hopes it is no Presumption to insist on this Natural Right of Judging for her self, and the rather, because by quitting it, we give up all the Means of Rational Conviction. Allow us then as many Glasses as you please to help our Sight, and as many good Arguments as you can afford to Convince our Understandings: But don't exact of us we beseech you, to affirm that we see such things as are only the Discovery of Men who have quicker Senses; or that we understand and Know what we have by Hearsay only, for to be so excessively Complaisant, is neither to see nor to understand.

That the Custom of the World has put Women, generally speaking, into a State of Subjection, is not deny'd; but the Right can no more be prov'd from the Fact, than the Predominancy of Vice can justifie it. A certain great Man has endeavour'd to prove by Reasons not contemptible, that in the Original State of things the Woman was the Superior, and that her Subjection to the Man is an Effect of the Fall, and the Punishment of her Sin. And that Ingenious Theorist Mr. *Whiston*[3] asserts, That before the Fall there was a greater equality between the two Sexes. However this be 'tis certainly no Arrogance in a Woman to conclude, that she was made for the Service of GOD, and that this is her End. Because GOD

---

[3] William Whiston (1667–1752), divine, mathematician and Newtonian. Author of many works including *A New Theory of the Earth* (1696). He succeeded Newton as the Lucasian Professor and did much to popularise Newton's ideas. In 1710 he was deprived of his chair for casting doubt on the doctrine of the Trinity.

made all Things for Himself, and a Rational Mind is too noble a Being to be Made for the Sake and Service of any Creature. The Service she at any time becomes oblig'd to pay to a Man, is only a Business by the Bye. Just as it may be any Man's Business and Duty to keep Hogs; he was not Made for this, but if he hires himself out to such an Employment, he ought conscientiously to perform it. Nor can anything be concluded to the contrary from St. *Paul's* Argument, *I Cor. II.* For he argues only for Decency and Order, according to the present Custom and State of things. Taking his Words strictly and literally, they prove too much, in that *Praying and Prophecying in the Church* are allow'd the Women, provided they do it with their Head Cover'd, as well as the Men; and no inequality can be inferr'd from hence, their Reverence to the Sacred Oracles who engage them in such Disputes. And therefore the blame be theirs, who have unnecessarily introduc'd them in the present Subject, and who by saying that the *Reflections* were not agreeable to Scripture, oblige the Reflector to shew that those who affirm it must either mistake her Meaning, or the Sense of Holy Scripture, or both, if they think what they say, and do not find fault merely because they resolve to do so. For had she ever writ any thing contrary to those sacred Truths, she wou'd be the first in pronouncing its Condemnation.

But what says the Holy Scripture? It speaks of Women as in a State of Subjection, and so it does of the *Jews* and *Christians* when under the Dominion of the *Chaldeans* and *Romans*, requiring of the one as well as of the other a quiet submission to them under whose Power they liv'd. But will any one say that these had a *Natural Superiority* and Right to Dominion? that they had a superior Understanding, or any Pre-eminence, except what their greater Strength acquir'd? Or that the other were subjected to their Adversaries for any other Reason but the Punishment of their sins, and in order to their Reformation? Or for the Exercise of their Vertue, and because the Order of the World and the Good of Society requir'd it?

If Mankind had never sinn'd, Reason wou'd always have been obey'd, there wou'd have been no struggle for Dominion, and Brutal Power wou'd not have prevail'd. But in the laps'd State of Mankind, and now that Men will not be guided by their Reason but by their Appetites, and do not what they *ought* but what they *can*, the Reason, or that which stands for it, the Will and Pleasure of the Governor is to be the Reason of those who will not be guided by their own, and must take place for Order's sake, altho' it shou'd not be conformable to right Reason. Nor can there be any Society great or little, from Empires down to private Families, with a last Resort, to determine the Affairs of that Society by an irresistible Sentence. Now unless this Supremacy be fix'd somewhere, there will be a perpetual Contention about it, such is the love of Dominion, and let the Reason of things be what it may, those who have least Force, or Cunning to supply it, will have the Disadvantage. So that since Women are acknowledg'd to have least Bodily strength, their being commanded to obey is in pure kindness to them and for their Quiet and Security, as well as for the Exercise of their Vertue. But does it follow that Domestic Governors have more Sense than their Subjects, any more than that other Governors have? We do not find that any Man thinks the worse of his own Understanding because another has superior Power; or concludes himself less capable of a Post of Honour and Authority, because he is not Prefer'd to it. How much time wou'd lie on Men's hands, how empty wou'd the Places of Concourse be, and how silent most Companies, did Men forbear to Censure their Governors, that is in effect to think themselves Wiser. Indeed Government wou'd be much more desirable than it is, did it invest the Possessor with a superior Understanding as well as Power. And if mere Power gives a Right to Rule, there can be no such thing as Usurpation; but a Highway-Man so long as he has strength to force, has also a Right to require our Obedience.

Again, if Absolute Sovereignty be not necessary in a State, how comes it to be so in a family? or if in a Family why not in a State; since no Reason can be alledg'd for the one that will not hold more strongly for the other? If the Authority of the Husband so far as it extends, is sacred and inalienable, why not of the Prince? The Domestic Sovereign is without Dispute Elected, and the Stipulations and Contract are mutual, is it not then partial in Men to the last degree, to contend for, and practise that Arbitrary Dominion in their Families, which they abhor and exclaim against in the State? For if Arbitrary Power is evil in itself, and an improper Method of Governing Rational and Free Agents, it ought not to be Practis'd any where; Nor is it less, but rather more mischievous in Families than in Kingdoms, by how much 100000 Tyrants are worse than one. What tho' a Husband can't deprive a Wife of Life without being responsible to the Law, he may however do what is much more grievous to a generous Mind, render Life miserable, for which she has no Redress, scarce Pity which is afforded to every other Complainant. It being thought a Wife's Duty to suffer everything without Complaint. *If all Men are born free*, how is it that all Women are born slaves? as they must be if the being subjected to the *inconstant, uncertain, unknown, arbitrary Will* of Men, be the *perfect Condition of Slavery?* and if the Essence of Freedom consists, as our Masters say it does, in having a *standing Rule to live by?* And why is Slavery so much condemn'd and strove against in one Case, and so highly applauded, and held so necessary and so sacred in another?

DISCUSSION QUESTIONS

1. According to Mary Astell, what is women's customary status in society, and why?
2. What evidence does Astell present to challenge this status?
3. What does the language Astell uses reveal about her style of thinking and basic intellectual beliefs?
4. Why do you think scholars characterize *Reflections upon Marriage* as a "feminist" work?

COMPARATIVE QUESTIONS

1. Both Louis XIV and Peter I have been described as "absolute" rulers. Do the documents support this claim? If so, how?
2. In what ways does Astell's discussion of the evils of arbitrary power foreshadow Montesquieu's concerns?
3. Although *Persian Letters* and *Equiano's Travels* belong to different literary genres, how do they adopt similar methods to describe eighteenth-century Europeans and their customs?

The Promise of Enlightenment
1740–1789

S UMMARY   The following documents allow us to hear some of the many voices of the Enlightenment, an intellectual and cultural movement in the eighteenth century that captured the minds of middle- and upper-class people across Europe and British North America. Enlightenment writers were united by their belief that reason was the key to humanity's advancement as the basis of truth, liberty, and justice. They cultivated and disseminated their ideals through letters, published works, and personal exchanges, particularly at gatherings known as *salons,* which were organized by upper-class women. By mid-century, people as diverse as the king of Prussia and a French artisan began to echo the Enlightenment principle that progress depended on destroying all barriers to reason, including religious intolerance. As the fourth document reveals, the Enlightenment's message spread further still into the North American colonies, where it had revolutionary consequences.

1
Marie-Thérèse Geoffrin and M. d'Alembert
The Salon of Madame Geoffrin
1765

From its beginnings as an intellectual movement against absolutism, the Enlightenment had become a formidable force of change by the mid-eighteenth century. The role of salons was crucial in this regard. By bringing innovative intellectuals, writers, and artists together in private homes on a regular basis, salons provided an arena for the discussion and dissemination of Enlightenment ideas. Madame Marie-Thérèse Geoffrin (1699–1777) presided over the most influential salon in Paris at the time, as described in the memoirs of a beneficiary of her patronage, M. d'Alembert. In addition to nurturing the intellectual scene in Paris, Madame de Geoffrin also cultivated it abroad by corresponding with important European leaders, including King

Stanislaw of Poland, to whom she wrote the following letter in 1765. Together, these two documents elucidate the life of a woman who was actively engaged in Enlightenment thinking.

Much has been said respecting Madame Geoffrin's goodness, to what a point it was active, restless, obstinate. But it has not been added, and which reflects the greatest honour upon her, that, as she advanced in years, this habit constantly increased. For the misfortune of society, it too often happens that age and experience produce a directly contrary effect, even in very virtuous characters, if virtue be not in them a powerful sentiment indeed, and of no common stamp. The more disposed they have been at first to feel kindness towards their fellow creatures, the more, finding daily their ingratitude, do they repent of having served them, and even consider it almost as a reproach to themselves to have loved them. Madame Geoffrin had learnt, from a more reflected study of mankind, from taking a view of them more *enlightened* by reason and justice, that they are more weak and vain than wicked; that we ought to compassionate their weakness, and bear with their vanity, that they may bear with ours. . . .

The passion of *giving*, which was an absolute necessity to her, seemed born with her, and tormented her, if I may say so, even from her earliest years. While yet a child, if she saw from the window any poor creature asking alms, she would throw whatever she could lay her hands upon to them; her bread, her linen, and even her clothes. She was often scolded for this *intemperance* of charity, sometimes even punished, but nothing could alter the disposition, she would do the same the very next day. . . .

Always occupied with those whom she loved, always anxious about them, she even anticipated every thing which might interrupt their happiness. A young man,[1] for whom she interested herself very much, who had till that moment been wholly absorbed in his studies, was suddenly seized with an unfortunate passion, which rendered study, and even life itself insupportable to him. She succeeded in curing him. Some time after she observed that the same young man, mentioned to her, with great interest, an amiable woman with whom he had recently become acquainted. Madame Geoffrin, who knew the lady, went to her. "I am come," she said, "to intreat a favour of you. Do not evince too much friendship for * * * * or too much desire to see him, he will be soon in love with you, he will be unhappy, and I shall be no less so to see him suffer; nay, you yourself will be a sufferer, from consciousness, of the sufferings you occasion him." This woman, who was truly amiable, promised what Madame Geoffrin desired, and kept her word.

As she had always among the circle of her society persons of the highest rank and birth, as she appeared even to seek an acquaintance with them, it was sup-

---

[1] This young man was M. d'Alembert himself.

Correspondance inédite du roi Stanislaw-Auguste Poniatowski et de Madame Geoffrin, ed. Charles de Nouy (Geneva: Satine, 1970; reprint of 1875 edition); trans. by Lynn Hunt as published in *Connecting with the Past,* 164–68.

posed that this flattered her vanity. But here a very erroneous opinion was formed of her; she was in no respect the dupe of such prejudices, but she thought that by managing the humours of these people, she could render them useful to her friends. "You think," said she, to one of the latter, for whom she had a particular regard, "that it is for my own sake I frequent ministers and great people. Undeceive yourself,—it is for the sake of you, and those like you who may have occasion for them. . . ."

Mme. Geoffrin Writes to the King of Poland

I am sending to you a banker named Claudel who is returning to Warsaw. He will have with him a printed memoir on a new kind of mill. The more I have learned about it, the more I see that this machine is very well-known. Your Majesty is best advised to invite a miller to come from France; he will know how to set it up and show how to use it, and use of it can spread from there.

Prince Sulkowski [a Polish nobleman] met Mr. Hennin at my salon. Mr. Hennin had been for a long time in Warsaw, and they talked together about Poland. I see with pain that it has a very bad government [Stanislaw was elected king only in 1764]; it seems almost impossible to make it better. . . .

I sent you the catalogue of the diamonds of Madame de Pompadour [King Louis XV's mistress had died recently and her diamonds were auctioned off]. . . .

Do not forget, my dear son, to send the memoir on commerce to Mr. Riancourt when he returns. . . .

I cannot report any news yet on your project for paintings; I am very sad about the death of poor Carle Vanloo [a leading French painter who died in July 1765]. It was a horrible loss for the arts.

DISCUSSION QUESTIONS

1. Based on these documents, how would you describe Madame Geoffrin's personality? In what ways was she "enlightened"?

2. What impressions do the documents give of her salon and how it functioned?

3. What does Madame Geoffrin's letter to the king of Poland suggest about the range of her interests? How was this typical of Enlightenment thinkers?

2

Frederick II
Political Testament
1752

The Enlightenment's triumph is perhaps best reflected in the politics of the second half of the eighteenth century. Rather than working to suppress the philosophes' calls for change, rulers across continental Europe now embraced them as a means of enhancing their power and prestige. They did so at their own discretion, however, and often with an iron hand, as the case of Frederick II of Prussia (r. 1740–1786) vividly reveals. A devotee of the Enlightenment as well as an exemplary soldier and statesman, Frederick transformed Prussia into a leading European state during his reign. In his Political Testament *of 1752, he outlines his political philosophy, which blended Enlightenment ideals with an uncompromising view of his own power.*

One must attempt, above all, to know the special genius of the people which one wants to govern in order to know if one must treat them leniently or severely, if they are inclined to revolt . . . to intrigue. . . .

[The Prussian nobility] has sacrificed its life and goods for the service of the state, its loyalty and merit have earned it the protection of all its rulers, and it is one of the duties [of the ruler] to aid those [noble] families which have become impoverished in order to keep them in possession of their lands: for they are to be regarded as the pedestals and the pillars of the state. In such a state no factions or rebellions need be feared . . . it is one goal of the policy of this state to preserve the nobility.

A well conducted government must have an underlying concept so well integrated that it could be likened to a system of philosophy. All actions taken must be well reasoned, and all financial, political and military matters must flow towards one goal: which is the strengthening of the state and the furthering of its power. However, such a system can flow but from a single brain, and this must be that of the sovereign. Laziness, hedonism and imbecility, these are the causes which restrain princes in working at the noble task of bringing happiness to their subjects . . . a sovereign is not elevated to his high position, supreme power has not been confined to him in order that he may live in lazy luxury, enriching himself by the labor of the people, being happy while everyone else suffers. The sovereign is the first servant of the state. He is well paid in order that he may sustain the dignity of his office, but one demands that he work efficiently for the good of the state, and that he, at the very least, pay personal attention to the most important problems. . . .

You can see, without doubt, how important it is that the King of Prussia govern personally. Just as it would have been impossible for Newton to arrive at his system of attractions if he had worked in harness with Leibnitz and Descartes, so a system of politics cannot be arrived at and continued if it has not sprung from a single brain. . . . All parts of the government are inexorably linked with each other. Finance, politics and military affairs are inseparable; it does not suffice that one be well administered; they must all be . . . a Prince who governs personally, who has formed his [own] political system, will not be handicapped when occasions arise where he has to act swiftly: for he can guide all matters towards the end which he has set for himself. . . .

Catholics, Lutherans, Reformed, Jews and other Christian sects live in this state, and live together in peace: if the sovereign, actuated by a mistaken zeal, de-

George L. Mosse, Rondo E. Cameron, Henry Bertram Hill, and Michael B. Petrovich, eds.; *Europe in Review* (Chicago: Rand McNally and Company, 1957), 111–12.

clares himself for one religion or another, parties will spring up, heated disputes ensue, little by little persecutions will commence and, in the end, the religion persecuted will leave the fatherland and millions of subjects will enrich our neighbors by their skill and industry.

It is of no concern in politics whether the ruler has a religion or whether he has none. All religions, if one examines them, are founded on superstitious systems, more or less absurd. It is impossible for a man of good sense, who dissects their contents, not to see their error; but these prejudices, these errors and mysteries were made for men, and one must know enough to respect the public and not to outrage its faith, whatever religion be involved.

DISCUSSION QUESTIONS

1. Based on this excerpt, in what ways does the term *enlightened despot* apply to Frederick II? How is he enlightened? How is he despotic?
2. What reasons does Frederick advance in favor of religious tolerance?
3. According to Frederick, what should the one goal of government be?

3

Jacques-Louis Ménétra
Journal of My Life
1764–1802

Although the philosophes *directed their message to the educated elite, Jacques-Louis Ménétra's* Journal of My Life *suggests that at least some people from the lower classes heard it, too. Born in Paris in 1738, Ménétra learned to read and write in local parish schools. Following his father's example, he became a master glazier. He begins his* Journal *in 1764 and organizes it principally around his recollections of his journeyman's "tour de France" from 1757 to 1764. Here he reveals not only his quick wit and sense of adventure, but also his affinity for the intellectual spirit of criticism that characterized the Enlightenment. As the following excerpt demonstrates, alongside the tales of his amusements, Ménétra commented on many of the fundamental issues of the day, including the question of religious tolerance. The excerpt is printed as it was originally written, without punctuation.*

I went to Paris to see Denongrais   Madame la Police had been interfering with business   she made up her mind to sell her property and to retire with her cuckold of a husband to her native village for she'd put by quite a bit in the course of her work   I was all for it   She said to me   I see clearly from what you've just said

Jacques-Louis Ménétra, *Journal of My Life*, intro. Daniel Roche, trans. Arthur Goldhammer (New York: Columbia University Press, 1986), 129–30.

that you never loved me She was right for never had a woman touched my heart except for sensual pleasure and nothing else I promised her to come say my farewells and they've yet to be said

Since it was the good season we went to Champigny and went with some friends of mine to what are called *guinguettes* [open-air cafés with music and dancing—Trans.] Sundays and holidays we went to dance in front of the castle and other days usually with the people from the *guinguette* we played tennis or went visiting the local festivals One holiday in a village one league from Montigny people were playing tennis on the square when Du Tillet showed up accompanied by the lord the magistrate or sheriff and the priest I heard somebody say That's the Parisian over there I wondered what this was all about It's because they know you're good at tennis said my friend they're going to propose a match In fact six young men came and politely gave each of us a racket My friend said no since he didn't know how to play but he said But as for my friend he'll give you a good show I declined They insisted the lord the sheriff and the priest joined in I played applause hands were heard to clap They took us to the castle (and) gave us refreshment

I was greatly applauded I promised again that the fellows from Montigny and I would be waiting for them next Sunday People came from all around I was all over the court and we had a good time we won and whatever else they were well entertained My friend went all out because M Trudaine had wanted to see me play and when I passed in front of him he and the people around him said to me Courage So I answered that that was one thing I wasn't lacking

One day I followed the game warden Since I had no rifle I let him run all over the fields and went to a village where I had seen the curate pay his respects to M Trudaine who recognized me and said I was pretty nimble at tennis and took me to his presbytery for a drink

After some idle talk we finally got onto the subject of religion We talked about the mysteries of the sacraments. . . . I spoke passionately about the sufferings that had been inflicted on men who worshiped the same God except for a few matters of opinion And (I said that) the Roman religion should be tolerant if it followed the maxims of its lawgiver that because of its mysteries it was absurd and that all mysteries were in my opinion nothing but lies And that so long as they sold indulgences and gave remission for sins in exchange for money fear of hell which was like purgatory just an invention of the first impostors that Jesus had never spoken of purgatory And that all those sacraments were nothing but pure inventions to make money and impress the vulgar And that he himself who was a very intelligent man was not capable of making his God chewing him and then swallowing him That we mistreated those peoples who did not share our belief (and who) according to the Church should have been damned because all the priests went around saying Outside the Church there is no salvation And that we accused those who worship idols of being idolators when we prostrate ourselves before statues We even worship a piece of dough which we eat in the firm belief that it is God And those idolators only worship all those things to keep from being hurt by them and other things in the hope of getting some good out of them while we on the other hand we were real man-eaters After praying to him and worshipping him in order to satisfy him we've got to eat him too

He answered me with objections as many others had answered me His one and only response was to say to me All these mysteries must be believed because the Church believes them he said to me My friend you are enlightened It is necessary that for the sake of government nations live always in ignorance and credulity I answered him So be it. . . .

DISCUSSION QUESTIONS

1. Why is Ménétra so critical of the Catholic Church?
2. How do his criticisms echo those of the great Enlightenment thinkers?
3. What does the priest mean when he describes Ménétra as enlightened?
4. How would you characterize Ménétra's style of writing?

4

Thomas Jefferson
Letter to Colonel Edward Carrington
1787

Even while calling for change, the philosophes *preferred to work within established institutions rather than abolish them altogether. Nonetheless, their ideals could have a revolutionary impact, as they did in Britain's North American colonies. Since the early 1760s, many colonists had come increasingly to resent British rule and turned to Enlightenment writings to build a case for independence. Tensions came to a head in 1775, and war quickly ensued. In 1783, Britain declared defeat, and the American republic was born. Deeply imbued with Enlightenment thought, Thomas Jefferson (1743–1826) was an eloquent spokesman of the fledgling nation as it struggled to craft a government that would preserve the achievements of the revolution without undermining its principles. He wrote the following letter while serving as minister to France at the very moment this struggle was unfolding. In this letter, he echoes Jean-Jacques Rousseau's belief that government should derive its authority from the people— an idea that would soon be enshrined in the Preamble to the U.S. Constitution.*

The tumults in America I expected would have produced in Europe an unfavorable opinion of our political state. But it has not. On the contrary, the small effect of these tumults seems to have given more confidence in the firmness of our governments. The interposition of the people themselves on the side of government has had a great effect on the opinion here. I am persuaded myself that the good sense of the people will always be found to be the best army. They may be led astray for a moment, but will soon correct themselves. The people are the only

Albert Ellery Bergh, ed., *The Writings of Thomas Jefferson,* Vol. VI (Washington, D.C.: The Thomas Jefferson Memorial Association, 1907), 57–59.

censors of their governors; and even their errors will tend to keep these to the true principles of their institution. To punish these errors too severely would be to suppress the only safeguard of the public liberty. The way to prevent these irregular interpositions of the people, is to give them full information of their affairs through the channel of the public papers, and to contrive that those papers should penetrate the whole mass of the people. The basis of our governments being the opinion of the people, the very first object should be to keep that right; and were it left to me to decide whether we should have government without newspapers, or newspapers without a government, I should not hesitate a moment to prefer the latter. But I should mean that every man should receive those papers, and be capable of reading them. I am convinced that those societies (as the Indians) which live without government, enjoy in their general mass an infinitely greater degree of happiness than those who live under the European governments. Among the former, public opinion is in the place of law, and restrains morals as powerfully as laws ever did anywhere. Among the latter, under pretence of governing, they have divided their nations into two classes, wolves and sheep. I do not exaggerate. This is a true picture of Europe. Cherish, therefore, the spirit of our people, and keep alive their attention. Do not be too severe upon their errors, but reclaim them by enlightening them. If once they become inattentive to the public affairs, you and I, and Congress and Assemblies, Judges and Governors, shall all become wolves. It seems to be the law of our general nature, in spite of individual exceptions; and experience declares that man is the only animal which devours his own kind; for I can apply no milder term to the governments of Europe, and to the general prey of the rich on the poor. The want of news has led me into disquisition instead of narration, forgetting you have every day enough of that. I shall be happy to hear from you sometimes, only observing that whatever passes through the post is read, and that when you write what should be read by myself only, you must be so good as to confide your letter to some passenger, or officer of the packet. I will ask your permission to write to you sometimes, and to assure you of the esteem and respect with which I have honor to be, dear Sir, your most obedient, and most humble servant.

DISCUSSION QUESTIONS
1. Why is Jefferson so critical of European governments?
2. What role does Jefferson think the people should play in government, and why?
3. According to Jefferson, why are newspapers especially important to this role?

COMPARATIVE QUESTIONS
1. How do Ménétra's and Frederick II's attitudes toward organized religion overlap?
2. What similarities and differences do you see between Frederick II's and Jefferson's views on the basis of good government?
3. What do both Madame Geoffrin and Jefferson reveal about the means by which Enlightenment ideas spread? Why is this significant to understanding the Enlightenment's development?

The Cataclysm of Revolution
1789–1800

S U M M A R Y   When the Estates General convened at Versailles in May 1789, no one could have foreseen what lie ahead: ten years of upheaval that established the model of modern revolution and set the course of modern politics. The following documents illuminate the French Revolution in the making, from the politically charged months preceding the convocation of the Estates General to the formation of a republic and a government of terror designed to destroy enemies of the Revolution from both within and without. At each stage, the revolutionaries remained committed to the Enlightenment principle of using reason to reshape society and government. Even so, they were not always in control of events either in France or beyond, as peasants, working-class city folk, and even slaves from the French colony of Saint Domingue (modern-day Haiti) rose up with their own demands, taking the Revolution in even more radical directions.

1
Abbé Sieyès
What Is the Third Estate?
1789

Although in 1788 Louis XVI agreed to call the Estates General, he left a thorny procedural question for the deputies to answer: Would the assembly vote by order or by head? The debate over this question galvanized the nation in the months preceding the opening of the Estates General in May 1789, thanks in part to pamphlets like the one that follows. Written by a middle-class clergyman, Abbé Emmanuel Joseph Sieyès (1748–1836), this pamphlet's message was clear: the privileged few should not determine the nation's future, as a traditional vote by order would ensure by allowing the clergy and nobility to join forces to block any decision contrary to their liking. Rather, government should rest in the hands of the people whose labor and skills sustain society, the Third Estate. In forging his argument, Sieyès forcefully condemned traditional political and social structures while granting the Third Estate a voice on the national stage.

The plan of this work is quite simple. We must ask ourselves three questions.

1. What is the Third Estate? Everything.
2. What has it been until now in the political order? Nothing.
3. What does it want? To become something. . . .

What does a Nation require to survive and prosper? *Private* employment and *public* offices.

Private employment includes four classes of work:

1. Since the land and water provide the raw material for the needs of mankind, the first class, in logical order, includes all those families attached to work in the countryside.

2. Between the initial sale of raw materials and their consumption or usage as finished goods, labor of various sorts adds more value to these goods. In this way human industry manages to improve on the blessings of Nature and to multiply the value of the raw materials two, ten, or a hundredfold. Such is the second class of work.

3. Between production and consumption, as also between the different stages of production, there are a host of intermediary agents, useful both to producers and consumers; these are the merchants and wholesale traders. Wholesale traders constantly weigh demand according to place and time and speculate on the profit that they can make on storage and transport; merchants actually sell the goods on the markets, whether wholesale or retail. This type of utility designates the third class of work.

4. Besides these three classes of hard-working and useful Citizens who occupy themselves with the *things* fit to be consumed or used, society also needs a multitude of private occupations and services *directly* useful or agreeable to the *person*. This fourth class embraces all those occupations from the most distinguished scientific and liberal professions down to the least esteemed domestic servants.

These are the kinds of work that sustain society. Who carries them out? The Third Estate.

Lynn Hunt, ed. and trans., *The French Revolution and Human Rights: A Brief Documentary History* (Boston: Bedford/St. Martin's, 1996), 65–70.

In the present state of affairs public offices can also be ranked in four well-known categories: the Sword [the army], the Robe [the courts], the Church, and the Administration. Detailed analysis is not necessary to show that the Third Estate makes up everywhere $\frac{19}{20}$ths of their number, except that it is charged with all the really hard work, all the work that the privileged order refuses to perform. Only the lucrative and most honored places are taken by the members of the privileged order. Should we praise them for this? We could do so only if the Third [Estate] was unwilling or unable to fill these offices. We know the truth of the matter, but the Third Estate has nonetheless been excluded. They are told, "Whatever your services, whatever your talents, you will only go so far and no further. Honors are not for your sort." A few rare exceptions, noteworthy as they are bound to be, are only a mockery, and the language encouraged on these exceptional occasions is but an additional insult.

If this exclusion is a social crime committed against the Third Estate, can we say at least that it is useful to the public good? Ah! Are the effects of monopoly now known? If it discourages those whom it pushes aside, does it not also render those it favors less competent? Is it not obvious that every piece of work kept out of free competition will be made more expensively and less well?

When any office is deemed the prerogative of a separate order among the citizens, has no one noticed that a salary has to be paid not only to the man who does the work but also to all those of the same caste who do not and even to entire families of both those who work and those who do not? Has no one noticed that this state of affairs, so abjectly respected among us, nonetheless seems contemptible and shameful in the history of ancient Egypt and in the stories of voyages to the Indies? But let us leave aside those considerations which though broadening our purview and perhaps enlightening would only slow our pace. It suffices here to have made the point that the supposed usefulness of a privileged order to the public service is nothing but a mirage; that without that order, all that is most arduous in this service is performed by the Third Estate; that without the privileged the best places would be infinitely better filled; that such places should naturally be the prize and reward for recognized talents and services; and that if the privileged have succeeded in usurping all the lucrative and honored posts, this is at once an odious iniquity committed against the vast majority of the citizenry and an act of treason against the public good.

Who therefore dares to say that the Third Estate does not contain within itself all that is needed to form a complete Nation? The Third Estate is like a strong and robust man with one arm still in chains. If we remove the privileged order, the Nation will not be something less but something more. Thus, what is the Third Estate? All, but an all that is shackled and oppressed. What would it be without the privileged order? All, but an all that is free and flourishing. Nothing can be done without it [the Third Estate]; everything would be infinitely better without the other two orders.

It does not suffice to have demonstrated that the privileged, far from being useful to the Nation, can only weaken and harm it; it must be proved further that the noble order[1] is not even part of society itself: It may very well be a burden for the Nation but it cannot be a part of it.

First, it is not possible to assign a place to the caste of nobles among the many elements that make up a Nation. I know that there are too many individuals whose infirmities, incapacity, incurable laziness, or excessively bad morals make them essentially foreigners to the work of society. The exception and the abuse always accompany the rule, especially in a vast empire. But at least we can agree that the fewer the abuses, the better ordered the state. The worst-off state of all would be the one in which not only isolated individual cases but also an entire class of citizens would glory in inactivity amidst the general movement and would contrive to consume the best part of what is produced without having contributed anything to its making. Such a class is surely foreign to the Nation because of its *idleness*.

The noble order is no less foreign amongst us by reason of its *civil* and *public* prerogatives.

What is a Nation? A body of associates living under a *common* law and represented by the same *legislature*.

Is it not more than certain that the noble order has privileges, exemptions, and even rights that are distinct from the rights of the great body of citizens? Because of this, it does not belong to the common order, it is not covered by the law common to the rest. Thus its civil rights already make it a people apart inside the great Nation. It is truly *imperium in imperio* [a law unto itself].

As for its *political* rights, the nobility also exercises them separately. It has its own representatives who have no mandate from the people. Its deputies sit separately, and even when they assemble in the same room with the deputies of the ordinary citizens, the nobility's representation still remains essentially distinct and separate: it is foreign to the Nation by its very principle, for its mission does not emanate from the people, and by its purpose, since in consists in defending, not the general interest, but the private interests of the nobility.

The Third Estate therefore contains everything that pertains to the Nation and nobody outside of the Third Estate can claim to be part of the Nation. What is the Third Estate? EVERYTHING. . . .

---

[1] [Sieyès's own note] I do not speak of the clergy here. In my way of thinking, the clergy is not an order but rather a profession charged with a public service. In the clergy, it is not the person who is privileged but the office, which is very different. . . . The word caste refers to a class of men who, without functions and without usefulness and by the sole fact that they exist, enjoy the privileges attached to their person. From this point of view, which is the true one in my opinion, there is only one order, that of the nobility. They are truly a people apart but a false people, which not being able to exist by itself by reason of its lack of useful organs, attaches itself to a real Nation like those plant growths which can only survive on the sap of the plants that they tire and suck dry. The Clergy, the Robe, the Sword, and the Administration are four classes of public trustees that are necessary everywhere. Why are they accused in France of *aristocraticism?* It is because the noble caste has usurped all the good positions; it has done so as if this was a patrimonial property exploited for its personal profit rather than in the spirit of social welfare.

By Third Estate is meant the collectivity of citizens who belong to the common order. Anybody who holds a legal privilege of any kind leaves that common order, stands as an exception to the common law, and in consequence does not belong to the Third Estate. . . . It is certain that the moment a citizen acquires privileges contrary to common law, he no longer belongs to the common order. His new interest is opposed to the general interest; he has no right to vote in the name of the people. . . .

What is the will of a Nation? It is the result of individual wills, just as the Nation is the aggregate of the individuals who compose it. It is impossible to conceive of a legitimate association that does not have for its goal the common security, the common liberty, in short, the public good. No doubt each individual also has his own personal aims. He says to himself, "protected by the common security, I will be able to peacefully pursue my own personal projects, I will seek my happiness where I will, assured of encountering only those legal obstacles that society will prescribe for the common interest, in which I have a part and with which my own personal interest is so usefully allied." . . .

Advantages which differentiate citizens from one another lie outside the purview of citizenship. Inequalities of wealth or ability are like the inequalities of age, sex, size, etc. In no way do they detract from the *equality* of citizenship. These individual advantages no doubt benefit from the protection of the law; but it is not the legislator's task to create them, to give privileges to some and refuse them to others. The law grants nothing; it protects what already exists until such time that what exists begins to harm the common interest. These are the only limits on individual freedom. I imagine the law as being at the center of a large globe; we the citizens, without exception, stand equidistant from it on the surface and occupy equal places; all are equally dependent on the law, all present it with their liberty and their property to be protected; and this is what I call the *common rights* of citizens, by which they are all alike. All these individuals communicate with each other, enter into contracts, negotiate, always under the common guarantee of the law. If in this general activity somebody wishes to get control over the person of his neighbor or usurp his property, the common law goes into action to repress this criminal attempt and puts everyone back in their place at the same distance from the law. . . .

It is impossible to say what place the two privileged orders ought to occupy in the social order: this is the equivalent of asking what place one wishes to assign to a malignant tumor that torments and undermines the strength of the body of a sick person. It must be *neutralized*. We must re-establish the health and working of all the organs so thoroughly that they are no longer susceptible to these fatal schemes that are capable of sapping the most essential principles of vitality.

DISCUSSION QUESTIONS

1. What is the traditional status of the Third Estate? How does Sieyès want to change it, and why?
2. Why is Sieyès so critical of nobility in particular?
3. What do these criticisms reveal about his political principles?
4. How effective do you think this pamphlet is as a work of political propaganda, and why?

2

National Assembly
The Declaration of the Rights of Man and of the Citizen
1789

Promulgated by the fledgling National Assembly in August 1789, The Declaration of the Rights of Man and of the Citizen *gave the Revolution a clear sense of purpose and direction after the dizzying series of events of that summer. In it, the delegates set forth the guiding principles of the new government, echoing many of the ideals of influential eighteenth-century thinkers. The document also marked the definitive end of the old regime by presenting the protection of individual rights, not royal prerogative, as the cornerstone of political authority. The deputies did not regard the declaration as an end in and of itself, however, but rather as a preliminary step toward their primary goal: to write a constitution for the country that would transform it into an enlightened constitutional monarchy. This goal was met with the Constitution of 1791, to which the declaration was attached.*

The representatives of the French people, organized as a National Assembly, believing that the ignorance, neglect, or contempt of the rights of man are the sole cause of public calamities and of the corruption of governments, have determined to set forth in a solemn declaration the natural, inalienable, and sacred rights of man, in order that this declaration, being constantly before all the members of the social body, shall remind them continually of their rights and duties; in order that the acts of the legislative power, as well as those of the executive power, may be compared at any moment with the objects and purposes of all political institutions and may thus be more respected; and, lastly, in order that the grievances of the citizens, based hereafter upon simple and incontestable principles, shall tend to the maintenance of the constitution and redound to the happiness of all. Therefore the National Assembly recognizes and proclaims, in the presence and under the auspices of the Supreme Being, the following rights of man and of the citizen:

Article 1. Men are born and remain free and equal in rights. Social distinctions may be founded only upon the general good.

2. The aim of all political association is the preservation of the natural and imprescriptible rights of man. These rights are liberty, property, security, and resistance to oppression.

3. The principle of all sovereignty resides essentially in the nation. No body nor individual may exercise any authority which does not proceed directly from the nation.

James Harvey Robinson, *Readings in European History,* Vol. II (Boston: Ginn and Company, 1906), 409–11.

4. Liberty consists in the freedom to do everything which injures no one else; hence the exercise of the natural rights of each man has no limits except those which assure to the other members of the society the enjoyment of the same rights. These limits can only be determined by law.

5. Law can only prohibit such actions as are hurtful to society. Nothing may be prevented which is not forbidden by law, and no one may be forced to do anything not provided for by law.

6. Law is the expression of the general will. Every citizen has a right to participate personally, or through his representative, in its formation. It must be the same for all, whether it protects or punishes. All citizens, being equal in the eyes of the law, are equally eligible to all dignities and to all public positions and occupations, according to their abilities, and without distinction except that of their virtues and talents.

7. No person shall be accused, arrested, or imprisoned except in the cases and according to the forms prescribed by law. Any one soliciting, transmitting, executing, or causing to be executed, any arbitrary order, shall be punished. But any citizen summoned or arrested in virtue of the law shall submit without delay, as resistance constitutes an offense.

8. The law shall provide for such punishments only as are strictly and obviously necessary, and no one shall suffer punishment except it be legally inflicted in virtue of a law passed and promulgated before the commission of the offense.

9. As all persons are held innocent until they shall have been declared guilty, if arrest shall be deemed indispensable, all harshness not essential to the securing of the prisoner's person shall be severely repressed by law.

10. No one shall be disquieted on account of his opinions, including his religious views, provided their manifestation does not disturb the public order established by law.

11. The free communication of ideas and opinions is one of the most precious of the rights of man. Every citizen may, accordingly, speak, write, and print with freedom, but shall be responsible for such abuses of this freedom as shall be defined by law.

12. The security of the rights of man and of the citizen requires public military forces. These forces are, therefore, established for the good of all and not for the personal advantage of those to whom they shall be intrusted.

13. A common contribution is essential for the maintenance of the public forces and for the cost of administration. This should be equitably distributed among all the citizens in proportion to their means.

14. All the citizens have a right to decide, either personally or by their representatives, as to the necessity of the public contribution; to grant this freely; to know to what uses it is put; and to fix the proportion, the mode of assessment and of collection and the duration of the taxes.

15. Society has the right to require of every public agent an account of his administration.

16. A society in which the observance of the law is not assured, nor the separation of powers defined, has no constitution at all.

17. Since property is an inviolable and sacred right, no one shall be deprived thereof except where public necessity, legally determined, shall clearly demand it, and then only on condition that the owner shall have been previously and equitably indemnified.

DISCUSSION QUESTIONS

1. In delineating the rights of the individual, how did the National Assembly respond to Enlightenment writers' calls for reforms?
2. According to the document, what are the fundamental roles of government and the individual citizen?
3. How does the document define political sovereignty, and how is this definition related to the deputies' collective sense of identity and purpose?

3

Olympe de Gouges
Letters on the Trial
1793

Despite the momentous events of the first two years of the Revolution, even more radical changes were yet to come. With pressures mounting at home and the threat of war looming abroad, in 1792 the National Convention abolished the monarchy and established the first French republic. A year later the government instituted a set of policies known as the "Terror" to crush all its enemies. The following excerpts from the trial record of French author and activist Olympe de Gouges illuminate the instruments and ideals of the Terror in action. De Gouges, the daughter of a butcher, had already gained fame by protesting women's exclusion from full political participation in the Revolution in her 1791 tract, Declaration of the Rights of Woman. *In 1793, she aimed the power of her pen at the Terror. Having caught the attention of the police, de Gouges was imprisoned, and upon her interrogation before the Revolutionary Tribunal in November, she met the same fate as thousands of others at the time: death by guillotine.*

Audience of . . . 12 Brumaire, Year II of the Republic.
Case of Olympe de Gouges.

Questioned concerning her name, surname, age, occupation, place of birth, and residence. Replied that her name was Marie Olympe de Gouges, age thirty-eight, *femme de lettres*, a native of Montauban, living in Paris, rue du Harlay, Section Pont-Neuf.

Darline Gay Levy, Harriet Branson Applewhite, Mary Durham Johnson, eds. and trans., *Women in Revolutionary Paris, 1789–1795* (Urbana: University of Illinois Press, 1979), 255–59.

The clerk read the act of accusation, the tenor of which follows.

Antoine-Quentin Fouquier-Tinville, public prosecutor before the Revolutionary Tribunal, etc.

States that, by an order of the administrators of police, dated last July 25, signed Louvet and Baudrais, it was ordered that Marie Olympe de Gouges, widow of Aubry, charged with having composed a work contrary to the expressed desire of the entire nation, and directed against whoever might propose a form of government other than that of a republic, one and indivisible, be brought to the prison called l'Abbaye, and that the documents be sent to the public prosecutor of the Revolutionary Tribunal. Consequently, the accused was brought to the designated prison and the documents delivered to the public prosecutor on July 26. The following August 6, one of the judges of the Revolutionary Tribunal proceeded with the interrogation of the above-mentioned de Gouges woman.

From the examination of the documents deposited, together with the interrogation of the accused, it follows that against the desire manifested by the majority of Frenchmen for republican government, and in contempt of laws directed against whoever might propose another form of government, Olympe de Gouges composed and had printed works which can only be considered as an attack on the sovereignty of the people because they tend to call into question that concerning which it [the people] formally expressed its desire; that in her writing, entitled *Les Trois urnes, ou le Salut de la patrie*, there can be found the project of the liberty-killing faction which wanted to place before the people the approbation of the judgment of the tyrant condemned by the people itself; that the author of this work openly provoked civil war and sought to arm citizens against one another by proposing the meeting of primary assemblies to deliberate and express their desire concerning either monarchical government, which the national sovereignty had abolished and proscribed; concerning the one and indivisible republican [form], which it had chosen and established by the organ of its representatives; or, finally, concerning the federative [form], which would be the source of incalculable evils and which would destroy liberty infallibly.

. . . The public prosecutor stated next that it is with the most violent indignation that one hears the de Gouges woman say to men who for the past four years have not stopped making the greatest sacrifices for liberty; who on August 10, 1792, overturned both the throne and the tyrant; who knew how to bravely face the arms and frustrate the plots of the despot, his slaves, and the traitors who had abused the public confidence—to men who have submitted tyranny to the avenging blade of the law—that Louis Capet[1] still reigns among them.

There can be no mistaking the perfidious intentions of this criminal woman, and her hidden motives, when one observes her in all the works to which, at the very least, she lends her name, calumniating and spewing out bile in large doses against the warmest friends of the people, their most intrepid defender. . . .

---

[1] **Louis Capet:** Louis XVI

On the basis of the foregoing exposé the public prosecutor drew up this accusation against Marie Olympe de Gouges, widow Aubry, for having maliciously and purposefully composed writings attacking the sovereignty of the people (whose desire, when these were written, had been pronounced for republican government, one and indivisible) and tending towards the reestablishment of the monarchical government (which it [the people] had formally proscribed) as well as the federative [form] (against which it [the people] had forcefully protested); for having had printed up and distributed several copies of one of the cited works tending towards these ends, entitled, *Les Trois urnes, ou le Salut de la patrie*; for having been stopped in her distribution of a greater number of copies as well as in her posting of the cited work only by the refusal of the bill-poster and by her prompt arrest; for having sent this work to her son, employed in the army of the Vendée as *officier de l'état major*; for having, in other manuscripts and printed works—notably, in the manuscript entitled *La France sauvée, ou le Tyran détrôné* as well as in the poster entitled *Olympe de Gouges au Tribunal Révolutionnaire*—sought to degrade the constituted authorities, calumniate the friends and defenders of the people and of liberty, and spread defiance among the representatives and the represented, which is contrary to the laws. . . .

Consequently, the public prosecutor asks that he be given official notice by the assembled Tribunal of this indictment, etc., etc.

In this case only three witnesses were heard, one of whom was the citizen bill-poster, who stated that, having been asked to post a certain number of copies of printed material with the title *Les Trois urnes*, he refused when he found out about the principles contained in this writing.

When the accused was questioned sharply about when she composed this writing, she replied that it was some time last May, adding that what motivated her was that seeing the storms arising in a large number of *départements* . . . she had the idea of bringing all parties together by leaving them all free in the choice of the kind of government which would be most suitable for them; that furthermore, her intentions had proven that she had in view only the happiness of her country.

Questioned about how it was that she, the accused, who believed herself to be such a good patriot, had been able to develop, in the month of June, means which she called conciliatory concerning a fact which could not longer be in question because the people, at that period, had formally pronounced for republican government, one and indivisible, she replied that this was also the [form of government] she had voted for as the preferable one; that for a long while she had professed only republican sentiments. . . .

Asked to declare whether she acknowledged authorship of a manuscript work found among her papers entitled *La France sauvée ou le Tyran détrôné*, she replied yes.

Asked why she had placed injurious and perfidious declamations against the most ardent defenders of the rights of the people in the mouth of the person who in this work was supposed to represent the Capet woman,[2] she replied that she

---

[2] **Capet woman:** Marie Antoinette

had the Capet woman speaking the language appropriate for her; that besides, the handbill for which she was brought before the Tribunal had never been posted; that to avoid compromising herself she had decided to send twenty-four copies to the Committee of Public Safety, which, two days later, had her arrested.

The public prosecutor pointed out to the accused, concerning this matter, that if her placard entitled *Les Trois urnes* had not been made public, this was because the bill-poster had not been willing to take it upon himself. The accused was in agreement with this fact.

Questioned about whether, since her detention, she had not sent a copy to her son along with a letter, she said that the fact was exact and that her intention concerning this matter had been to apprise him of the cause of her arrest; that besides, she did not know whether her son had received it, not having heard from him in a long while and not knowing at all what could have become of him.

Asked to speak concerning various phrases in the placard entitled *Olympe de Gouges, défenseur de Louis Capet*, a work written by her at the time of the former's trial, and concerning the placard entitled *Olympe de Gouges au Tribunal Révolutionnaire* as well, she responded only with oratorical phrases and persisted in saying that she was and always had been a good *citoyenne*, that she had never intrigued.

Asked to express herself and to reply precisely concerning her sentiments with respect to the faithful representatives of the people whom she had insulted and calumniated in her writings, the accused replied that she had not changed, that she still held to her same opinion concerning them, and that she had looked upon them as ambitious persons.

In her defense the accused said that she had ruined herself in order to propagate the principles of the Revolution and that she was the founder of popular societies of her sex, etc.

During the résumé of the charge brought by the public prosecutor, the accused, with respect to the facts she was hearing articulated against her, never stopped her smirking. Sometimes she shrugged her shoulders; then she clasped her hands and raised her eyes towards the ceiling of the room; then, suddenly, she moved on to an expressive gesture, showing astonishment; then gazing next at the court, she smiled at the spectators, etc.

Here is the judgment rendered against her.

The Tribunal, based on the unanimous declaration of the jury, stating that (1) it is a fact that there exist in the case writings tending towards the reestablishment of a power attacking the sovereignty of the people [and] (2) that Marie Olympe de Gouges, calling herself widow Aubry, is proven guilty of being the author of these writings, and admitting the conclusions of the public prosecutor, condemns the aforementioned Marie Olympe de Gouges, widow Aubry, to the punishment of death in conformity with Article One of the law of last March 29, which was read, which is conceived as follows: "Whoever is convicted of having composed or printed works or writings which provoke the dissolution of the national representation, the reestablishment of royalty, or of any other power attacking the sovereignty of the people, will be brought before the Revolutionary

Tribunal and punished by death," and declares the goods of the aforementioned Marie Olympe de Gouges acquired for the republic. . . .

. . . The execution took place the same day [13 Brumaire] towards 4 P.M.; while mounting the scaffold, the condemned, looking at the people, cried out: "Children of the Fatherland, you will avenge my death." Universal cries of "Vive la République" were heard among the spectators waving hats in the air.

DISCUSSION QUESTIONS

1. What was the basis of the charges against de Gouges?
2. What do these charges and the ensuing judgment reveal about the political principles of the Terror?
3. How were these ideals at odds with those of de Gouges?
4. Do you think that de Gouges's gender influenced the tribunal's attitudes toward her?

4

François Dominique Toussaint L'Ouverture
Revolution in the Colonies
1794–1795

In declaring that all men are born free and equal, the National Convention unleashed a debate with momentous consequences. Did blacks fall within the category of "all men"? This question proved explosive in the French colony of Saint Domingue. News of the Revolution's progress traveled quickly to the island, prompting slaves in the north to launch an insurrection against their white masters in August 1791. Their revolt sparked more than a decade of war. The former slave François Dominique Toussaint L'Ouverture (1743–1803) became the most prominent black leader of the revolution. Allied first with Spain in 1793, which controlled much of the island, he and his troops joined the French the following year, for reasons he explained in the letter excerpted here to the chief French commander in northern Saint Domingue. The letter is followed by extracts from two proclamations made by Toussaint to local dissenters in 1795 that further illuminate his revolutionary principles and actions.

Toussaint L'Ouverture to General Etienne Laveaux
May 1794

It is very true, general, that I was led into error by the enemies of the Republic [of France] and of mankind, but who is the man who can hope to avoid all the traps of the wicked? Indeed, I fell into their nets, but not without reason . . . the Spanish

Gérard M. Laurent, *Toussaint L'Ouverture à travers sa correspondance (1794–1798)* (Madrid, 1953), 103–04, 169–72. Translated by Katharine J. Lualdi.

offered me their protection, and freedom for all those who fought for the kings' cause[1]; and having always fought to possess this same freedom, I clung to their offer, seeing myself abandoned by the French, my brothers.[2] But an experience a little later opened my eyes to these treacherous protectors; and being aware of their deceit and villainy, I saw clearly that their intentions were to make us cut each other's throats in order to reduce our numbers and oppress those remaining in chains and cause them to sink back into their former slavery. No, they never would reach their base goal! And in our turn we will avenge ourselves of these wretched beings in every respect. Thus let us unite forever and, forgetting the past, henceforth concern ourselves only with crushing our enemies. . . .

Toussaint L'Ouverture to the French Citizens
Encamped in Motet
March 1795

Frenchmen, the alarm rings, wake up, return from the deadly errors where you have been thrown; the opportunity for it is offered to you for the last time. The chains of the despot of England were not made for you; recover your dignity as French citizens, recover your national character. The heroic trumpet must have instructed you about the great feats of your country, which is cloaked in glory before the eyes of the universe. I was sent by Laveaux . . . to bring you words of peace. If, cured by time and experience, you return under the benevolent laws of the Republic, say the word, and nothing will be neglected to spare you from the deplorable fate which awaits you if you persist in your dreadful rebellion.

I exhort you to return to the nation . . . Like all republicans, I am motivated by an ardent desire to find only brothers and friends wherever I have the troops under my command march. Humanity is one of the sacred duties that will make us surpass all other peoples. It is also among our principles to rescue our brothers from their error and to hold out a helping hand to them. . . .

After this outpouring of my heart for you, I can call upon you, in the name of the Republic, to join me within an hour. Once this hour is up, I will deploy force against you and I will conquer you.

---

[1] The royalist governments of both Britain and Spain participated in the war. Spain already controlled much of the island, and jumped at the opportunity to expand its holdings once the slave revolts had begun. To this end, they joined forces with Britain, which had been at war with France since February 1793, to destroy France's hold on the colony.

[2] In 1793, Toussaint wrote to Laveaux, offering to join the French in exchange for a full amnesty for black rebels and freedom for all slaves. Laveaux rejected the offer, and Toussaint continued fighting for royalist Spain. By spring 1794, the situation had changed radically. Not only had British and Spanish forces gained control of most of the island, making Laveaux desperate for Toussaint's support, but the National Convention had also sanctioned the abolition of slavery.

Toussaint L'Ouverture to the People of Verrettes
March 1795

Brothers and sisters,

The moment has arrived when the thick veil that was blocking the light must fall. One must no longer forget the decrees of the National Convention. Its principles, its love of liberty, are unchanging, and henceforth, there can be no hope of this sacred edifice crumbling. . . .

I have learned with infinite joy about the return of some citizens of Verrettes to the bosom of the Republic; they will find the happiness that eluded them at the instigation of the soldiers of tyranny and royalty.

. . . To give them help, console them regarding past faults and prompt them to abjure the errors in which they were insidiously nourished, is an absolute duty and the sacred maxim of the French for all republicans.

This is why not only by virtue of the powers entrusted by General Laveaux, but also animated by the feelings of humanity and brotherhood with which I am filled, I must remind the citizens of Verrettes of their errors; but as much as they are detrimental to the interests of the Republic, as much I feel that their return, if sincere, can be advantageous to the growth of our success. . . .

The French are brothers; the English, the Spanish, and royalists are ferocious beasts who caress them only in order to suck their blood, that of their wives, and of their children at leisure, until satiation.

Citizens, I am not searching here to make a show of your faults. . . . You have returned to the bosom of the Republic, and well! Since then the past is forgotten; your duty is now to unite all of your physical and moral means to revive your parish and let the principles of sacred liberty germinate.

DISCUSSION QUESTIONS

1. What links can you find between the ideals of the French Revolution and those of Toussaint as expressed in the preceding documents?
2. What was Toussaint's ultimate goal as a leader in the revolution, whether fighting for the Spanish or the French?
3. What do these documents reveal about his strategies for achieving this goal?

COMPARATIVE QUESTIONS

1. How does the *Declaration of the Rights of Man and of the Citizen* address the concerns raised by Sieyès in his pamphlet?
2. Based on the trial record of Olympe de Gouges, in what ways did the Terror undermine the basic tenets of the *Declaration of the Rights of Man*?
3. In what ways were de Gouges and Toussaint fighting a similar battle?
4. Taken collectively, how do these documents allow us to chart the course the Revolution took between 1789 and 1795?

CHAPTER

21

Napoleon and the
Revolutionary Legacy
1800–1830

S U M M A R Y   The end of the Terror in 1794 opened a new chapter in
European history—one marked by the extraordinary rise of Napoleon
Bonaparte (1769–1821). Between 1795 and 1799, Napoleon transformed
himself from a humble artillery officer in the Revolutionary Army into the ruler
of France. The first document describes a key stage in this transformation,
Napoleon's invasion of Egypt in 1798. Although the campaign ultimately failed,
it foreshadowed Napoleon's subsequent attempts to colonize large parts of Europe along similar lines. When Napoleon finally met his match on the battlefield
in 1813, peace now seemed within reach. As the other documents reveal, however, voices of unrest continued to reverberate across Europe. Not only was the
revolutionary legacy still powerful, but another force was at work: industrialization. This "dual revolution" prompted people to search for new ways of understanding the changes unfolding around them. Their quest gave rise to new
ideologies that ultimately sounded the death knell of the conservative order.

1
Abd al-Rahman al-Jabartî
Napoleon in Egypt
1798

*While the Directory government that came to power in 1795 worked to establish order
in France, Napoleon continued the Revolution's policy of conquest and annexation
abroad, first in Italy (1796–1797) and then in Egypt (1798–1801). At the time,
Egypt was France's most important trading partner outside of the Caribbean; it
was also a key base for challenging British interests in Asia. Egyptian historian Abd
al-Rahman al-Jabartî's (1753–c. 1826) account of the first six months of the French*

60

invasion allows us to see Napoleon from a native's perspective. In the excerpt below, Jabartî views Napoleon's actions skeptically through the lens of his own culture. His skepticism proved well founded, for Napoleon failed to colonize Egypt. Even so, he retained his reputation as a great military leader, preparing the way for his mastery of France and much of Europe through a similar blend of authoritarian policies and revolutionary principles as that used in Egypt.

On Monday news arrived that the French had reached Damanhūr and Rosetta, bringing about the flight of their inhabitants to Fuwwa and its surroundings. Contained in this news was mention of the French sending notices throughout the country demanding impost for the upkeep of the military. Furthermore they printed a large proclamation in Arabic, calling on the people to obey them and to raise their "Bandiera." In this proclamation were inducements, warnings, all manner of wiliness and stipulations. Some copies were sent from the provinces to Cairo and its text is:

In the name of God, the Merciful, the Compassionate. There is no god but God. He has no son, nor has He an associate in His Dominion.

On behalf of the French Republic which is based upon the foundation of liberty and equality, General Bonaparte, Commander-in-Chief of the French armies makes known to all the Egyptian people that for a long time the Sanjaqs[1] who lorded it over Egypt have treated the French community basely and contemptuously and have persecuted its merchants with all manner of extortion and violence. Therefore the hour of punishment has now come.

Unfortunately this group of Mamlūks,[2] imported from the mountains of Circassia and Georgia have acted corruptly for ages in the fairest land that is to be found upon the face of the globe. However, the Lord of the Universe, the Almighty, has decreed the end of their power.

O ye Egyptians, they may say to you that I have not made an expedition hither for any other object than that of abolishing your religion; but this is a pure falsehood and you must not give credit to it, but tell the slanderers that I have not come to you except for the purpose of restoring your rights from the hands of the oppressors and that I more than the Mamlūks, serve God. . . .

And tell them also that all people are equal in the eyes of God and the only circumstances which distinguish one from the other are reason, virtue, and knowledge. But amongst the Mamlūks, what is there of reason, virtue, and knowledge, which would distinguish them from others and qualify them alone to possess everything which sweetens life in this world? Wherever fertile land is found it is

---

Shmuel Moreh, trans. *Napoleon in Egypt: Al-Jabartî's Chronicle of the French Occupation, 1798* (Princeton: Markus Wiener, 1993), 24–33.

[1] **Sanjaqs:** Provincial governors in the Ottoman Empire.

[2] **Mamlūks:** Descendants of medieval slave-soldiers who enjoyed considerable political power until the French invasion.

appropriated to the Mamlūks; and the handsomest female slaves, and the best horses, and the most desirable dwelling-places, all these belong to them exclusively. If the land of Egypt is a fief of the Mamlūks, let them then produce the title-deed, which God conferred upon them. But the Lord of the Universe is compassionate and equitable toward mankind, and with the help of the Exalted, from this day forward no Egyptian shall be excluded from admission to eminent positions nor from acquiring high ranks, therefore the intelligent and virtuous and learned ('*ulamā*') amongst them, will regulate / their affairs, and thus the state of the whole population will be rightly adjusted. . . .

Blessing on blessing to the Egyptians who will act in concert with us, without any delay, for their condition shall be rightly adjusted, and their rank raised. Blessing also, upon those who will abide in their habitations, not siding with either of the two hostile parties, yet when they know us better, they will hasten to us with all their hearts. But woe upon woe to those who will unite with the Mamlūks and assist them in the war against us, for they will not find the way of escape, and no trace of them shall remain. . . .

Here is an explanation of the incoherent words and vulgar constructions which he put into this miserable letter.

His statement "In the name of God, the Merciful, the Compassionate. There is no god but God. He has no son, nor has He an associate in His Dominion." In mentioning these three sentences there is an indication that the French agree with the three religions, but at the same time they do not agree with them, not with any religion. They are consistent with the Muslims in stating the formula "In the name of God," in denying that He has a son or an associate. They disagree with the Muslims in not mentioning the two Articles of Faith, in rejecting the mission of Muhammad, and the legal words and deeds which are necessarily recognized by religion. They agree with the Christians in most of their words and deeds, but disagree with them by not mentioning the Trinity, and denying the mission and furthermore in rejecting their beliefs, killing the priests and destroying the churches. Then, their statement "On behalf of the French Republic, etc.," that is, this proclamation is sent from their Republic, that means their body politic, because they have no chief or sultan with whom they all agree, like others, whose function is to speak on their behalf. For when they rebelled against their sultan six years ago and killed him, the people agreed unanimously that there was not to be a single ruler but that their state, territories, laws, and administration of their affairs, should be in the hands of the intelligent and wise men among them. They appointed persons chosen by them and made them heads of the army, and below them generals and commanders of thousands, two hundreds, and tens, administrators and advisers, on condition that they were all to be equal and none superior to any other in view of the equality of creation and nature. They made this the foundation and basis of their system. This is the meaning of their statement "based upon the foundation of liberty and equality." . . . They follow this rule: great and small, high and low, male and female are all equal. Sometimes they break this rule according to their whims and inclinations or reasoning. Their women do not veil themselves and have no modesty; they do not care whether they uncover their private parts. Whenever a Frenchman has to perform an act of nature he does so wherever he happens to be, even in full view of people, and he goes away as he is, without washing his private parts after defecation. If he is a man of taste and refinement he wipes himself with whatever he finds, even with a paper with writing on it, otherwise he remains as he is. They have intercourse with any woman who pleases them and vice versa. Sometimes one of their women goes into a barber's shop, and invites him to shave her pubic hair. If he wishes he can take his fee in kind. It is their custom to shave both their moustaches and beard. Some of them leave the hair of their cheeks only. . . .

His saying *qad hattama* etc. (has decreed) shows that they are appointing themselves controllers of God's secrets, but there is no disgrace worse than disbelief. . . .

His statement *wa-qūlū li 'l-muftariyīn* (but tell the slanderers) is the plural of *muftari* (slanderer) which means liar, and how worthy of this description they are. The proof of that is his saying "I have not come to you except for the purpose of restoring your rights from the hands of the oppressors," which is the first lie he uttered and a falsehood which he invented. Then he proceeds to something even worse than that, may God cast him into perdition, with his words: "I more than the Mamlūks serve God. . . ." There is no doubt that this is a derangement of his mind, and an excess of foolishness. . . .

His saying [all people] are equal in the eyes of God the Almighty, this is a lie and stupidity. How can this be when God has made some superior to others as is testified by the dwellers in the Heavens and on the Earth? . . .

May God hurry misfortune and punishment upon them, may He strike their tongues with dumbness, may He scatter their hosts, and disperse them, confound their intelligence, and cause their breath to cease. He has the power to do that, and it is up to Him to answer.

Discussion Questions

1. What strategy did Napoleon use in his proclamation to garner the support of the Egyptian people?
2. What does this strategy suggest about his personal ambitions and method of rule?
3. Why is Jabartî critical of Napoleon's intentions as stated in his proclamation?
4. What do Jabartî's criticisms suggest about the differences between French and Egyptian culture?

2

T. B. Macaulay
Speech on Parliamentary Reform
1831

Upon Napoleon's defeat in 1813, the allied powers worked to erase the imprint that the French Revolution and Napoleon's conquests had left on European society and politics. They faced many obstacles, however, including the new ideology of liberalism. Unlike their political rivals, liberals heralded individual rights and the need for broader political representation, two hallmarks of the French Revolution. Even so,

they shared conservatives' fear of popular unrest. British politician Thomas B.
Macaulay (1800–1859) sought to capitalize on this common ground in a speech he
delivered to Parliament in support of a bill for electoral reform at the very moment
when mass unrest gripped Europe. His words struck a chord, for the bill passed a
year later, expanding the British electorate to more than 800,000. Although this rep-
resented a tiny fraction of the country's growing population, which reached more
than 20 million by 1850, it marked a triumph over exclusive aristocratic politics and
opened the door to yet more sweeping changes.

It is a circumstance, Sir, of happy augury for the motion before the House, that
almost all those who have opposed it have declared themselves hostile on principle to parliamentary reform. . . . For what I feared was, not the opposition of
those who are averse to all reform, but the disunion of reformers. I knew that,
during three months, every reformer had been employed in conjecturing what
the plan of the government would be. I knew that every reformer had imagined
in his own mind a scheme. . . . I felt therefore great apprehension that one person
would be dissatisfied with one part of the bill, that another person would be dissatisfied with another part, and that thus our whole strength would be wasted in
internal dissensions. That apprehension is now at an end. I have seen with delight
the perfect concord which prevails among all who deserve the name of reformers
in this House. . . . I will not, Sir, at present express any opinion as to the details of
the bill; but, having during the last twenty-four hours given the most diligent
consideration to its general principles, I have no hesitation in pronouncing it a
wise, noble, and comprehensive measure, skilfully framed for the healing of great
distempers, for the securing at once of the public liberties and of the public re-
pose, and for the reconciling and knitting together of all the orders of the state.

The honorable Baronet who has just sat down[1] has told us, that the Ministers
have attempted to unite two inconsistent principles in one abortive measure.
Those were his very words. He thinks, if I understand him rightly, that we ought
either to leave the representative system such as it is, or to make it perfectly sym-
metrical. I think, Sir, that the Ministers would have acted unwisely if they had
taken either course. Their principle is plain, rational, and consistent. It is this, to
admit the middle class to a large and direct share in the representation, without
any violent shock to the institutions of our country. . . . The government has, in
my opinion, done all that was necessary for the removal of a great practical evil,
and no more than was necessary.

I consider this, Sir, as a practical question. I rest my opinion on no general
theory of government. I distrust all general theories of government. I will not
positively say, that there is any form of polity which may not, in some conceiv-
able circumstances, be the best possible. I believe that there are societies in which

---

T. B. Macaulay, *Miscellanies*, vol. I (Boston: Houghton Mifflin, 1901), 1–19.
[1] Sir John Walsh.

every man may safely be admitted to vote. Gentlemen may cheer, but such is my opinion. I say, Sir, that there are countries in which the condition of the laboring classes is such that they may safely be entrusted with the right of electing Members of the Legislature. If the laborers of England were in that state in which I, from my soul, wish to see them, if employment were always plentiful, wages always high, food always cheap, if a large family were considered not as an encumbrance but as a blessing, the principal objection to Universal Suffrage would, I think, be removed. Universal Suffrage exists in the United States without producing any very frightful consequences; and I do not believe that the people of those States, or of any part of the world, are in any good quality naturally superior to our own countrymen. But, unhappily, the laboring classes in England, and in all old countries, are occasionally in a state of great distress. Some of the causes of this distress are, I fear, beyond the control of the government. We know what effect distress produces, even on people more intelligent than the great body of the laboring classes can possibly be. . . . It is therefore no reflection on the poorer class of Englishmen, who are not, and who cannot in the nature of things be, highly educated, to say that distress produces on them its natural effects, those effects which it would produce on the Americans, or on any other people, that it blinds their judgment, that it inflames their passions, that it makes them prone to believe those who flatter them, and to distrust those who would serve them. For the sake, therefore, of the whole society, for the sake of the laboring classes themselves, I hold it to be clearly expedient that, in a country like this one, the right of suffrage should depend on a pecuniary qualification.

But, Sir, every argument which would induce me to oppose Universal Suffrage induces me to support the plan which is now before us. I am opposed to Universal Suffrage, because I think that it would produce a destructive revolution. I support this plan, because I am sure that it is our best security against a revolution. . . . I do in my conscience believe that, unless the plan proposed, or some similar plan, be speedily adopted, great and terrible calamities will befall us. Entertaining this opinion, I think myself bound to state it, not as a threat, but as a reason. I support this bill because it will improve our institutions; but I support it also because it tends to preserve them. That we may exclude those whom it is necessary to exclude, we must admit those whom it may be safe to admit. At present we oppose the schemes of revolutionists with only one half, with only one quarter of our proper force. We say, and we say justly, that it is not by mere numbers, but by property and intelligence, that the nation ought to be governed. Yet, saying this, we exclude from all share in the government great masses of property and intelligence, great numbers of those who are most interested in preserving tranquillity, and who know best how to preserve it. We do more. We drive over to the side of revolution those whom we shut out from power. Is this a time when the cause of law and order can spare one of its natural allies? . . .

If it be said that there is an evil in change as change, I answer that there is also an evil in discontent as discontent. This, indeed, is the strongest part of our case. It is said that the system works well. I deny it. I deny that a system works well, which the people regard with aversion. We may say here, that it is a good system and a perfect system. But if any man were to say so to any six hundred and fifty-eight respectable farmers or shopkeepers, chosen by lot in any part of England, he would be hooted down, and laughed to scorn. Are these the feelings with which any part of the government ought to be regarded? Above all, are these the feelings with which the popular branch of the legislature ought to be regarded? It is almost as essential to the utility of a House of Commons, that it should possess the confidence of the people, as that it should deserve that confidence. Unfortunately, that which is in theory the popular part of our government is in practice the unpopular part. Who wishes to dethrone the King? Who wishes to turn the Lords out of their House? Here and there a crazy radical, whom the boys in the street point at as he walks along. Who wishes to alter the constitution of this House? The whole people. It is natural that it should be so. . . .

Now, . . . if I were convinced that the great body of the middle class in England look with aversion on monarchy and aristocracy, I should be forced, much against my will, to come to this conclusion, that monarchical and aristocratical institutions are unsuited to my country. Monarchy and aristocracy, valuable and useful as I think them, are still valuable and useful as means, and not as ends. The end of government is the happiness of the people: and I do not conceive that, in a country like this, the happiness of the people can be promoted by a form of government in which the middle classes place no confidence, and which exists only because the middle classes have no organ by which to make their sentiments known. But, Sir, I am fully convinced that the middle classes sincerely wish to uphold the Royal prerogatives and the constitutional rights of the Peers. . . .

Now therefore while everything at home and abroad forebodes ruin to those who persist in a hopeless struggle against the spirit of the age, now, while the crash of the proudest throne of the Continent is still resounding in our ears, now, while the roof of a British palace affords an ignominious shelter to the exiled heir of forty kings, now, while we see on every side ancient institutions subverted, and great societies dissolved, now, while the heart of England is still sound, now, while old feelings and old associations retain a power and a charm which may too soon pass away, now, in this your accepted time, now, in this your day of salvation, take counsel, not of prejudice, not of party spirit, not of the ignominious pride of a fatal consistency, but of history, of reason, of the ages which are past, of the signs of this most portentous time. Pronounce in a manner worthy of the expectation with which this great debate has been anticipated, and of the long remembrance which it will leave behind. Renew the youth of the state. Save property, divided against itself. Save the multitude, endangered by its own ungovernable passions. Save the aristocracy, endangered by its own unpopular power. Save the greatest, and fairest, and most highly civilized community that ever existed, from calamities which may in a few days sweep away all the rich heritage of so many ages of wisdom and glory. The danger is terrible. The time is short. If this bill should be rejected, I pray to God that none of those who concur in rejecting it may ever remember their votes with unavailing remorse, amidst the wreck of laws, the confusion of ranks, the spoliation of property, and the dissolution of social order.

DISCUSSION QUESTIONS

1. What, according to Macaulay, is the main goal of the reform bill?
2. Why is he against universal manhood suffrage?
3. What strategy does Macaulay use to sway opponents of the bill to support it?
4. In what ways does Macaulay's speech reflect liberal principles?

3

Robert Owen
Constitution of the Preliminary Society of New Harmony
1825

Socialism was not simply the newest ideology of the 1820s; it was potentially the most threatening to the status quo. The ideas and actions of the founder of British socialism, Robert Owen (1771–1858), help us to understand why. As a wealthy manufacturer, he knew the problems caused by industrialization. His solution was not parliamentary action but total social reorganization. Having been informed of a unique real estate opportunity in Indiana, he arrived in the United States in 1824 to transform this goal into a reality. Soon thereafter he purchased the Indiana property, where he planned to establish a community of complete equality called New Harmony. News about his project spread quickly, and hundreds of settlers arrived. On May 1, 1825, the community adopted a preliminary constitution prepared by Owen, much of which is excerpted here. The document is an eloquent testimony to Owen's beliefs, which, despite their ultimate failure in New Harmony, shaped the future of socialism.

This Preliminary Society is particularly formed to improve the character and conditions of its own members, and to prepare them to become associates in independent communities, having common property.

The sole objects of these communities will be to procure for all their members the greatest amount of happiness, to secure it to them, and to transmit it to their children to the latest posterity.

Persons of all ages and descriptions, exclusive of persons of color, may become members of the preliminary society. Persons of color may be received as helpers to the society, if necessary; or it may be found useful to prepare and enable them to become associates in communities in Africa, or in some other country, or in some other part of this country.

The members of the Preliminary Society are all of the same rank, no artificial inequality being acknowledged; precedence to be given only to age and experience, and to those who may be chosen to offices of trust and utility.

George Browning Lockwood, *The New Harmony Communities* (Marion, Ind.: The Chronicle Company, 1902), 105–09.

The Committee—As the proprietor of the settlement, and founder of the system, has purchased the property, paid for it, and furnished the capital, and has consequently subjected himself to all the risk of the establishment, it is necessary for the formation of the system, and for its security, that he should have the appointment of the committee which is to direct and manage the affairs of the society.

This committee will conduct all the affairs of the society. It will be, as much as possible, composed of men of experience and integrity, who are competent to carry the system into effect, and to apply impartial justice to all the members of the society.

The number of the committee will be augmented from time to time, according as the proprietor may secure the assistance of other valuable members.

At the termination of one year from the establishment of the settlement, which shall be dated from the first day of May, the members of the society shall elect, by ballot, from among themselves, three additional members of the committee. Their election is for the purpose of securing to all the members a full knowledge of the proceedings of the committee, and of the business of the society; but it is delayed for one year, in order to afford time for the formation of the society, and to enable the members to become acquainted with the characters and abilities of those who are proper to be elected.

It is expected that at the termination of the second year, or between that period and the end of the third year, an association of members may be formed to constitute a community of equality and independence to be governed according to the rules and regulations contained in the printed paper entitled: "Mr. Owen's Plan for the Permanent Relief of the Working Classes," with such alterations as experience may suggest and the localities of the situation may require.

The independent community will be established upon property purchased by the associated members.

The Preliminary Society will continue to receive members, preparatory to their removal into other independent communities.

Admission of Members

Every individual, previous to admission as a member, must sign the constitution, which signature shall be regularly witnessed. The members must join the society at their own expense.

The society shall not be answerable for the debts of any of its members, nor in any manner for their conduct, no partnership whatsoever existing between the members of the Preliminary Society.

The members shall occupy the dwellings which the committee may provide for them.

The live stock possessed by members will be taken and placed to their credit, if wanted for the society, but if not required, it shall not be received.

All members must provide their own household and kitchen furniture, and their small tools, such as spades, hoes, axes, rakes, etc., and they may bring such provisions as they have already provided.

The General Duties of Members

All the members shall willingly render their best services for the good of the society, according to their age, experience and capacity, and if inexperienced in that which is requisite for its welfare, they shall apply diligently to acquire the knowledge of some useful occupation or employment.

They shall enter the society with a determination to promote its peace, prosperity and harmony, and, never, under any provocation whatever, act unkindly or unjustly towards, not speak in an unfriendly manner of, any one either in or out of the society.

Members shall be temperate, regular and orderly in their whole conduct, and they shall be diligent in their employments, in proportion to their age, capacity and constitution.

They shall show a good example, it being a much better instructor than precept.

They shall watch over, and endeavor to protect, the whole property from every kind of injury.

General Privileges of Members

The members shall receive such advantages, living, comfort and education for their children as this society, and the present state of New Harmony affords.

The living shall be upon equal terms for all, with the exceptions hereafter to be mentioned.

In old age, in sickness, or when an accident occurs, care shall be taken of all parties, medical aid shall be afforded, and every attention shown to them that kindness can suggest.

Each member shall, within a fixed amount in value, have the free choice of food and clothing; to effect this, a credit (to be hereafter fixed by the committee), will be opened in the store for each family, in proportion to the number of its useful members, also for each single member, but beyond this amount, no one will be permitted to draw on credit. . . .

Each family and individual member shall have a credit and debit account, in which they will be charged with what they receive, at the prices the Harmonists usually received for the same articles and credits by the value of their services, to be estimated by the committee, assisted by the persons at the head of the departments in which the respective individuals may be employed; the value of their services over their expenditure, shall be placed at the end of each year to their credit in the books of the society, but no part of this credit shall be drawn out, except in the productions of the establishment, or in store goods, and with the consent of the committee.

Members may visit their friends, or travel whenever they please, provided the committee can conveniently supply their places in the departments in which they may be respectively employed. . . .

Members may receive their friends to visit them, provided they be answerable that such visitors, during their stay, do not transgress the rules of the society.

The children will be located in the best possible manner in day schools, and will board and sleep in their parents' houses. Should any members, however, prefer placing their children in the boarding school, they must make a particular and individual engagement with the committee; but no members shall be permitted to bind themselves nor their children to the society for a longer period than one week.

All the members shall enjoy complete liberty of conscience, and be afforded every facility for exercising those practices of religious worship and devotion which they may prefer.

Should the arrangements formed for the happiness of the members, fail to effect their object, any of them by giving a week's notice, can quit the society, taking with them, in the productions of the establishment, the value of what they brought, which value shall be ascertained and fixed by the committee. The members may also, in the same manner, take out the amount of what appears to their credit in the books of the society, at the end of the year immediately preceding their removal, provided that amount still remain to their credit.

Dismission of Members

Any families or members contravening any of the articles of this constitution, or acting in any way improperly, shall be dismissed by the committee from the society and settlement, upon giving them the same notice by which they are at liberty to quit the society.

Persons who possess capital, and who do not wish to be employed, may partake of the benefits of this society, by paying such sum annually as may be agreed upon between them and the committee, always paying a quarter in advance.

Persons wishing to invest capital on interest in the funds of the society, may do so by making a particular agreement with the committee.

DISCUSSION QUESTIONS
1. What were the fundamental principles governing life at New Harmony?
2. What were the responsibilities of each of its members?
3. In what ways do you think Owen designed the community to counteract what he saw as the ills of industrial society?
4. Based on this document, why do you think that some people described Owen's plans as "utopian"?

4

Joseph Mazzini
Life and Writings of Joseph Mazzini
1805–1872

The son of a Genoese doctor, Joseph Mazzini (1805–1872) embodied the growing force of nationalist sentiment in post-Napoleonic Europe. Politically fragmented, Italy had long been a battleground for European rulers, including Napoleon. Napoleon's annexation of Italian territories and establishment of satellite kingdoms sparked local resistance, sowing the seeds of the movement for Italian unification that emerged later in the century. Mazzini dedicated his life to nourishing these seeds after the failed political revolts of 1820–21. Indeed, as he recounts in this excerpt, from that point on, the quest to free Italy from foreign rule and establish a republic consumed his very soul. France was no longer the target, however; instead it was Austria, which had regained a political foothold in the region upon Napoleon's defeat.

One Sunday in April 1821, while I was yet a boy, I was walking in the Strada Nuova of Genoa with my mother, and an old friend of our family named Andrea Gambini. The Piedmontese insurrection had just been crushed; partly by Austria, partly through treachery, and partly through the weakness of its leaders.

The revolutionists, seeking safety by sea, had flocked to Genoa, and, finding themselves distressed for means, they went about seeking help to enable them to cross into Spain, where the revolution was yet triumphant. The greater number of them were crowded in S. Pier d'Arena, awaiting a chance to embark; but not a few had contrived to enter the city one by one, and I used to search them out from amongst our own people, detecting them either by their general appearance, by some peculiarity of dress, by their warlike air, or by the signs of a deep and silent sorrow on their faces.

The population were singularly moved. Some of the boldest had proposed to the leaders of the insurrection—Santarosa and Ansaldi, I think—to concentrate themselves in, and take possession of the city, and organize a new resistance; but Genoa was found to be deprived of all means of successful defence; the fortresses were without artillery, and the leaders had rejected the proposition, telling them *to preserve themselves for a better fate.*

Presently we were stopped and addressed by a tall black-bearded man, with a severe and energetic countenance, and a fiery glance that I have never since forgotten. He held out a white handkerchief towards us, merely saying, *For the refugees of Italy.* My mother and friend dropped some money into the handkerchief, and he turned from us to put the same request to others. I afterwards learned his name. He was one Rini, a captain in the National Guard, which had been instituted at the commencement of the movement. He accompanied those for whom he had thus constituted himself collector, and, I believe, died—as so many of ours have perished—for the cause of liberty in Spain.

That day was the first in which a confused idea presented itself to my mind— I will not say of country or of liberty—but an idea that we Italians *could* and therefore *ought* to struggle for the liberty of our country. I had already been unconsciously educated in the worship of equality by the democratic principles of my parents, whose bearing towards high or low was ever the same. Whatever the position of the individual, they simply regarded the *man*, and sought only the honest man. And my own natural aspirations towards liberty were fostered by constantly hearing my father and the friend already mentioned speak of the recent republican era in France; by the study of the works of Livy and Tacitus, which my Latin master had given me to translate; and by certain old French newspapers, which I discovered half-hidden behind my father's medical books. Amongst these last were some numbers of the *Chronique du Mois*, a Girondist publication belonging to the first period of the French Revolution.

But the idea of an existing wrong in my own country, against which it was a duty to struggle, and the thought that I too must bear my part in that struggle, flashed before my mind on that day for the first time, never again to leave me. The remembrance of those refugees, many of whom became my friends in after life, pursued me where-ever I went by day, and mingled with my dreams by night. I would have given I know not what to follow them. I began collecting names and facts, and studied, as best I might, the records of that heroic struggle, seeking to fathom the causes of its failure.

They had been betrayed and abandoned by those who had sworn to concentrate every effort in the movement; the new king[1] had invoked the aid of Austria; part of the Piedmontese troops had even preceded the Austrians at Novara; and the leaders had allowed themselves to be overwhelmed at the first encounter, without making an effort to resist. All the details I succeeded in collecting led me to think that they *might* have conquered, if all of them had done their duty;— then why not renew the attempt? . . .

Discussion Questions

1. Why, according to Mazzini, did the 1820-21 revolts fail?
2. How did this failure shape the course of Mazzini's life?
3. What were some of the other influences at work?

Comparative Questions

1. In what ways did the legacy of the French Revolution shape the development of liberalism and nationalism as represented by Macaulay and Mazzini, respectively?
2. Macaulay and Owen both recognized the difficulties faced by the working class in the industrial age. Yet how were their responses to this recognition diametrically opposed? What does this suggest about the differences between liberal and socialist doctrines?
3. What common experience molded Mazzini's and Jabartî's political perspectives?

---

[1] Carlo Felice.

Industrialization, Urbanization, and Revolution

1830–1850

S U M M A R Y   The nineteenth century was a time of momentous economic and social change as factories sprang up across much of Europe and railroad tracks crisscrossed the landscape. Although Britain initially led the way in industrial growth, the continent soon began to catch up. For the middle classes, industrialization opened the door to new riches and prestige. By contrast, for the men, women, and children who labored in the new factories, it meant little more than a life of urban drudgery and extreme poverty. The first two documents that follow expose industrialization's effects on the everyday world, from the grueling regime of factory work to the demands of running the ideal middle-class household. The third document illuminates one of the most significant ideological consequences of the new age: the birth of communism. Although its immediate impact was far less visible than the fumes billowing from smokestacks, it ultimately changed the course of modern history. The final document shows the cultural response to the changing European landscape, romanticism, which strove to strip away artifice and expose truth as embodied in nature and daily life.

1

Factory Rules in Berlin
1844

Industrialization did not simply create new social classes, new jobs, and new problems; it also created new work habits regimented by the pace of machines and the time clock. It fell upon the factory owners and managers to instill these habits in their workforce to ensure efficient and consistent levels of production. This was no easy task, as most people, whether former peasants or skilled workers, were tradi-

73

tionally accustomed to controlling their own time. The list of rules distributed to the employees of the Foundry and Engineering Works of the Royal Overseas Trading Company in Berlin provides a telling example of one approach to this challenge. This document also illustrates the spread of industrialization eastward across continental Europe.

In every large works, and in the co-ordination of any large number of workmen, good order and harmony must be looked upon as the fundamentals of success, and therefore the following rules shall be strictly observed.

Every man employed in the concern named below shall receive a copy of these rules, so that no one can plead ignorance. Its acceptance shall be deemed to mean consent to submit to its regulations.

(1) The normal working day begins at all seasons at 6 a.m. precisely and ends, after the usual break of half an hour for breakfast, a hour for dinner and half an hour for tea, at 7 p.m., and it shall be strictly observed.

Five minutes before the beginning of the stated hours of work until their actual commencement, a bell shall ring and indicate that every worker employed in the concern has to proceed to his place of work, in order to start as soon as the bell stops.

The doorkeeper shall lock the door punctually at 6 a.m., 8.30 a.m., 1 p.m. and 4.30 p.m.

Workers arriving 2 minutes late shall lose half an hour's wages; whoever is more than 2 minutes late may not start work until after the next break, or at least shall lose his wages until then. Any disputes about the correct time shall be settled by the clock mounted above the gatekeeper's lodge.

These rules are valid both for time- and for piece-workers, and in cases of breaches of these rules, workmen shall be fined in proportion to their earnings. The deductions from the wage shall be entered in the wage-book of the gatekeeper whose duty they are; they shall be unconditionally accepted as it will not be possible to enter into any discussions about them.

(2) When the bell is rung to denote the end of the working day, every workman, both on piece- and on day-wage, shall leave his workshop and the yard, but is not allowed to make preparations for his departure before the bell rings. Every breach of this rule shall lead to a fine of five silver groschen to the sick fund. Only those who have obtained special permission by the overseer may stay on in the workshop in order to work. – If a workman has worked beyond the closing bell, he must give his name to the gatekeeper on leaving, on pain of losing his payment for the overtime.

(3) No workman, whether employed by time or piece, may leave before the end of the working day, without having first received permission from the over-

Sidney Pollard and C. Holmes, *Documents of European Economic History,* vol. I, *The Process of Industrialization, 1750–1870* (New York: St. Martin's Press, 1968), 534–36.

seer and having given his name to the gatekeeper. Omission of these two actions shall lead to a fine of ten silver groschen payable to the sick fund.

(4) Repeated irregular arrival at work shall lead to dismissal. This shall also apply to those who are found idling by an official or overseer, and refuse to obey their order to resume work.

(5) Entry to the firm's property by any but the designated gateway, and exit by any prohibited route, e.g. by climbing fences or walls, or by crossing the Spree, shall be punished by a fine of fifteen silver groschen to the sick fund for the first offences, and dismissal for the second.

(6) No worker may leave his place of work otherwise than for reasons connected with his work.

(7) All conversation with fellow-workers is prohibited; if any worker requires information about his work, he must turn to the overseer, or to the particular fellow-worker designated for the purpose.

(8) Smoking in the workshops or in the yard is prohibited during working hours; anyone caught smoking shall be fined five silver groschen for the sick fund for every such offence.

(9) Every worker is responsible for cleaning up his space in the workshop, and if in doubt, he is to turn to his overseer. – All tools must always be kept in good condition, and must be cleaned after use. This applies particularly to the turner, regarding his lathe.

(10) Natural functions must be performed at the appropriate places, and whoever is found soiling walls, fences, squares, etc., and similarly, whoever is found washing his face and hands in the workshop and not in the places assigned for the purpose, shall be fined five silver groschen for the sick fund.

(11) On completion of his piece of work, every workman must hand it over at once to his foreman or superior, in order to receive a fresh piece of work. Pattern makers must on no account hand over their patterns to the foundry without express order of their supervisors. No workman may take over work from his fellow-workman without instruction to that effect by the foreman.

(12) It goes without saying that all overseers and officials of the firm shall be obeyed without question, and shall be treated with due deference. Disobedience will be punished by dismissal.

(13) Immediate dismissal shall also be the fate of anyone found drunk in any of the workshops.

(14) Untrue allegations against superiors or officials of the concern shall lead to stern reprimand, and may lead to dismissal. The same punishment shall be meted out to those who knowingly allow errors to slip through when supervising or stocktaking.

(15) Every workman is obliged to report to his superiors any acts of dishonesty or embezzlement on the part of his fellow workmen. If he omits to do so, and it is shown after subsequent discovery of a misdemeanour that he knew about it at the time, he shall be liable to be taken to court as an accessory after the fact and the wage due to him shall be retained as punishment. Conversely, anyone denouncing a theft in such a way as to allow conviction of the thief shall receive a

reward of two Thaler, and, if necessary, his name shall be kept confidential.—Further, the gatekeeper and the watchman, as well as every official, are entitled to search the baskets, parcels, aprons etc. of the women and children who are taking dinners into the works, on their departure, as well as search any worker suspected of stealing any article whatever. . . .

(18) Advances shall be granted only to the older workers, and even to them only in exceptional circumstances. As long as he is working by the piece, the workman is entitled merely to his fixed weekly wage as subsistence pay; the extra earnings shall be paid out only on completion of the whole piece contract. If a workman leaves before his piece contract is completed, either of his own free will, or on being dismissed as punishment, or because of illness, the partly completed work shall be valued by the general manager with the help of two overseers, and he will be paid accordingly. There is no appeal against the decision of these experts.

(19) A free copy of these rules is handed to every workman, but whoever loses it and requires a new one, or cannot produce it on leaving, shall be fined 2½ silver groschen, payable to the sick fund.

Discussion Questions

1. As delineated here, what new modes of discipline did factory work require, and why?
2. What was the principal method used to encourage compliance to these rules?
3. Based on this document, how would you describe a typical day in this factory for the workers employed there?

2

Isabella Mayson Beeton
Book of Household Management
1861

As working-class women toiled in factories, the growing ranks of middle-class women faced their own strikingly different challenges. Many social commentators expected middle-class women to center their lives on their homes, thereby transforming them into bastions of order, tranquility, and proper behavior. Writers such as the English-woman Isabella Mayson Beeton (1836–1865) offered ample advice on the means of fulfilling such expectations. In her hugely successful Book of Household Management, *first published in 1861, Beeton discussed a range of topics, from domestic chores to meal planning, to help her female readers become masterful household managers, uncomplaining wives, and suitable mothers. Her words paint a picture of the ideal domestic sphere that in reality eluded many women, either by choice or circumstance. Even so, her book tells us much about changing attitudes toward women in the industrial age.*

As with the Commander of an Army, or the leader of any enterprise, so is it with the mistress of a house. Her spirit will be seen through the whole establishment; and just in proportion as she performs her duties intelligently and thoroughly, so will her domestics follow in her path. Of all those acquirements, which more particularly belong to the feminine character, there are none which take a higher rank, in our estimation, than such as enter into a knowledge of household duties; for on these are perpetually dependent the happiness, comfort, and well-being of a family. . . .

Having risen early, . . . and having given due attention to the bath, and made a careful toilet, it will be well at once to see that the children have received their proper ablutions, and are in every way clean and comfortable. . . .

After breakfast is over, it will be well for the mistress to make a round of the kitchen and other offices, to see that all are in order, and that the morning's work has been properly performed by the various domestics. The orders for the day should then be given, and any questions which the domestics desire to ask, respecting their several departments, should be answered, and any special articles they may require, handed to them from the store-closet. In those establishments where there is a housekeeper, it will not be so necessary for the mistress, personally, to perform the above-named duties.

After this general superintendence of her servants, the mistress, if a mother of a young family, may devote herself to the instruction of some of its younger members, or to the examination of the state of their wardrobe, leaving the later portion of the morning for reading, or for some amusing recreation. . . . Unless the means of the mistress be very circumscribed, and she be obliged to devote a great deal of her time to the making of her children's clothes, and other economical pursuits, it is right that she should give some time to the pleasure of literature, the innocent delights of the garden, and to the improvement of any special abilities for music, painting, and other elegant arts, which she may, happily, possess. . . .

After luncheon, morning calls and visits may be made and received. . . . Visits of ceremony, or courtesy . . . are uniformly required after dining at a friend's house, or after a ball, picnic, or any other party. These visits should be short, a stay of from fifteen to twenty minutes being quite sufficient. A lady paying a visit may remove her boa or neckerchief; but neither her shawl nor bonnet. . . .

The morning calls being paid or received, and their etiquette properly attended to, the next great event of the day in most establishments is "The Dinner." . . .

The half-hour before dinner has always been considered as the great ordeal through which the mistress, in giving a dinner-party, will either pass with flying colours, or, lose many of her laurels. The anxiety to receive her guests, her hope that all will be present in due time, her trust in the skill of her cook, and the attention of the other domestics, all tend to make these few minutes a trying time.

Janet Horowitz Murray, *Strong-Minded Women and Other Lost Voices from Nineteenth-Century England* (New York: Pantheon Books, 1982), 84–85.

The mistress, however, must display no kind of agitation, but show her tact in suggesting light and cheerful subjects of conversation. . . .

When fruit has been taken, and a glass or two of wine passed round, the time will have arrived when the hostess will rise, and thus give the signal for the ladies to leave the gentlemen, and retire to the drawing-room. . . .

Of the manner of passing evenings at home, there is none pleasanter than in such recreative enjoyments as those which relax the mind from its severer duties, whilst they stimulate it with a gentle delight. Where there are young people forming a part of the evening circle, interesting and agreeable pastime should especially be promoted. . . . It ought . . . to enter into the domestic policy of every parent, to make her children feel that home is the happiest place in the world; that to imbue them with this delicious home-feeling is one of the choicest gifts a parent can bestow.

Light or fancy needlework often forms a portion of the evening's recreation for the ladies of the household, and this may be varied by an occasional game at chess or backgammon. It has often been remarked, too, that nothing is more delightful to the feminine members of a family, than the reading aloud of some good standard work or amusing publication. . . .

In retiring for the night, it is well to remember that early rising is almost impossible, if late going to bed be the order, or rather disorder, of the house. The younger members of a family should go early and at regular hours to their beds, and the domestics as soon as possible after a reasonably appointed hour. Either the master or the mistress of a house should, after all have gone to their separate rooms, see that all is right with respect to the lights and fires below; and no servants should, on any account, be allowed to remain up after the heads of the house have retired.

Discussion Questions

1. What does Beeton mean when she compares the mistress of a house to an army commander and business owner?
2. According to Beeton, what are a woman's principal daily duties as a wife and mother?
3. What do these duties suggest about the status of middle-class women in English society at the time?

3

Frederich Engels
Draft of a Communist Confession of Faith
1847

When Frederich Engels (1820–1895) composed this draft of a communist "confession of faith" in 1847, the Industrial Revolution was in full swing in Great Britain and rapidly gaining ground on the continent. Engels observed the impact of this process on the working class with a critical eye. Two years earlier, he had joined forces with another critic of industrialization, Karl Marx (1818–1883), and together they launched an ideological revolution with the publication of the Communist Manifesto *in 1848. Here they set forth a new understanding of industrial society and its problems and proposed a new set of solutions centered on the abolition of capitalist, "private" property. Engels's "confession of faith" illuminates key landmarks on his and Marx's intellectual journey, for it was among the materials Marx used to compose the* Manifesto. *The confession was debated and approved in 1847 at the first congress of the Communist League. Although the first six questions reveal Engels's debt to the utopian principle of the community of property, those remaining reflect his and Marx's distinct historical vision.*

A Credo for the Communist League

This draft of a programmatic "confession of faith" by Frederich Engles was discussed and approved at the Communist League's first congress in London on June 2–9, 1847. The program was distributed to League members for discussion after the congress and revised by Engels in late October for renewed discussion at the second congress in November–December. Its full text was discovered in Hamburg in 1968 among the papers of a former member of the Communist League and translated into English in 1971. The first six questions reflect the more traditional utopian socialist ideas of many members of the League, but the remainder of the document reveals how effective Engles was in shifting the program toward an affirmation of his own and Marx's more "historical" positions.

Draft of a Communist Confession of Faith

June 9, 1847

QUESTION 1:   *Are you a Communist?*

ANSWER: Yes.

QUESTION 2:   *What is the aim of the Communists?*

ANSWER: To organise society in such a way that every member of it can develop and use all his capabilities and powers in complete freedom and without thereby infringing the basic conditions of this society.

QUESTION 3:   *How do you wish to achieve this aim?*

ANSWER: By the elimination of private property and its replacement by community of property.

QUESTION 4:   *On what do you base your community of property?*

ANSWER: Firstly, on the mass of productive forces and means of subsistence resulting from the development of industry, agriculture, trade and colonisation, and on the possibility inherent in machinery, chemical and other resources of their infinite extension.

John E. Toews, ed., *The Communist Manifesto with Related Documents* (Boston: Bedford/ St. Martin's, 1999), 99–104.

Secondly, on the fact that in the consciousness or feeling of every individual there exist certain irrefutable basic principles which, being the result of the whole of historical development, require no proof.

QUESTION 5: *What are such principles?*

ANSWER: For example, every individual strives to be happy. The happiness of the individual in inseparable from the happiness of all, etc.

QUESTION 6: *How do you wish to prepare the way for your community of property?*

ANSWER: By enlightening and uniting the proletariat.

QUESTION 7: *What is the proletariat?*

ANSWER: The proletariat is that class of society which lives exclusively by its labour and not on the profit from any kind of capital; that class whose weal and woe, whose life and death, therefore, depend on the alternation of times of good and bad business; in a word, on the fluctuations of competition.

QUESTION 8: *Then there have not always been proletarians?*

ANSWER: No. There have always been poor and working classes; and those who worked were almost always the poor. But there have not always been proletarians, just as competition has not always been free.

QUESTION 9: *How did the proletariat arise?*

ANSWER: The proletariat came into being as a result of the introduction of the machines which have been invented since the middle of the last century and the most important of which are: the steam-engine, the spinning machine and the power loom. These machines, which were very expensive and could therefore only be purchased by rich people, supplanted the workers of the time, because by the use of machinery it was possible to produce commodities more quickly and cheaply than could the workers with their imperfect spinning wheels and hand-looms. The machines thus delivered industry entirely into the hands of the big capitalists and rendered the workers' scanty property which consisted mainly of their tools, looms, etc., quite worthless, so that the capitalist was left with everything, the worker with nothing. In this way the factory system was introduced. Once the capitalists saw how advantageous this was for them, they sought to extend it to more and more branches of labour. They divided work more and more between the workers so that workers who formerly had made a whole article now produced only a part of it. Labour simplified in this way produced goods more quickly and therefore more cheaply and only now was it found in almost every branch of labour that here also machines could be used. As soon as any branch of labour went over to factory production it ended up, just as in the case of spinning and weaving, in the hands of the big capitalists, and the workers were deprived of the last remnants of their independence. We have gradually arrived at the position where almost *all* branches of labour are run on a factory basis. This has increasingly brought about the ruin of the previously existing middle class, especially of the small master craftsmen, completely transformed the previous position of the workers, and two new classes which are gradually swallowing up all other classes have come into being, namely:

I. The class of the big capitalists, who in all advanced countries are in almost exclusive possession of the means of subsistence and those means (machines, factories, workshops, etc.) by which these means of subsistence are produced. This is the *bourgeois* class, or the *bourgeoisie.*

II. The class of the completely propertyless, who are compelled to sell their labour to the first class, the bourgeois, simply to obtain from them in return their means of subsistence. Since the parties to this trading in labour are not *equal,* but the bourgeois have the advantage, the propertyless must submit to the bad conditions laid down by the bourgeois. This class, dependent on the bourgeois, is called the class of the *proletarians* or the *proletariat.*

QUESTION 10:   *In what way does the proletarian differ from the slave?*

ANSWER: The slave is sold once and for all, the proletarian has to sell himself by the day and by the hour. The slave is the property of one master and for that very reason has a guaranteed subsistence, however wretched it may be. The proletarian is, so to speak, the slave of the entire bourgeois *class,* not of one master, and therefore has no guaranteed subsistence, since nobody buys his labour if he does not need it. The slave is accounted a *thing* and not a member of civil society. The proletarian is recognised as a *person,* as a member of civil society. The slave *may,* therefore, have a better subsistence than the proletarian but the latter stands at a higher stage of development. The slave frees himself by *becoming a proletarian,* abolishing from the totality of property relationships *only* the relationship of slavery. The proletarian can free himself only by abolishing *property in general.*

QUESTION 11:   *In what way does the proletarian differ from the serf?*

ANSWER: The serf has the piece of land, that is, of an instrument of production, in return for handing over a greater or lesser portion of the yield. The proletarian works with instruments of production which belong to someone else who, in return for his labour, hands over to him a portion, determined by competition, of the products. In the case of the serf, the share of the labourer is determined by his own labour, that is, by himself. In the case of the proletarian it is determined by competition, therefore in the first place by the bourgeois. The serf has guaranteed subsistence, the proletarian has not. The serf frees himself by driving out his feudal lord and becoming a property owner himself, thus entering into competition and joining for the time being the possessing class, the privileged class. The proletarian frees himself by doing away with property, competition, and all class differences.

QUESTION 12:   *In what way does the proletarian differ from the handicraftsman?*

ANSWER: As opposed to the proletarian, the so-called handicraftsman, who still existed nearly everywhere during the last century and still exists here and there, is at most a *temporary* proletarian. His aim is to acquire capital himself and so to exploit other workers. He can often achieve this aim where the craft guilds still exist or where freedom to follow a trade has not yet led to the organisation of handwork on a factory basis and to intense competition. But as soon as the factory system is introduced into handwork and competition is in full swing, this prospect is eliminated and the handicraftsman becomes more and more a proletarian. The handicraftsman therefore frees himself *either* by becoming a bourgeois or in general passing over into the middle class, *or,* by becoming a proletarian as a result of competition (as now happens in most cases) and join-ing the movement of the proletariat—i.e., the more or less conscious commu-nist movement.

QUESTION 13: *Then you do not believe that community of property has been pos-sible at any time?*

ANSWER: No. Communism has only arisen since machinery and other inven-tions made it possible to hold out the prospect of an all-sided development, a happy existence, for all members of society. Communism is the theory of a liber-ation which was not possible for the slaves, the serfs, or the handicraftsmen, but only for the proletarians and hence it belong of necessity to the 19th century and was not possible in any earlier period.

QUESTION 14: *Let us go back to the sixth question. As you wish to prepare for community of property by the enlightening and uniting of the proletariat, then you reject revolution?*

ANSWER: We are convinced not only of the uselessness but even of the harm-fulness of all conspiracies. We are also aware that revolutions are not made delib-erately and arbitrarily but that everywhere and at all times they are the necessary consequence of circumstances which are not in any way whatever dependent either on the will or on the leadership of individual parties or of whole classes. But we also see that the development of the proletariat in almost all countries of the world is forcibly repressed by the possessing classes and that thus a revolution is being forcibly worked for by the opponents of communism. If, in the end, the oppressed proletariat is thus driven into a revolution, then we will defend the cause of the proletariat just as well by our deeds as now by our words.

QUESTION 15: *Do you intend to replace the existing social order by community of property at one stroke?*

ANSWER: We have no such intention. The development of the masses cannot be ordered by decree. It is determined by the development of the conditions in which these masses live, and therefore proceeds gradually.

QUESTION 16: *How do you think the transition from the present situation to com-munity of property is to be effected?*

ANSWER: The first, fundamental condition for the introduction of commu-nity of property is the political liberation of the proletariat through a democratic constitution.

QUESTION 17: *What will be your first measure once you have established democracy?*

ANSWER: Guaranteeing the subsistence of the proletariat.

QUESTION 18: *How will you do this?*

ANSWER: I. By limiting private property in such a way that it gradually pre-pares the way for its transformation into social property, e.g., by progressive taxation, limitation of the right of inheritance in favour of the state, etc., etc.

    II. By employing workers in national workshops and factories and on national estates.

   III. By educating all children at the expense of the state.

QUESTION 19: *How will you arrange this kind of education during the period of transition?*

ANSWER: All children will be educated in state establishments from the time when they can do without the first maternal care.

QUESTION 20: *Will not the introduction of community of property be accompanied by the proclamation of the community of women?*

ANSWER: By no means. We will only interfere in the personal relationship between men and women or with the family in general to the extent that the maintenance of the existing institution would disturb the new social order. Besides, we are well aware that the family relationship has been modified in the course of history by the property relationships and by periods of development, and that consequently the ending of private property will also have a most important influence on it.

QUESTION 21: *Will nationalities continue to exist under communism?*

ANSWER: The nationalities of the peoples who join together according to the principle of community will be just as much compelled by this union to merge with one another and thereby supersede themselves as the various differences between estates and classes disappear through the superseding of their basis—private property.

QUESTION 22: *Do Communists reject the existing religions?*

ANSWER: All religions which have existed hitherto were expressions of historical stages of development of individual peoples or groups of peoples. But communism is that stage of historical development which makes all existing religions superfluous and supersedes them.

DISCUSSION QUESTIONS

1. According to the confession, what were the central goals of the communists, and how did they aim to achieve them?
2. How does Engels define the proletariat, and what sets it apart from other types of workers?
3. How does the confession explicitly link communist ideology to industrialization? What place did revolution have in this ideology?

4

Victor Hugo
Preface to Cromwell
1827

The economic and political changes sweeping across Europe in the first half of the nineteenth century found cultural expression in the reigning artistic movement of the period: romanticism. As a whole, the movement shunned the rules and models of the past and embraced freedom, creative genius, and originality instead. Victor

Marie, Count Hugo (1802–1885), was among the most celebrated romantic French poets and novelists of his day. In this excerpt from the preface to one of his early works, the play Cromwell, *published in 1827, he paints a colorful picture of his artistic ideals. His passionate vision helped shape the explosion of culture after 1830 when painters, poets, playwrights, and authors turned not only to nature for inspiration but also to the gritty realities of everyday life in an increasingly industrial and urban society.*

Let us then speak boldly. The time for it has come, and it would be strange if, in this age, liberty, like the light, should penetrate everywhere except to the one place where freedom is most natural—the domain of thought. Let us take the hammer to theories and poetic systems. Let us throw down the old plastering that conceals the façade of art. There are neither rules nor models; or, rather, there are no other rules than the general laws of nature, which soar above the whole field of art, and the special rules which result from the conditions appropriate to the subject of each composition. The former are of the essence, eternal, and do not change; the latter are variable, external, and are used but once. The former are the framework that supports the house; the latter the scaffolding which is used in building it, and which is made anew for each building. In a word, the former are the flesh and bones, the latter the clothing, of the drama. But these rules are not written in the treatises on poetry. Richelet has no idea of their existence. Genius, which divines rather than learns, devises for each work the general rules from the general plan of things, the special rules from the separate *ensemble* of the subject treated; not after the manner of the chemist, who lights the fire under his furnace, heats his crucible, analyzes and destroys; but after the manner of the bee, which flies on its golden wings, lights on each flower and extracts its honey, leaving it as brilliant and fragrant as before.

The poet—let us insist on this point—should take counsel therefore only of nature, truth and inspiration, which is itself both truth and nature. *"Quando he,"* says Lope de Vega:

> Quando he de escrivir una comedia,
> Encierro los preceptos con seis llaves.[1]

To secure these precepts "six keys" are none too many, in very truth. Let the poet beware especially of copying anything whatsoever—Shakespeare no more than Molière, Schiller no more than Corneille. If genuine talent could abdicate its own nature in this matter, and thus lay aside its original personality, to transform itself into another, it would lose everything by playing this role of its own double. It is as if a god should turn valet. We must draw our inspiration from the original sources. . . .

The Dramatic Works of Victor Hugo, vol. III, (New York: The Athenaeum Society, 1909), 3–54.

[1] When I have to write a comedy, / I enclose the precepts with six keys.

Let there be no misunderstanding: if some of our poets have succeeded in being great, even when copying, it is because, while forming themselves on the antique model, they have often listened to the voice of nature and to their own genius—it is because they have been themselves in some one respect. Their branches became entangled in those of the near-by tree, but their roots were buried deep in the soil of art. They were the ivy, not the mistletoe. Then came imitators of the second rank, who, having neither roots in the earth, nor genius in their souls, had to confine themselves to imitation. As Charles Nodier says: "After the school of Athens, the school of Alexandria." Then there was a deluge of mediocrity; then there came a swarm of those treatises on poetry, so annoying to true talent, so convenient for mediocrity. We were told that everything was done, and God was forbidden to create more Molières or Corneilles. Memory was put in place of imagination. Imagination itself was subjected to hard-and-fast rules, and aphorisms were made about it: "To imagine," says La Harpe, with his naive assurance, "is in substance to remember, that is all."

But nature! Nature and truth!—And here, in order to prove that, far from demolishing art, the new ideas aim only to reconstruct it more firmly and on a better foundation, let us try to point out the impassable limit which in our opinion, separates reality according to art from reality according to nature. It is careless to confuse them as some ill-informed partisans of *romanticism* do. Truth in art cannot possibly be, as several writers have claimed, *absolute* reality. Art cannot produce the thing itself. Let us imagine, for example, one of those unreflecting promoters of absolute nature, of nature viewed apart from art, at the performance of a romantic play, say *Le Cid*. "What's that?" he will ask at the first word. "The Cid speaks in verse? It isn't *natural* to speak in verse."—"How would you have him speak, pray?"—"In prose." Very good. A moment later, "How's this!" he will continue, if he is consistent; "the Cid is speaking French!"—"Well?"—"Nature demands that he speak his own language; he can't speak anything but Spanish."

We shall fail entirely to understand but again—very good. You imagine that this is all? By no means: before the tenth sentence in Castilian, he is certain to rise and ask if the Cid who is speaking is the real Cid, in flesh and blood. By what right does the actor, whose name is Pierre or Jacques, take the name of the Cid? That is *false*. There is no reason why he should not go on to demand that the sun should be substituted for the footlights, *real* trees and *real* houses for those deceitful wings. For, once started on that road, logic has you by the collar, and you cannot stop.

We must admit therefore, or confess ourselves ridiculous, that the domains of art and of nature are entirely distinct. Nature and art are two things—were it not so, one or the other would not exist. Art, in addition to its idealistic side, has a terrestrial, material side. Let it do what it will, it is shut in between grammar and prosody, between Vaugelas and Richelet. For its most capricious creations, it has formulae, methods of execution, a complete apparatus to set in motion. For genius there are delicate instruments, for mediocrity, tools.

It seems to us that someone has already said that the drama is a mirror wherein nature is reflected. But if it be an ordinary mirror, a smooth and polished surface, it will give only a dull image of objects, with no relief—faithful, but colourless; everyone knows that colour and light are lost in a simple reflection. The drama, therefore, must be a concentrating mirror, which, instead of weakening, concentrates and condenses the coloured rays, which make a mere gleam a light, and of a light a flame. Then only is the drama acknowledged by art.

The stage is an optical point. Everything that exists in the world—in history, in life, in man—should be and can be reflected therein, but under the magic wand of art. Art turns the leaves of the ages, of nature, studies chronicles, strives to reproduce actual facts (especially in respect to manners and peculiarities, which are much less exposed to doubt and contradiction than are concrete facts), restores what the chroniclers have lopped off, harmonises what they have collected, divines and supplies their omissions, fills their gaps with imaginary scenes which have the colour of the time, groups what they have left scattered about, sets in motion anew the threads of Providence which work the human marionettes, clothes the whole with a form at once poetical and natural, and imparts to it that vitality of truth and brilliancy which gives birth to illusion, that prestige of reality which arouses the enthusiasm of the spectator, and of the poet first of all, for the poet is sincere. Thus the aim of art is almost divine: to bring to life again if it is writing history, to create if it is writing poetry. . . .

It will readily be imagined that, for a work of this kind, if the poet must *choose* (and he must), he should choose, not the *beautiful*, but the *characteristic*. Not that it is advisable to "make local colour," as they say to-day; that is, to add as an afterthought a few discordant touches here and there to a work that is at best utterly conventional and false. The local colour should not be on the surface of the drama, but in its substance, in the very heart of the work, whence it spreads of itself, naturally, evenly, and, so to speak, into every corner of the drama, as the sap ascends from the root to the tree's topmost leaf. The drama should be thoroughly impregnated with this colour of the time, which should be, in some sort, in the air, so that one detects it only on entering the theatre, and that on going forth one finds one's self in a different period and atmosphere. It requires some study, some labour, to attain this end; so much the better. It is well that the avenues of art should be obstructed by those brambles from which everybody recoils except those of powerful will. Besides, it is this very study, fostered by an ardent inspiration, which will ensure the drama against a vice that kills it—the *commonplace*. To be commonplace is the failing of short-sighted, short-breathed poets. In this tableau of the stage, each figure must be held down to its most prominent, most individual, most precisely defined characteristic. Even the vulgar and the trivial should have an accent of their own. Like God, the true poet is present in every part of his work at once. Genius resembles the die which stamps the king's effigy on copper and golden coins alike. . . .

Discussion Questions

1. According to Hugo, why should artists turn to nature for guidance and inspiration?

2. As described here, what is the relationship between art and reality?

3. Why does Hugo think that it is especially important for poets to include "local color" in their works?
4. What links do you see between Hugo's ideas and the broader political and social context?

COMPARATIVE QUESTIONS

1. How do both Beeton's book and the Berlin factory rules reflect the regimentation of daily life that characterized industrial society?
2. In what ways was Engels reacting against the picture of working- and middle-class life painted by the first two documents?
3. How is the idea of liberty central to both Hugo's and Engels's discussions?

23

Politics and Culture of the Nation-State
c. 1850–1870

S U M M A R Y   The late nineteenth century marked the dawning of a new age in European politics and culture. After the failed revolutions of 1848–49, politicians, artists, intellectuals, and the general public cast aside the promises of idealists and claimed to see society as it really was: combative, competitive, and inherently disordered. The first two documents elucidate how European leaders sought to master this unruly scene and strengthen state power from above. The making of the modern nation-state also assumed global proportions as governments expanded their empires abroad. The third document illuminates the human scope of such efforts by the greatest colonial power of the day, Great Britain. The biological research of Charles Darwin reflected the scientific dimensions of the new age, as the final document reveals. To some observers, his work suggested that just as in politics, only the hardiest survived in the natural world. The social applications of Darwin's theories supported industrial Europe's march toward world dominance.

1
Rudolf von Ihering
Two Letters
1866

Among the most skilled practitioners of Realpolitik *in late-nineteenth-century Europe was Prussian prime minister Otto von Bismarck (1815–1898). Through his military and diplomatic strategies, Bismarck took advantage of the collapse of the concert of Europe and made the dream of a united Germany a reality. Bismarck had many detractors, however, including liberals like the jurist Rudolf von Ihering (1818–1892). In two letters he wrote in 1866, von Ihering provides a contemporary assessment of*

Realpolitik in action during a pivotal period in Bismarck's quest for German unification: the war with Austria. The war erupted in June, and by early July, Prussia was triumphant. At first, Bismarck's tactics shocked von Ihering. Yet the allure of German unity proved irresistible to him and other liberals, and they soon embraced the sense of military superiority that came to define German nationalism.

(*To J. Glaser, Giessen, 1 May.*) . . . Never, probably, has a war been incited so shamelessly and with such horrifying frivolity as the one that Bismarck is currently trying to start against Austria. My innermost feelings are revolted by this violation of every legal and moral principle. God knows I am no friend of Austria; on the contrary, I have always been regarded as one of her enemies—that is to say of her political system, not of the Austrian people whom I have learned to love . . .—; I am devoted to the idea of Prussian influence in north Germany, even though I have little sympathy for the present political system in Prussia. But I would rather cut off my hand than to use it in such a disgusting operation as Prussian policy is now launching against Austria—the common sense of any honest man cannot even comprehend the depths of this perfidy. We ask ourselves in amazement: is it really true that what the whole world knows to be lies can be proclaimed from on high as the truth? Austria is supposed to be mobilizing against Prussia! Any child knows that the opposite is the case. . . . The saddest thing about it all is that once the struggle is under way principles of right and wrong must come in absolutely tragic conflict with interests. Whom should we wish victorious, Austria or Prussia? We have no choice, we must come down on the side of the *unjust* cause, because we cannot tolerate the possibility of Austria gaining the upper hand in Germany. Everyone here detests this war, nobody can be comfortable with the idea that it will have the result that we *must* desire—the hegemony of Prussia. That is our situation. Germans taking up arms against Germans, civil war, a plot of three or four Powers against one, with not even an appearance of legality, without popular participation, created by a few diplomats alone, a conspiracy against your poor country, which causes even the enemies of Austria to sympathize with her and in which they would have to desire her victory—if this victory did not mean our own ruin! . . . The war would be unthinkable if Austria had not for decades been doing everything to make it impossible even for her friends in Germany to take sides with her and putting the most menacing weapons in the hands of her enemies. . . . Everyone agrees on the crying injustice that is being done to Austria, and yet, as I say, thousands here would not lift a finger for her cause, people feel that that would mean turning against one's own cause; for with very few exceptions the general opinion here is that the free development of Germany would be incompatible with Austrian supremacy. This may be wrong, but I am merely stating the fact. There is just as little affection for

---

Walter Michael Simon, *Germany in the Age of Bismarck* (London: George Allen and Unwin, 1968), 110–13.

the German princes: here also one finds the same collision between undoubted historical justice and a total inability to work up any enthusiasm for it. It is sad to be in conflict with one's own feelings—we ought to desire victory for the just cause in this instance too, but we cannot! . . .

(*To B. Windscheid, Giessen, 19 August.*) . . . I think I must be dreaming when I think of how much has happened in the short space of a few weeks; it seems that it must be years. I am only now gradually coming to my senses again; at one time I was quite dizzy from the pace of events. What a surging of emotions—of deep fear, anxious hesitation, joyous exultation, apprehensive suspense, furious indignation, profound pity, and in the end once more a rejoicing of the soul, an ecstasy of happiness such as my heart has never before known! Oh, my dear friend, what enviable luck to be living at this time, to have seen this turning-point in German history with which there has been nothing to compare for a thousand years. For years I have envied the Italians that they succeeded in what seemed for us to lie only in the distant future, I have wished for a German Cavour and Garibaldi as Germany's political messiah. And overnight he has appeared in the person of the much-abused Bismarck. Should we not think we are dreaming if the impossible becomes possible? Like you I was afraid at the prospect of war, I was convinced of the notion that the Austrians, experienced in the practical school of war, would be superior to the Prussians. Has intelligence and moral energy ever in history celebrated such a triumph over crude force? There is something wonderful about this spirit that animates little Prussia, this spirit that lifts us all out of a state of impotence and ignominy and gives to the name of Germany in Europe a lustre and a tone that it has not had for a thousand years. I bow before the genius of Bismarck, who has achieved a masterpiece of political planning and action such as are only rarely to be found in history. How marvelously the man spun all the threads of the great web, how firmly and safely so that none of them broke, how precisely he knew and used all the ways and means—his king, Napoleon, his army, the administration, Austria and her forces—in short, a masterpiece of calculation. I have forgiven the man everything he has done up to now, more, I have convinced myself that it was necessary; what seemed to us, the uninitiated, as criminal arrogance has turned out in the end to have been an indispensable means to the goal. He is one of the greatest men of the century; it is a real revelation to have lived at the same time as such a man; a man of action like that, not heedless action but action inspired and prepared both politically and morally, is worth a hundred men of liberal principles and of powerless honesty!

Nine weeks ago I should not have believed that I would write a paean of praise to Bismarck, but I cannot help myself! I leave it to my stubborn colleagues from Swabia and Bavaria to abuse him, to concentrate everything disgusting they can think of on the name of Bismarck. Incorrigible doctrinaires! For years, they have yelled and drunk themselves hoarse for German unity, and when someone comes on the scene and achieves the impossible by transferring German unity from a book of student songs into reality they cry "crucify him." . . .

DISCUSSION QUESTIONS

1. What does von Ihering reveal about Bismarck's political methods in these two letters?
2. Why is he conflicted in his attitudes about these methods?
3. How do his opinions change between the time he wrote the first and second letters, and why?

2

Alexander II
Address in the State Council
1861

Russia's defeat in the Crimean War (1853–1856) blatantly revealed its inability to compete in the rapidly changing industrial world. Among its greatest liabilities was the institution of serfdom, which, by binding the peasant population to the land, inhibited the growth of a modern labor force while fostering widespread discontent. To combat these problems, Alexander II chose a momentous solution: the emancipation of the serfs. After years of discussion and debate, drafts of the reform were presented at a meeting of the State Council on January 28, 1861. The tsar began the meeting with the following speech, in which he underscores the importance of emancipation to Russia's future. His audience clearly shared his sense of urgency, for the general statute on the emancipation of the serfs was approved less than a month later.

The matter of the liberation of the serfs, which has been submitted for the consideration of the State Council, I consider to be a vital question for Russia, upon which will depend the development of her strength and power. I am sure that all of you, gentlemen, are just as convinced as I am of the benefits and necessity of this measure. I have another conviction, which is that this matter cannot be postponed; therefore I demand that the State Council finish with it in the first half of February so that it can be announced before the start of work in the fields; . . . I repeat—and this is my absolute will—that this matter should be finished right away.

For four years now it has dragged on and has been arousing various fears and anticipations among both the estate owners and the peasants. Any further delay could be disastrous to the state. I cannot help being surprised and happy, and I am sure all of you are happy, at the trust and calm shown by our good people in this matter. Although the apprehensions of the nobility are to a certain extent understandable, for the closest and material interests of each are involved, notwithstanding all this, I have not forgotten and shall never forget that the approach to the matter was made on the initiative of the nobility itself, and I am

A Source Book for Russian History, vol. III, (New Haven: University Press, Yale, 1972), 599–600.

happy to be able to be a witness to this before posterity. In my private conversations with the guberniia marshals of the nobility, and during my travels about Russia, when receiving the nobility, I did not conceal the trend of my thoughts and opinions on the question that occupies us all and said everywhere that this transformation cannot take place without certain sacrifices on their part and that all my efforts consist in making these sacrifices as little weighty and burdensome as possible for the nobility. I hope, gentlemen, that on inspection of the drafts presented to the State Council, you will assure yourselves that all that can be done for the protection of the interests of the nobility has been done; if on the other hand you find it necessary in any way to alter or to add to the presented work, then I am ready to receive your comments; but I ask you only not to forget that the basis of the whole work must be the improvement of the life of the peasants—an improvement not in words alone or on paper but in actual fact.

Before proceeding to a detailed examination of this draft itself, I would like to trace briefly the historical background of this affair. You are acquainted with the origin of serfdom. Formerly it did not exist among us; this law was established by autocratic power and only autocratic power can abolish it, and that is my sincere will.

My predecessors felt all the evils of serfdom and continually endeavored, if not to destroy it completely, to work toward the gradual limitation of the arbitrary power of the estate owners.

. . . My late father [Nicholas I] was continuously occupied with the thought of freeing the serfs. Sympathizing completely with this thought, already in 1856, before the coronation, while in Moscow I called the attention of the leaders of the nobility of the Moscow guberniia to the necessity for them to occupy themselves with improving the life of the serfs, adding that serfdom could not continue forever and that it would therefore be better if the transformation took place from above rather than from below. . . .

The Editorial Commissions worked for a year and seven months and, notwithstanding all the reproaches, perhaps partly just, to which the commissions were exposed, they finished their work conscientiously and presented it to the Main Committee. The Main Committee, under the chairmanship of my brother [Grand Duke Konstantin Nikolaevich], toiled with indefatigable energy and zeal. I consider it my duty to thank all the members of the committee, especially my brother, for their conscientious labors in this matter.

There may be various views on the draft presented, and I am willing to listen to all the different opinions. But I have the right to demand one thing from you: that you, putting aside all personal interests, act not like estate owners but like imperial statesmen invested with my trust. Approaching this important matter I have not concealed from myself all those difficulties that awaited us and I do not conceal them now; but, firmly believing in the grace of God and being convinced of the sacredness of this matter, I trust that God will not abandon us but will bless us to finish it for the future prosperity of our beloved fatherland.

DISCUSSION QUESTIONS

1. What were Alexander's principal goals in granting the serfs freedom?
2. How did Alexander consider emancipation to be an expression of his power as tsar?
3. In calling for emancipation, did Alexander seek to undermine the existing social hierarchy?

Krupa Sattianadan
Saguna: A Story of Native Christian Life
1887–1888

Along with strengthening state power at home in the late nineteenth century, European leaders expanded their empires abroad and tightened their control therein. Great Britain's decision to assume direct control of India in 1858 provides a dramatic example of this shift in colonial policy. In her autobiographical novel Saguna, *Krupa Sattianadan (1862–1894) illuminates the everyday dimensions of British imperialism. She was born to Christian parents in the Bombay Presidency, an administrative unit of the colonial administration. While in her teens, the death of her beloved brother, Bhasker, gravely affected her physical and emotional health. She was sent to a nearby mission school to recover, and describes her experiences there in the following passage. As she recounts, her white teachers strove to mold her according to English tastes, morals, and behavior, thereby exposing the racist attitudes underlying British rule. Her book found a ready audience and was published both in English and Tamil, a language widely used in southern India.*

My sister paid a visit to the city, not long after Bhasker's death. She noticed my retired ways and my peculiar moods and took me to her home. One day as I was sitting in the hall, puzzling my head over some books that I found in the study, two ladies were announced, and before I had time to run away, they were in the hall. The first grasped my sister's hand in hers and gave her a hearty kiss. Her appearance at once attracted my notice. She seemed fresh coloured, tall, as she looked with a good-humoured smile at me over sister's shoulder. There was a twinkle in her eye, as if she wished every one to be a partaker of her high spirits. She was certainly strikingly different from other ladies, I thought, and I listened with great attention to what she had to say. . . . Then she turned round toward me, and, catching hold of both of my hands, put question after question to me in such a way that I could not but answer. She had large light brown eyes, a fine, full

Susie Tharu and K. Lalita, eds., *Women Writing in India: 600 B.C. to the Present,* vol. I, *600 B.C. to the Early Twentieth Century* (New York: The Feminist Press, 1991), 277–81.

long face, a nose rather blunt, and a broad, high forehead. I liked her. Presently she turned toward my sister and talked aside for a few minutes while her companion smiled to me and drew me toward her. But before we could talk much the other turned toward me, and said, "So that's settled; you are to come next month and stay with me. You will learn to your heart's content there, but mind you are to be very free with me and tell me everything. I mean to quarrel with you very often. Ah! you critical thing. Don't I know what you are thinking?" and with a warm, but rather rough hug and a brushing kiss she left me. My sister said I must go and stay with the two ladies for some time. I liked the idea and made up my mind to go. The first thing that I was told on going to Miss Roberts'—for that was the name of the lady who took charge of me—was that I was a little girl; that in England girls of fourteen and fifteen were considered mere chits, and that I was to lay aside all solemnity of manner and behave as a girl. When it came to the lessons I was asked what I was learning.

I said: "History, geography, &c."

"What in history?"

"I have finished *Landmarks of the History of Greece*, and am reading—"

"Greece! Greece! What have you to do with Greece?"

I had loved this little book. It was like a storybook, and I thought that she would have been pleased, but she only murmured, "Well! I will see. I must get something more suited to you. What about English? Can you read fluently?"

Longfellow's poems were put into my hand. The volume opened at "Pleasant it was when woods were green." I read this fast enough.

"Too fast."

"Oh I know it by heart," I exclaimed, anxious to show my cleverness. I shut the book and repeated the whole thing to her. I had once learnt it in a fit of study, and it had given me much pleasure.

"Well! I tell you what," she said, shutting the book, "you know a little too much. When a horse goes too fast, what does his master do?"

I did not know what he did, but I thought the comparison was not a good one, and I exclaimed abruptly, "I am not a horse."

"Well! Well!" she said laughing, "we won't discuss that point. I think you want occupation. You must teach in my little school this afternoon. Now we have done with our lessons for one day."

To my great surprise she shut up the books and put them by. When dinner time came I saw the other lady for the first time. She gave me a smile and pointed to my place by her side, but Miss Roberts never left me alone. She began by saying to her neighbour, "Girls in England never sit at the table with their elders, but of course we shall allow this one." In my sister's house I had learned to some extent how to use spoon and fork, but when I found the lady's eyes fixed on me my fingers trembled, and I thought I was sure to make all kinds of mistakes to her amusement. Already her eyes were twinkling with fun and laughter. I refused many a tempting thing that was offered, while she kept on remarking: "That's right, don't eat if you don't care. Girls in England don't eat these things." At last came curry and rice, of which I took a little, and enjoyed it. . . .

During the day, the school was my delight. This Miss Roberts managed. She instructed me in the art of teaching, in which I found a great delight. I was astonished at the explanations which I was able to give, and the way in which a knowledge of things seemed to spring into existence when it was required. I was in a whirl of delight with the blackboards, the large maps and the pictures, and the new dignity that all these conferred on me. Miss Roberts smiled at my eagerness, and forgot to say that I was only a child. I loved to think myself grown up and important. Miss Roberts used to quarrel with me as impetuously and passionately as if she had been of my own age, and then make it up by giving me a hearty hug and a kiss. She had very peculiar views, and we often had little fights with each other. I can hardly help thinking that she sometimes gave expression to her views for the sole purpose of teasing me. "Oh, Miss D., what made you receive the Bible woman in the drawing room?" she said one day, alluding to a very respectable person, a great friend of our family. "In England we receive them in the kitchen. She is no better than a servant, I assure you."

"In the kitchen?" I said, in amazement and indignation. I was angry, and thought of many grievances that I had heard spoken of. I had also heard that we were the real aristocrats of our country, and that the English ladies who came to India only belonged to the middle class, and I resolved to tell her that, so I boldly added: "What do you think of us? We are real aristocrats of this place." Unfortunately I pronounced the big word wrongly, and she burst out laughing and repeated it again and again, as I had done. "I don't care. Anyhow, you are middle-class people. She is a brahmin, and only takes money from the Mission because she is poor. She is no servant. In your country you are no brahmins. You are sudras." Tears fell from my eyes, and I felt as if I should choke.

"Miss D.," exclaimed the angry lady, now quite beside herself, "do girls ever talk at table like this? I protest against this. I can't have it. I tell you I can't,"—this with so much emphasis that I was quite frightened. Miss D. looked at me and shook her head. The tears that were rolling from my eyes I hastily wiped. "What can I do?" I said, while a shower of words, such as "rude," "bad," "naughty," "disrespectful," &c., fell on my head. Tiffin over, Miss Roberts went with a bounce to her room and I went to mine and began to cry. "Natives," I said to myself, "we are natives. Tomorrow she will say that my mother was a Bible woman too. Oh! I will go away from her," and I began to cry more. About five minutes afterward the door behind me opened, and Miss Roberts rushed in, took hold of me, and kissed me profusely. "Now it is all right," she said smiling and wonderfully changed. "We won't talk about it."

"And you won't send Bible women to the kitchen?" I said.

She shook her head and rushed away from me laughing.

In the evenings we generally sat together in the lobby. It was our free time, and I was told to say anything I liked. I used to sit far back on the deep seat with my hands on my lap, although there was a table in front. I liked to draw my own pictures, with the stars and shadows outside, and often my thoughts were with Bhasker; but I was always disturbed and told to talk. Generally the ladies had some fancy work in their hands; but I never brought any. One day Miss Roberts rebuked me and said: "Why did you not bring some work?"

I felt guilty, but still as I rose I said somehow, "I thought we were expected to be free at this time."

"Yes, but we must not appear so. I hate laziness."

Something in this remark caught my attention. I stood near the table and looked out. All my pictures vanished. I looked into her face and said, "It is only for appearance, is it? What is the good of that? Won't it be acting falsely?"

She flew into a passion, and when I tried to escape to my room, she forced me down. "Falsely! Sit and be lazy," she said, "and let everyone of us put you to shame."

The second lady, however, calmed her, saying, "Really I don't do anything. I had better sit quietly too."

"Sit, sit," said Miss Roberts, who had by this time nearly spent her wrath and was in a little pet.

The other lady had on various occasions whispered to me, "She is Irish and means nothing," and now she looked and smiled at me.

My greatest trials always came through my tongue. I had got into the habit of thinking loudly. Bhasker had encouraged it, and the discussions carried on by my other brothers, in which I often took part, had made me quite an adept in defending my views. I had had to stand up for my rights from my childhood. I had not then learnt the beauty of silence. One day I was sitting in the lobby in my usual half-sleepy, half-dreamy state, when I heard a visitor announced. As soon as Miss Roberts heard the name, she broke out abruptly, "Oh, how disgusting! What a bore she is! and she wants me, that is true enough." So saying she walked out, and an elderly lady met her near the lobby.

"Oh! I am so glad to see you. How do you do?" Miss Roberts said in a hearty tone as she brought in the visitor. Surely this is somebody else, and I am glad that it is a surprise for Miss Roberts, I said to myself. The talk evidently was cheerful and genial, but as soon as it was over, I was rather taken aback to hear Miss Roberts say, "Oh, what a bore to be sure! How glad I am she is gone! We must really not have visitors at this time."

"She! she!" I said, "was not she a surprise to you?"

"What do you mean?" said Miss Roberts, turning abruptly round on me.

"No! I thought the lady was a surprise to you. You said you were so glad to see her."

"Oh! Oh!" she said, lifting her voice and her hands.

"Miss D., I tell you I can't have this imper—"

"You said free speech was allowed here," I answered, interrupting her.

"Free speech, but not to your superiors, not to me," this with a thump on the table. "You naughty girl."

But it was a little overdone, and there was a burst from the other lady in which Miss Roberts found herself heartily joining.

Later on I came to know that they did not mean anything. It was only the custom, and they used the few set phrases that etiquette compelled them to use. But my readers will understand from this what a boor I was. I loved these two ladies and stayed with them for months, and in spite of little quarrels now and then, I lived very happily with them. Not long after I was attacked with fever, and my sister was compelled to take me away.

DISCUSSION QUESTIONS

1. How would you describe the attitudes of Sattianadan's teachers toward her, and vice versa?

2. As described by Sattianadan, in what ways did the mission school further the goals of British colonial policy?

3. What does this passage suggest about both the benefits and drawbacks of this policy?

4
Charles Darwin
The Descent of Man
1871

As Bismarck and other Realpolitikers *were transforming European political views in the late nineteenth century, the English naturalist Charles Darwin (1809–1882) was transforming their scientific ones. In 1859 he published* On the Origin of Species, *which argued that animal species evolved over time through a process of natural selection by which the strongest, and most well adapted to any given environment, survived. The biblical story of creation had no place in Darwin's conclusions, and this incited considerable debate. The debate intensified twelve years later when Darwin applied his theory of evolution directly to humans in* The Descent of Man. *The ramifications of this work extended beyond the field of biology when some people began to use evolutionary principles to understand, justify, and perpetuate the social and political inequalities of the day.*

The main conclusion here arrived at, and now held by many naturalists who are well competent to form a sound judgment, is that man is descended from some less highly organised form. The grounds upon which this conclusion rests will never be shaken, for the close similarity between man and the lower animals in embryonic development, as well as in innumerable points of structure and constitution, both of high and of the most trifling importance,—the rudiments which he retains, and the abnormal reversions to which he is occasionally liable,—are facts which cannot be disputed. They have long been known, but until recently they told us nothing with respect to the origin of man. Now when viewed by the light of our knowledge of the whole organic world, their meaning is unmistakable. The great principle of evolution stands up clear and firm, when these groups of facts are considered in connection with others such as the mutual affinities of the members of the same group, their geographical distribution in past and present times, and their geological succession. It is incredible that all these facts should speak falsely. He who is not content to look, like a savage, at the phenomena of nature as disconnected, cannot any longer believe that man is the work of a

Charles Darwin, *The Descent of Man and Selection in Relation to Sex* (New York: D. Appleton and Company, 1896), 606–19.

separate act of creation. He will be forced to admit that the close resemblance of the embryo of man to that, for instance, of a dog—the construction of his skull, limbs and whole frame on the same plan with that of other mammals, independently of the uses to which the parts may be put—the occasional re-appearance of various structures, for instance of several muscles, which man does not normally possess, but which are common to the Quadrumana—and a crowd of analogous facts—all point in the plainest manner to the conclusion that man is the co-descendant with other mammals of a common progenitor.

We have seen that man incessantly presents individual differences in all parts of his body and in his mental faculties. These differences or variations seem to be induced by the same general causes, and to obey the same laws as with the lower animals. In both cases similar laws of inheritance prevail. Man tends to increase at a greater rate than his means of subsistence; consequently he is occasionally subjected to a severe struggle for existence, and natural selection will have effected whatever lies within its scope. A succession of strongly-marked variations of a similar nature is by no means requisite; slight fluctuating differences on the individual suffice for the work of natural selection; not that we have any reason to suppose that in the same species, all parts of the organisation tend to vary to the same degree. . . .

Through the means just specified, aided perhaps by others as yet undiscovered, man has been raised to his present state. But since he attained to the rank of manhood, he has diverged into distinct races, or as they may be more fitly called, subspecies. Some of these, such as the Negro and European, are so distinct that, if specimens had been brought to a naturalist without any further information, they would undoubtedly have been considered by him as good and true species. Nevertheless all the races agree in so many unimportant details of structure and in so many mental peculiarities, that these can be accounted for only by inheritance from a common progenitor; and a progenitor thus characterised would probably deserve to rank as man.

It must not be supposed that the divergence of each race from the other races, and of all from a common stock, can be traced back to any one pair of progenitors. On the contrary, at every stage in the process of modification, all the individuals which were in any way better fitted for their conditions of life, though in different degrees, would have survived in greater numbers than the less well-fitted. The process would have been like that followed by man, when he does not intentionally select particular individuals, but breeds from all the superior individuals, and neglects the inferior. He thus slowly but surely modifies his stock, and unconsciously forms a new strain. So with respect to modifications acquired independently of selection, and due to variations arising from the nature of the organism and the action of the surrounding conditions, or from changed habits of life, no single pair will have been modified much more than the other pairs inhabiting the same country, for all will have been continually blended through free intercrossing.

By considering the embryological structure of man, —the homologies which he presents with the lower animals,—the rudiments which he retains,—and the reversions to which he is liable, we can partly recall in imagination the former condition of our early progenitors; and can approximately place them in their proper place in the zoological series. We thus learn that man is descended from a hairy, tailed quadruped, probably arboreal in its habits, and an inhabitant of the Old World. This creature, if its whole structure had been examined by a naturalist, would have been classed amongst the Quadrumana, as surely as the still more ancient progenitor of the Old and New World monkeys. The Quadrumana and all the higher mammals are probably derived from an ancient marsupial animal, and this through a long line of diversified forms, from some amphibian-like creature, and this again from some fish-like animals. In the dim obscurity of the past we can see that the early progenitor of all the Vertebrata must have been an aquatic animal, provided with branchiae, with the two sexes united in the same individual, and with the most important organs of the body (such as the brain and heart) imperfectly or not at all developed. This animal seems to have been more like the larvae of the existing marine Ascidians than any other known form.

The high standard of our intellectual powers and moral disposition is the greatest difficulty which presents itself, after we have been driven to this conclusion on the origin of man. But every one who admits the principle of evolution, must see that the mental powers of the higher animals, which are the same in kind with those of man, though so different in degree, are capable of advancement. Thus the interval between the mental powers of one of the higher apes and of a fish, or between those of an ant and scale-insect, is immense; yet their development does not offer any special difficulty; for with our domesticated animals, the mental faculties are certainly variable, and the variations are inherited. No one doubts that they are of the utmost importance to animals in a state of nature. Therefore the conditions are favourable for their development through natural selection. The same conclusion may be extended to man; the intellect must have been all-important to him, even at a very remote period, as enabling him to invent and use language, to make weapons, tools, traps, &c., whereby with the aid of his social habits, he long ago became the most dominant of all living creatures. . . .

The belief in God has often been advanced as not only the greatest, but the most complete of all the distinctions between man and the lower animals. It is however impossible, as we have seen, to maintain that this belief is innate or instinctive in man. On the other hand a belief in all-pervading spiritual agencies seems to be universal; and apparently follows from a considerable advance in man's reason, and from a still greater advance in his faculties of imagination, curiosity and wonder. I am aware that the assumed instinctive belief in God has been used by many persons as an argument for His existence. But this is a rash argument, as we should thus be compelled to believe in the existence of many cruel and malignant spirits, only a little more powerful than man; for the belief in them is far more general than in a beneficent Deity. The idea of a universal and beneficent Creator does not seem to arise in the mind of man, until he has been elevated by long-continued culture. . . .

I am aware that the conclusions arrived at in this work will be denounced by some as highly irreligious; but he who denounces them is bound to show why it is more irreligious to explain the origin of man as a distinct species by descent from some lower form, through the laws of variation and natural selection, than to explain the birth of the individual through the laws of ordinary reproduction. The birth both of the species and of the individual are equally parts of that grand sequence of events, which our minds refuse to accept as the result of blind chance. The understanding revolts at such a conclusion, whether or not we are able to believe that every slight variation of structure,—the union of each pair in marriage,—the dissemination of each seed,—and other such events, have all been ordained for some special purpose. . . .

The main conclusion arrived at in this work, namely that man is descended from some lowly organised form, will, I regret to think, be highly distasteful to many. But there can hardly be a doubt that we are descended from barbarians. The astonishment which I felt on first seeing a party of Fuegians on a wild and broken shore will never be forgotten by me, for the reflection at once rushed into my mind—such were our ancestors. These men were absolutely naked and bedaubed with paint, their long hair was tangled, their mouths frothed with excitement, and their expression was wild, startled, and distrustful. They possessed hardly any arts, and like wild animals lived on what they could catch; they had no government, and were merciless to every one not of their own small tribe. He who has seen a savage in his native land will not feel much shame, if forced to acknowledge that the blood of some more humble creature flows in his veins. For my own part I would as soon be descended from that heroic little monkey, who braved his dreaded enemy in order to save the life of his keeper, or from that old baboon, who descending from the mountains, carried away in triumph his young comrade from a crowd of astonished dogs—as from a savage who delights to torture his enemies, offers up bloody sacrifices, practises infanticide without remorse, treats his wives like slaves, knows no decency, and is haunted by the grossest superstitions.

Man may be excused for feeling some pride at having risen, though not through his own exertions, to the very summit of the organic scale; and the fact of his having thus risen, instead of having been aboriginally placed there, may give him hope for a still higher destiny in the distant future. But we are not here concerned with hopes or fears, only with the truth as far as our reason permits us to discover it; and I have given the evidence to the best of my ability. We must, however, acknowledge, as it seems to me, that man with all his noble qualities, with sympathy which feels for the most debased, with benevolence which extends not only to other men but to the humblest living creature, with his god-like intellect which has penetrated into the movements and constitution of the solar system—with all these exalted powers—Man still bears in his bodily frame the indelible stamp of his lowly origin.

DISCUSSION QUESTIONS

1. What evidence does Darwin supply to support his theory of human evolution?

2. How does this evidence call into question the relationship between religion and science?

3. In what ways does Darwin voice the concern for realism and concrete facts that marked the general mood of his day?

COMPARATIVE QUESTIONS

1. What similarities and differences do you see in the political methods and goals of Bismarck and Alexander II?

2. How does Darwin's picture of nature lend support to these methods and goals?

3. In what ways do you think Darwin's theories might have shaped British attitudes toward colonial peoples as revealed in Sattianadan's story?

24

Industry, Empire, and Everyday Life
1870–1890

S U M M A R Y   The dual phenomena of industry and empire changed Europe and the world profoundly in the late nineteenth century. The first document reveals that with domestic industries booming, European leaders looked abroad for new markets and raw materials. The widespread belief that a nation's imperial holdings were an indication of its strength and racial superiority also fueled the quest for empire. Industrial growth went hand in hand with imperial expansion. In the second document, we see Germany's extraordinary success on these two fronts, which raised concerns throughout Europe, especially in Great Britain. The third document points to the political repercussions of industrial progress as workers joined together to fight for their rights. At the same time, many painters cast the people and scenery of the age in a new light, giving birth to the impressionist movement. As the final document reveals, impressionists were particularly inspired by Asian art, revealing Europe's increasing interconnectedness with the world.

1

Jules Ferry
Speech before the French National Assembly
1883

French politician Jules Ferry (1832–1893) fueled his country's quest to compete in the continent's race to conquer foreign territory in the closing decades of the nineteenth century. While serving two terms as premier during the Third Republic, Ferry took the lead in France's colonial expansion in Africa and Asia. Yet not everyone embraced his imperialist policies, including his conservative and socialist colleagues within the government. In the following speech, delivered before the National Assembly in July

1883, Ferry faced his opponents head on, defending not only the political and economic necessity of French expansionism but also its moral justness. At the same time, his critics voice their views, revealing the basis of their anticolonial sentiment.

M. JULES FERRY: Gentlemen, it embarrasses me to make such a prolonged demand upon the gracious attention of the Chamber, but I believe that the duty I am fulfilling upon this platform is not a useless one. It is as strenuous for me as for you, but I believe that there is some benefit in summarizing and condensing, in the form of arguments, the principles, the motives, and the various interests by which a policy of colonial expansion may be justified; it goes without saying that I will try to remain reasonable, moderate, and never lose sight of the major continental interests which are the primary concern of this country. What I wish to say, to support this proposition, is that in fact, just as in word, the policy of colonial expansion is a political and economic system; I wish to say that one can relate this system to three orders of ideas: economic ideas, ideas of civilization in its highest sense, and ideas of politics and patriotism.

In the area of economics, I will allow myself to place before you, with the support of some figures, the considerations which justify a policy of colonial expansion from the point of view of that need, felt more and more strongly by the industrial populations of Europe and particularly those of our own rich and hard working country: the need for export markets. Is this some kind of chimera? Is this a view of the future or is it not rather a pressing need, and, we could say, the cry of our industrial population? I will formulate only in a general way what each of you, in the different parts of France, is in a position to confirm. Yes, what is lacking for our great industry, drawn irrevocably on to the path of exportation by the [free trade] treaties of 1860, what it lacks more and more is export markets. Why? Because next door to us Germany is surrounded by barriers, because beyond the ocean, the United States of America has become protectionist, protectionist in the most extreme sense, because not only have these great markets, I will not say closed but shrunk, and thus become more difficult of access for our industrial products, but also these great states are beginning to pour products not seen heretofore onto our own markets. . . . It is not necessary to pursue this demonstration any farther. Yes, gentlemen, I am speaking to the economists, whose convictions and past services no one appreciates more than I do; I am speaking to the honorable M. Passy, whom I see here and who is one of the most authoritative representatives among us of the old school of economics [*smiles*]; I know very well what they will reply to me, what is at the bottom of their thoughts . . . the old school, the great school, gentlemen; one, M. Passy, which your name has embellished, which was led in France by Jean-Baptiste Say and by Adam Smith in England. I do not mean to treat you with any irony, M. Passy, believe me.

Ralph A. Austin, ed., *Modern Imperialism: Western Overseas Expansion and Its Aftermath, 1776–1965* (Lexington, Mass.: D. C. Heath, 1969), 69–74.

I say that I know very well the thoughts of the economists, whom I can call doctrinaires without offending M. Passy. They say to us, "The true export markets are the commercial treaties which furnish and assure them." Gentlemen, I do not look down upon commercial treaties: if we could return to the situation which existed after 1860, if the world had not been subjected to that economic revolution which is the product of the development of science and the speeding up of communications, if this great revolution had not intervened, I would gladly take up the situation which existed after 1860. It is quite true that in that epoch the competition of grain from Odessa did not ruin French agriculture, that the grain of America and of India did not yet offer us any competition; at that moment we were living under the regime of commercial treaties, not only with England, but with the other great powers, with Germany, which had not yet become an industrial power. I do not look down upon them, these treaties; I had the honor of negotiating some of less importance than those of 1860; but gentlemen, in order to make treaties, it is necessary to have two parties: one does not make treaties with the United States; this is the conviction which has grown among those who have attempted to open some sort of negotiations in this quarter, whether officially or officiously.

Gentlemen, there is a second point, a second order of ideas to which I have to give equal attention, but as quickly as possible, believe me; it is the humanitarian and civilizing side of the question. On this point the honorable M. Camille Pellatan has jeered in his own refined and clever manner; he jeers, he condemns, and he says "What is this civilization which you impose with cannonballs? What is it but another form of barbarism? Don't these populations, these inferior races, have the same rights as you? Aren't they masters of their own houses? Have they called upon you? You come to them against their will, you offer them violence, but not civilization." There, gentlemen, is the thesis; I do not hesitate to say that this is not politics, nor is it history: it is political metaphysics. ["Ah, Ah," *on far left*].

. . . Gentlemen, I must speak from a higher and more truthful plane. It must be stated openly that, in effect, superior races have rights over inferior races. [*Movement on many benches on the far left.*]

M. JULES MAIGNE: Oh! You dare to say this in the country which has proclaimed the rights of man!

M. DE GUILLOUTET: This is a justification of slavery and the slave trade!

M. JULES FERRY: If M. Maigne is right, if the declaration of the rights of man was written for the blacks of equatorial Africa, then by what right do you impose regular commerce upon them? They have not called upon you.

M. RAOUL DUVAL: We do not want to impose anything upon them. It is you who wish to do so!

M. JULES MAIGNE: To propose and to impose are two different things!

M. GEORGES PERIN: In any case, you cannot bring about commerce by force.

M. JULES FERRY: I repeat that superior races have a right, because they have a duty. They have the duty to civilize inferior races. . . . [*Approbation from the left. New interruptions from the extreme left and from the right*]

That is what I have to answer M. Pelletan in regard to the second point upon which he touched.

He then touched upon a third, more delicate, more serious, and upon which I ask your permission to express myself quite frankly. It is the political side of the question. The honorable M. Pelletan, who is a distinguished writer, always comes up with remarkably precise formulations. I will borrow from him the one which he applied the other day to this aspect of colonial policy.

"It is a system," he says, "which consists of seeking out compensations in the Orient with a circumspect and peaceful seclusion which is actually imposed upon us in Europe."

I would like to explain myself in regard to this. I do not like this word, "compensation," and, in effect, not here but elsewhere it has often been used in treacherous way. If what is being said or insinuated is that any government in this country, any Republican minister could possibly believe that there are in any part of the world compensations for the disasters which we have experienced, an injury is being inflicted . . . and an injury undeserved by that government. [*Applause at the center and left.*] I will ward off this injury with all the force of my patriotism! [*New applause and bravos from the same benches.*]

Gentlemen, there are certain considerations which merit the attention of all patriots. The conditions of naval warfare have been profoundly altered. ["Very true! Very true!"]

At this time, as you know, a warship cannot carry more than fourteen days' worth of coal, no matter how perfectly it is organized, and a ship which is out of coal is a derelict on the surface of the sea, abandoned to the first person who comes along. Thence the necessity of having on the oceans provision stations, shelters, ports for defense and revictualling. [*Applause at the center and left. Various interruptions.*] And it is for this that we needed Tunisia, for this that we needed Saigon and the Mekong Delta, for this that we need Madagascar, that we are at Diégo-Suarez and Vohemar [two Madagascar ports] and will never leave them! [*Applause from a great number of benches.*] Gentlemen, in Europe as it is today, in this competition of so many rivals which we see growing around us, some by perfecting their military or maritime forces, others by the prodigious development of an ever growing population; in a Europe, or rather in a universe of this sort, a policy of peaceful seclusion or abstention is simply the highway to decadence! Nations are great in our times only by means of the activities which they develop; it is not simply "by the peaceful shining forth of institutions" [*Interruptions on the extreme left and right*] that they are great at this hour.

As for me, I am astounded to find the monarchist parties becoming indignant over the fact that the Republic of France is following a policy which does not confine itself to that ideal of modesty, of reserve, and, if you will allow me the expression, of bread and butter [*Interruptions and laughter on the left*] which the representatives of fallen monarchies wish to impose upon France. [*Applause at the center.*]

... [The Republican Party] has shown that it is quite aware that one cannot impose upon France a political ideal conforming to that of nations like independent Belgium and the Swiss Republic; that something else is needed for France: that she cannot be merely a free country, that she must also be a great country, exercizing all of her rightful influence over the destiny of Europe, that she ought to propagate this influence throughout the world and carry everywhere that she can her language, her customs, her flag, her arms, and her genius. [*Applause at center and left.*]

DISCUSSION QUESTIONS

1. Why does Ferry consider colonial expansion to be an economic necessity?
2. Aside from its economic benefits, why, according to Ferry, is colonial expansion justified?
3. How does Ferry appeal to nationalist sentiment to defend his imperialist stance, and why?
4. What is the basis of his critics' arguments against imperialism?

2

Ernest Edwin Williams
Made in Germany
1896

In the closing decades of the nineteenth century, a new, seemingly unstoppable economic force appeared on the scene in Europe: Germany. It enjoyed astounding industrial growth throughout this period and gained a substantial share of European export markets. Many people in Great Britain observed these events with dismay, seeing Germany as a threat not simply to their country's long-standing industrial dominance but also to its national identity as a world power. Journalist Ernest Edwin Williams (1866–1935) fanned the flames of such fears in Made in Germany, *published in 1896. Drawing on a dizzying array of statistics, Williams painted a menacing picture of the omnipresence of German products in his readers' everyday lives. He hoped that his bleak portrait would prompt Parliament to adopt measures to protect and enhance British trade. Although his message went unheeded, it evidently struck a chord, for the book went through six editions in its first year.*

The Departing Glory
Preliminary

The Industrial Supremacy of Great Britain has been long an axiomatic commonplace; and it is fast turning into a myth, as inappropriate to fact as the Chinese Emperor's computation of his own status. This is a strong statement. But it is neither wide nor short of the truth. The industrial glory of England is departing,

Ernest Edwin Williams, *Made in Germany,* 4th ed. (London: William Heinemann, 1896), 1–2, 7–12, 18.

and England does not know it. There are spasmodic outcries against foreign competition, but the impression they leave is fleeting and vague. The phrase, "Made in Germany," is raw material for a jape at the pantomime, or is made the text for a homily by the official guardians of some particular trade, in so far as the matter concerns themselves. British Consuls, too, send words of warning home, and the number of these is increasing with significant frequency. But the nation at large is yet as little alive to the impending danger as to the evil already wrought. The man in the shop or the factory has plenty to say about the Armenian Question and the House of Lords, but about commercial and industrial matters which concern him vitally he is generally much less eloquent. The amount of interest evinced by the amateur politician seems invariably to advance with the remoteness of the matter from his daily bread. It is time to disturb the fatal torpor: even though the moment be, in one sense, unhappily chosen. The pendulum between depression and prosperity has swung to the latter, and manufacturers and merchants are flushed with the joyful contemplation of their order-books. Slackness has given way to briskness; the lean years have been succeeded by a term of fat ones. The prophet of evil commands his most attentive audiences when the times are with him. When they are good—though the good be fleeting—his words are apt to fall unheeded. . . .

As It Was

There was a time when our industrial empire was unchallenged. It was England which first emerged from the Small-Industry stage. She produced the Industrial Revolution about the middle of the last century, and well-nigh until the middle of this she developed her multitude of mills, and factories, and mines, and warehouses, undisturbed by war at home, and profiting by wars abroad. The great struggles which drained the energies of the Continental nations, sealed her industrial supremacy, and made her absolute mistress of the world-market. Thanks to them, she became the Universal Provider. English machinery, English pottery, English hardware, guns, and cutlery, English rails and bridge-work, English manufactures of well-nigh every kind formed the material of civilisation all over the globe. She covered the dry land with a network of railways, and the seas were alive with her own ships freighted with her own merchandise. Between 1793 and 1815 the value of her exports had risen from £17,000,000 to £58,000,000. Her industrial dominion was immense, unquestioned, unprecedented in the history of the human race; and not unnaturally we have come to regard her rule as eternal. But careless self-confidence makes not for Empire. While she was throwing wide her gates to the world at large, her sisters were building barriers of protection against her; and, behind those barriers, and aided often by State subventions, during the middle and later years of the century, they have developed industries of their own. Of course, this was to a certain extent inevitable. England could not hope for an eternal monopoly of the world's manufactures; and industrial growths abroad do not of necessity sound the knell of her greatness. But she must discriminate in her equanimity. And most certainly she must discriminate against Germany. For Germany has entered into a deliberate and deadly rivalry with her, and is battling with might and main for the extinction of her supremacy. . . .

The German Revolution

Up to a couple of decades ago, Germany was an agricultural State. Her manufactures were few and unimportant; her industrial capital was small; her export trade was too insignificant to merit the attention of the official statistician; she imported largely for her own consumption. Now she has changed all that. Her youth has crowded into English houses, has wormed its way into English manufacturing secrets, and has enriched her establishments with the knowledge thus purloined. She has educated her people in a fashion which has made it in some branches of industry the superior, and in most the equal of the English. Her capitalists have been content with a simple style, which has enabled them to dispense with big immediate profits, and to feed their capital. They have toiled at their desks, and made their sons do likewise; they have kept a strict controlling hand on all the strings of their businesses; they have obtained State aid in several ways—as special rates to shipping ports; they have insinuated themselves into every part of the world—civilised, barbarian, savage—learning the languages, and patiently studying the wants and tastes of the several peoples. Not content with reaping the advantages of British colonisation—this was accomplished with alarming facility—Germany has "protected" the simple savage on her own account, and the Imperial Eagle now floats on the breezes of the South Sea Islands, and droops in the thick air of the African littoral. Her diplomatists have negotiated innumerable commercial treaties. The population of her cities has been increasing in a manner not unworthy of England in the Thirties and Forties. Like England, too, she is draining her rural districts for the massing of her children in huge factory towns. Her yards (as well as those of England) too, are ringing with the sound of hammers upon ships being builded for the transport of German merchandise. Her agents and travelers swarm through Russia, and wherever else there is a chance of trade on any terms—are even supplying the foreigner with German goods *at a loss,* that they may achieve their purpose in the end. In a word, an industrial development, unparalleled, save in England a century ago, is now her portion. A gigantic commercial State is arising to menace our prosperity, and contend with us for the trade of the world. . . .

Made in Germany

The phrase is fluent in the mouth: how universally appropriate it is, probably no one who has not made a special study of the matter is aware. Take observations, Gentle Reader, in your own surroundings: the mental exercise is recommended as an antidote to that form of self-sufficiency which our candid friends regard as indigenous to the British climate. Your investigations will work out somewhat in this fashion. You will find that the material of some of your own clothes was probably woven in Germany. Still more probably is it that some of your wife's garments are German importations; while it is practically beyond a doubt that the magnificent mantles and jackets wherein her maids array themselves on their Sundays out are German-made and German-sold, for only so could they be done at the figure. Your governess's *fiancé* is a clerk in the City; but he also was made in Germany. The toys, and the dolls, and the fairy books which your children maltreat in the nursery are made in Germany: nay, the material of your favourite (patriotic) newspaper had the same birthplace as like as not. Roam the house over, and the fateful mark will greet you at every turn, from the piano in your drawing-room to the mug on your kitchen dresser, blazoned though it be with the legend, *A Present from Margate.* Descend to your domestic depths, and you shall find your very drain-pipes German made. You pick out of the grate the paper wrappings from a book consignment, and they also are "Made in Germany." You stuff them into the fire, and reflect that the poker in your hand was forged in Germany. As you rise from your hearthrug you knock over an ornament on your mantlepiece; picking up the pieces you read, on the bit that formed the base, "Manufactured in Germany." And you jot your dismal reflections down with a pencil that was made in Germany. At midnight your wife comes home from an opera which was made in Germany, has been here enacted by singers and conductor and players made in Germany, with the aid of instruments and sheets of music made in Germany. You go to bed, and glare wrathfully at a text on the wall; it is illuminated with an English village church, and it was "Printed in Germany." If you are imaginative and dyspeptic, you drop off to sleep only to dream that St. Peter (with a duly stamped halo round his head and a bunch of keys from the Rhineland) has refused you admission into Paradise, because you bear not the Mark of the Beast upon your forehead, and are not of German make. But you console yourself with the thought that it was only a Bierhaus Paradise any way; and you are awakened in the morning by the sonorous brass of a German band.

Is the picture exaggerated? Bear with me, while I tabulate a few figures from the Official Returns of Her Majesty's Custom House, where, at any rate, fancy and exaggeration have no play. In '95 Germany sent us linen manufactures to the value of £91,257; cotton manufactures to the value of £536,471; embroidery and needlework to the value of £11,309; leather gloves to the value of £27,934 (six times the amount imported six years earlier); and woollen manufactures to the value of £1,016,694. Despite the exceeding cheapness of toys, the value of German-made playthings for English nurseries amounted, in '95, to £459,944. In the same year she sent us books to the value of £37,218, and paper to the value of £586,835. For musical instruments we paid her as much as £563,018; for china and earthenware £216,876; for prints, engravings, and photographs, £111,825. This recital of the moneys which *in one year* have come out of John Bull's pocket for the purchase of his German-made household goods is, I submit disproof enough of any charge of alarmism. For these articles, it must be remembered, are not like oranges and guano. They are not products which we must either import or lack: — *they all belong to the category of English manufactures,* the most important of them, indeed, being articles in the preparation of which Great Britain is held pre-eminent. The total value of manufactured goods imported into the United Kingdom by Germany rose from £16,629,987 in '83 to £21,632,614 in '93: an increase of 30.08 per cent. . . .

The Significance of these Facts

These are the sober—to believers in our eternal rule, the sobering—facts. They are picked almost at random from a mass of others of like import, and I think they are sufficient to prove that my general statements are neither untrue nor unduly emphatic. And yet the data needed for the purpose of showing the parlous condition into which our trade is drifting are still largely to seek. Germany is yet in her industrial infancy; and the healthiest infant can do but poor battle against a grown man. England, with her enormous capital, and the sway she has wielded for a century over the world-market, is as that strong man. Now, to tell a strong man, conscious of his strength to an over-weening degree, that he is in peril from a half-grown youngster, is to invite his derision; and yet if a strong man, as the years advance on him, neglect himself and abuse his strength, he may fall before an energetic stripling. Germany has already put our trade in a bad way; but the worst lies in the future, and it is hard to convince the average Englishman of this. He will admit that Germany's trade has increased, and that at many points it hits our own; but her his robust insularity asserts itself. Germany has not the capital, he will tell you; here workmen are no workmen at all; her capitalists and her managers are poor bureaucratic plodders; the world will soon find out that her products are not of English make, and so forth. And he goes on vocalising *Rule Britannia* in his best commercial prose.

Discussion Questions

1. According to Williams, what are the secrets of Germany's economic "revolution"?
2. Why does he regard Germany's industrial success as a cause for alarm in Great Britain in particular?
3. What does this excerpt suggest about industrial growth in this period and its impact on international relations?

3

Margaret Bondfield
A Life's Work
1948

Despite the explosive industrial growth of the last third of the nineteenth century, life for European workers was still a struggle. They remained vulnerable to economic exploitation and fluctuations in the faster-paced, more competitive, and more complex marketplace. Workers began to take matters into their own hands by organizing formal unions to fight for better working conditions. Although men dominated the trade union movement, women found a place, too, as the following excerpt from the autobiography of Margaret Bondfield (1873–1954) reveals. The daughter of a lace factory worker, Bondfield went to work at fourteen as a draper's assistant. With the rise of consumer capitalism, shop assisting was among the fastest growing employment opportunities for women. The long days and low wages prompted Bondfield to join the newly established National Union for Shop Assistants in 1894, launching her lifelong commitment to political activism.

London: By dint of rigid economy, at the end of five years of shop life in Brighton I had saved £5, which seemed to me great wealth; but the material side of life did

Margaret Bondfield, *A Life's Work* (London: Hutchinson & Co., 1948), 27–29, 36.

not bother me much. I had reached a stage in my spiritual pilgrimage which I must needs travel alone. Religion had become something personal, to be accepted or rejected; at home it was like the air—it permeated our lives, but was not discussed. I could no longer passively accept contemporary opinion on business morality, to which I applied the harsh judgments of the very young. The outward and visible sign of my protest was a sudden move to London. It was undoubtedly *the* turning-point in my life. But for that I might have become a successful business woman!

For the next three months I was nearer to starvation than at any time since. I learned the bitterness of a hopeless search for work. The kindness of a landlady who trusted me kept me going when I was penniless, and until I got a job.

In those days the seekers after work had no Labour Exchange to help them. The best plan was to visit the wholesale firms in the City and get information about vacancies from the commercial travellers, and then journey as fast as the old horse buses allowed—perhaps right across London—only to find a queue of 150 to 200 applicants already there. Before we had stood in the queue for long a notice would be put up: "No good waiting any longer—placed filled."

I have taken the whole of Oxford Street, going into every shop walking West on the one side, and every shop on the other side coming back on the chance that there might be a vacancy. I was not tall enough. I remember one man saying to me, "We never engage anyone under five feet eight inches."

Even today those first months in the great city searching for work carry the shadow of a nightmare; but finally I got a job—only to find that conditions, which I had thought peculiar to the Brighton shop, were almost universal. . . .

A small thing led me to another adventure of faith. I was hungry and I went across to Fitzroy Street to buy a penn'orth of fish and a ha'p'orth of chips, served to me in a newspaper; munching my feast, I strolled around Fitzroy Square reading the paper, in which was a letter from James Macpherson, Secretary of the National Union of Shop Assistants, Warehousemen and Clerks, urging shop assistants to join together to fight against the wretched conditions of employment. I was working about sixty-five hours a week for between £15 and £25 per annum, living in. Here I felt was the right thing to do, and at once I joined up.

My brother Frank was in London, working at Clement's House Printing Works, where he was "Father of the Chapel" and a member of the Union committee to negotiate terms for the introduction of the Linotype. He encouraged my Trade Union activities. This was a happy time for me.

My Union officers gave me all the work I could do in my scant leisure, and every kind of encouragement. They elected me on to the district council, and once I attended a national conference. For the next two years the Union utilized me for platform work in an ever-increasing degree.

Encouraged by T. Spencer Jones, the editor of our little Union paper, I ventured first to undertake reports of meetings, and later to write a few short stories under the pen-name of Grace Dare. It was quite impossible for me to write in the presence of any who might know what I was doing, and as I had not one inch of space I could call my own, I would wait till one or two of my room-mates were asleep, and then stealthily, with the feeling of a conspirator, and knowing that I was committing an offence for which I could be heavily fined, I would light my halfpenny dip, hiding its glare by means of a towel thrown over the back of a chair, and set to work on my monthly article.

If my room-mates woke they were kind enough not to remember it the next morning, and although this surreptitious writing was kept up for about two years, I do not think any breach of rules was ever reported to the firm.

In those early days—1894 to 1896—executive committee meetings of my Union were called for Sundays, the only possible day. The committee members had often to travel long distances on night trains, arriving early on Sunday morning, sitting for the transaction of business in a stuffy room, clouded with tobacco smoke, starting back again on Sunday night to be in time for business at 7.30 or 8 a.m. on Monday; they were the pioneers, and to me they were heroes, for they had only bare expenses from the Union. . . . "Death to the Living-in System," "Abolish Fines and Deductions," "Reduce the Hours Worked in Shops," were the slogans. We had no delusions about the size of the job. We frankly told our audiences that we invited them to share in hard work for the next ten years in building up the membership. We were about 2,000 strong in a trade employing 750,000 people. "Come, pioneers! O pioneers!" we sang, and they were coming! . . .

From this time on I just lived for the Trade Union Movement. I concentrated on my job.

This concentration was undisturbed by love affairs. I had seen too much— too early—to have the least desire to join in the pitiful scramble of my work-mates. The very surroundings of shop life accentuated the desire of most shop girls to get married. Long hours of work and the living-in system deprived them of the normal companionship of men in their leisure hours, and the wonder is that so many of the women continued to be good and kind, and self-respecting, without the incentive of a great cause, or of any interest outside their job.

Many of them would toil after business hours to make their clothes, so that, from their small salaries, they could help some member of their family. Some women, much older than myself, would look forward to marriage with hope and dread—hope of economic security, and dread of the unknown ordeal of child-birth. Through what sex knowledge I was able to pass on, Mrs. Martindale re-solved their fears, but it was not at all easy to transmit to them the reverence for motherhood, which I had seen at its best and highest, but which to them was too often linked with the obscene.

I had no vocation for wifehood or motherhood, but an urge to serve the Union—an urge which developed into "a sense of oneness with our kind."

DISCUSSION QUESTIONS

1. According to Bondfield, what was life like for her and her coworkers?
2. What traditional female roles did she reject to devote herself fully to union activities?
3. What does Bondfield reveal about the role of literacy and the press in working-class collective action?

4

Emile Zola

Impressionism
1880

As Europe's economic and political frontiers expanded, so did its cultural ones. Impressionism, an avant-garde artistic movement based in France in the late nineteenth century, was especially important in this regard. Inspired in part by Asian art, impressionists broke free from the precise realism typical of studio painting and ventured outdoors instead. Here they strove to capture on canvas the scenery, colors, and mood of modern life as it unfolded before them, whether on busy city streets or in tranquil fields. Their unconventional style and subjects aroused considerable public debate. Among the impressionists' most ardent champions was French writer Emile-Edouard-Charles-Antoine Zola (1840–1902). A cultural innovator in his own right, Zola saw reflections of his own artistic ideals in impressionist paintings, as he revealed in the following article, which was published in the Paris newspaper Le Voltaire *in June 1880.*

These last few years something very interesting and instructive has been happening under our own eyes. I refer to the independent exhibitions put on by a group of painters that have been called "the Impressionists." . . . I use this term "Impressionist" here, because a label is really wanting to name the young artists who, in the wake of Courbet and of our great landscape painters, have devoted themselves to the study of nature. . . . When we come down to it, as a working painter Courbet himself is a magnificent classic. . . . The true revolutionaries of form appear with Mr. Edouard Manet, with the Impressionists, Messrs. Claude Monet, Renoir, Pissarro, Guillaumin, and still others. These propose to get out of the studio in which painters have shut themselves up for so many centuries, and go paint in the open. In the open, the light is no longer uniform, and this means a multiplicity of impressions. . . . This study of light in its thousand decompositions and recompositions is what has been called, more or less properly, Impressionism because by it a painting becomes the impression of a moment experienced in nature. The jokers of the press have started from there to caricature the Impressionist painter catching, so to speak, his impressions on the wing in half a dozen shapeless brush strokes; and it must be admitted that certain artists have unfortunately warranted these attacks by contenting themselves with sketches that are far too rudimentary. As far as I am concerned, it is true that one has to apprehend living nature in the expression of an instant; only, this instant must be fixed on the canvas for ever by a fully considered composition. In the end, nothing solid is possible without work. . . .

The public is dumbfounded when it comes face to face with certain canvases painted in the open at specific hours; it stands gaping before blue grasses, violet-

---

Eugen Weber, *Movements, Currents, Trends: Aspects of European Thought in the Nineteenth and Twentieth Centuries* (Lexington, Mass., 1992), 199–200.

113

colored soils, red trees, waters running with all the motley of the rainbow. And yet the artist has been conscientious; he has, perhaps, by reaction, slightly exaggerated the new tonalities his eye has noted; but, when it comes down to it, the observation is absolutely true, nature has never adhered to the simplified notation that the established schools use to treat it. [But it is this last to which the public is used.] Hence the laughter of the crowd faced with the Impressionist paintings, despite the good faith and the very honest, naïve efforts of the young painters.

They are taken for pranksters, humbugs, charlatans making fun of the public and drumming up publicity around their works, when they are, on the contrary, severe and principled observers. What seems to be ignored is that most of these contenders are poor men who work themselves to death, sometimes quite literally from misery and weariness. Strange humbugs, these martyrs for their beliefs!

This is, then, what the Impressionist painters have to offer: a more exact examination of the causes and effects of light, exerting its influence both on color and design. They have been justifiably accused of drawing their inspiration from Japanese prints. . . . It is certain that our dark schools of painting, the bituminous-minded work of our established schools, has been surprised and forced to rethink things when faced with the limpid horizons, the beautiful vibrant spots of the Japanese water-colorists. There was in these works a simplicity of means and an intensity of performance which struck our young artists and drove them on to this path of painting soaked in air and light—a path which all the talented newcomers take today. . . .

The great pity is that this new formula which they all bring scattered in their works, not one of the artists of the group has realized powerfully and definitively. The formula is there, endlessly divided; but nowhere, in any one of them, do we find it applied by a master. . . . Yet, while we can take objection to their personal incapacity, they remain none the less the true representatives of our time. They have plenty of gaps, their workmanship is too often slack, they are too easily satisfied, they show themselves to be incomplete, illogical, exaggerated, ineffectual. No matter: it is enough for them to apply themselves to contemporary naturalism in order to find themselves at the head of a movement and play a great part in our school of painting.

DISCUSSION QUESTIONS

1. How does Zola define impressionism as a movement?
2. Why does he describe impressionists as "revolutionaries"?
3. What does this document suggest about the relationship between art and the public at the time?

COMPARATIVE QUESTIONS

1. According to Ferry and Williams, what factors are key to a nation's strength, and why?
2. What do their views suggest about changes in Europe's place within the world at large?
3. What do Zola and Bondfield reveal about the impact of industrialization and imperialism on everyday life and culture?

CHAPTER

25

Modernity and the Road to War
c. 1890–1914

SUMMARY   As the twentieth century dawned, Europeans had cause for both elation and fear. On the one hand, many enjoyed unprecedented prosperity. Europe's industrial and technological forces continued to grow, and European nations controlled most of the world's surface. On the other, domestic and international tensions abounded. At home people struggled to navigate the hazards of modern life, while abroad nation-states faced mounting competition and dissent in their quest for imperial glory. The following documents illustrate that disorder and chaos seemed to lurk around every corner, such as in an individual's dream, a suffrage organization, an anti-imperialist placard, and a hate-filled newspaper article. Collectively, these documents reveal that the road of modernity was rocky and uncertain, casting a permanent shadow over the Enlightenment's faith in the inevitability of progress.

1
Sigmund Freud
The Interpretation of Dreams
1900

The fast-paced and conflict-ridden nature of life in industrial Europe undermined many people's optimism about their own and society's future. Austrian doctor Sigmund Freud (1856–1939) developed the method of psychoanalysis to tap into and cure such anxieties. After studying medicine in Vienna, in 1886 Freud opened his own practice to treat patients with nervous disorders. His clinical experience was the basis for his lifelong commitment to the scientific study of the human unconscious. He published his most well-known work, The Interpretation of Dreams, *in 1900. In it, he described dreams as windows into an individual's irrational desires and inner conflicts. Only by drawing out dreams' hidden meanings could a person expose the roots of his or her psychological problems. Psychoanalysis was designed to do just that, thereby laying the foundation of modern psychology.*

In the following pages, I shall demonstrate that there is a psychological technique which makes it possible to interpret dreams, and that on the application of this technique, every dream will reveal itself as a psychological structure, full of significance, and one which may be assigned to a specific place in the psychic activities of the waking state. Further, I shall endeavor to elucidate the processes which underlie the strangeness and obscurity of dreams, and to deduce from these processes the nature of the psychic forces whose conflict or co-operation is responsible for our dreams. . . .

I am proposing to show that dreams are capable of interpretation; and any contributions to the solution of the problem which have already been discussed will emerge only as possible by-products in the accomplishment of my special task. On the hypothesis that dreams are susceptible of interpretation, I at once find myself in disagreement with the prevailing doctrine of dreams . . . for "to interpret a dream" is to specify its "meaning," to replace it by something which takes its position in the concatenation of our psychic activities as a link of definite importance and value. But, as we have seen, the scientific theories of the dream leave no room for a problem of dream-interpretation; since, in the first place, according to these theories, dreaming is not a psychic activity at all, but a somatic process which makes itself known to the psychic apparatus by means of symbols. Lay opinion has always been opposed to these theories. It asserts its privilege of proceeding illogically, and although it admits that dreams are incomprehensible and absurd, it cannot summon up the courage to deny that dreams have any significance. Led by a dim intuition, it seems rather to assume that dreams have a meaning, albeit a hidden one; that they are intended as a substitute for some other thought-process, and that we have only to disclose this substitute correctly in order to discover the hidden meaning of the dream.

The unscientific world, therefore, has always endeavored to "interpret" dreams, and by applying one or the other of two essentially different methods. The first of these methods envisages the dream-content as a whole, and seeks to replace it by another content, which is intelligible and in certain respects analogous. This is symbolic dream-interpretation; and of course it goes to pieces at the very outset in the case of those dreams which are not only unintelligible but confused. The construction which the biblical Joseph placed upon the dream of Pharaoh furnishes an example of this method. The seven fat kine, after which came seven lean ones that devoured the former, were a symbolic substitute for seven years of famine in the land of Egypt, which according to the prediction

A. A. Brill, trans. and ed., *The Basic Writings of Sigmund Freud* (New York: The Modern Library, 1938), 183, 188–94, 208–09, 217–18.

were to consume all the surplus that seven fruitful years had produced. Most of the artificial dreams contrived by the poets are intended for some such symbolic interpretation, for they reproduce the thought conceived by the poet in a guise not unlike the disguise which we are wont to find in our dreams.

The idea that the dream concerns itself chiefly with the future, whose form it surmises in advance—a relic of the prophetic significance with which dreams were once invested—now becomes the motive for translating into the future the meaning of the dream which has been found by means of symbolic interpretation.

A demonstration of the manner in which one arrives at such a symbolic interpretation cannot, of course, be given. Success remains a matter of ingenious conjecture, of direct intuition, and for this reason dream-interpretation has naturally been elevated into an art which seems to depend upon extraordinary gifts. The second of the two popular methods of dream-interpretation entirely abandons such claims. It might be described as the "cipher method," since it treats the dream as a kind of secret code in which every sign is translated into another sign of known meaning, according to an established key. For example, I have dreamt of a letter and also of a funeral or the like; I consult a "dream-book," and I find that "letter" is to be translated by "vexation" and "funeral" by "engagement." It now remains to establish a connection, which I am again to assume as pertaining to the future, by means of the rigmarole which I have deciphered. . . .

The worthlessness of both these popular methods of interpretation does not admit of discussion. As regards the scientific treatment of the subject, the symbolic method is limited in its application, and is not susceptible of a general exposition. In the cipher method everything depends upon whether the "key," the dream-book, is reliable, and for that all guarantees are lacking. So that one might be tempted to grant the contention of the philosophers and psychiatrists, and to dismiss the problem of dream-interpretation as altogether fanciful.

I have, however, come to think differently. I have been forced to perceive that here, once more, we have one of those not infrequent cases where an ancient and stubbornly retained popular belief seems to have come nearer to the truth of the matter than the opinion of modern science. I must insist that the dream actually does possess a meaning, and that a scientific method of dream-interpretation is possible. I arrived at my knowledge of this method in the following manner:

For years I have been occupied with the solution of certain psychopathological structures—hysterical phobias, obsessional ideas, and the like—with therapeutic intentions. . . . In the course of these psychoanalytic studies, I happened upon the question of dream-interpretation. My patients, after I had pledged them to inform me of all the ideas and thoughts which occurred to them in connection with a given theme, related their dreams, and thus taught me that a dream may be interpolated in the psychic concatenation, which may be followed backwards from a pathological idea into the patient's memory. The next step was to treat the dream itself as a symptom, and to apply to it the method of interpretation which had been worked out for such symptoms.

For this a certain psychic preparation on the part of the patient is necessary. A twofold effort is made, to stimulate his attentiveness in respect of his psychic perceptions, and to eliminate the critical spirit in which he is ordinarily in the habit of viewing such thoughts as come to the surface. For the purpose of self-observation with concentrated attention it is advantageous that the patient should take up a restful position and close his eyes; he must be explicitly instructed to renounce all criticism of the thought-formations which he may perceive. He must also be told that the success of the psychoanalysis depends upon his noting and communicating everything that passes through his mind, and that he must not allow himself to suppress one idea because it seems to him unimportant or irrelevant to the subject, or another because it seems nonsensical. He must preserve an absolute impartiality in respect to his ideas; for if he is unsuccessful in finding the desired solution of the dream, the obsessional idea, or the like, it will be because he permits himself to be critical of them. . . .

As will be seen, the point is to induce a psychic state which is in some degree analogous, as regards the distribution of psychic energy (mobile attention), to the state of the mind before falling asleep—and also, of course, to the hypnotic state. On falling asleep the "undesired ideas" emerge, owing to the slackening of a certain arbitrary (and, of course, also critical) action, which is allowed to influence the trends of our ideas; we are accustomed to speak of fatigue as the reason of this slackening; the emerging undesired ideas are changed into visual and auditory images. In the condition which it utilized for the analysis of dreams and pathological ideas, this activity is purposely and deliberately renounced, and the psychic energy thus saved (or some part of it) is employed in attentively tracking the undesired thoughts which now come to the surface—thoughts which retain their identity as ideas (in which the condition differs from the state of falling asleep). *"Undesired ideas" are thus changed into "desired" ones.* . . .

The first step in the application of this procedure teaches us that one cannot make the dream as a whole the object of one's attention, but only the individual components of its content. If I ask a patient who is as yet unpractised: "What occurs to you in connection with this dream?" he is unable, as a rule, to fix upon anything in his psychic field of vision. I must first dissect the dream for him; then, in connection with each fragment, he gives me a number of ideas which may be described as the "thoughts behind" this part of the dream. In this first and important condition, then, the method of dream-interpretation which I employ diverges from the popular, historical and legendary method of interpretation by symbolism and approaches more nearly to the second or "cipher method." Like this, it is an interpretation in detail, not *en masse;* like this, it conceives the dream, from the outset, as something built up, as a conglomerate of psychic formations. . . .

When, after passing through a narrow defile, one suddenly reaches a height beyond which the ways part and a rich prospect lies outspread in different directions, it is well to stop for a moment and consider whither one shall turn next. We are in somewhat the same position after we have mastered this first interpretation of a dream. We find ourselves standing in the light of a sudden discovery. The dream is not comparable to the irregular sounds of a musical instrument, which, instead of being played by the hand of a musician, is struck by some external force; the dream is not meaningless, not absurd, does not presuppose that one part of our store of ideas is dormant while another part begins to awake. It is a perfectly valid psychic phenomenon, actually a wish-fulfilment; it may be enrolled in the continuity of the intelligible psychic activities of the waking state; it is built up by a highly complicated intellectual activity. . . .

It is easy to show that the wish-fulfilment in dreams is often undisguised and easy to recognize, so that one may wonder why the language of dreams has not long since been understood. There is, for example, a dream which I can evoke as often as I please, experimentally, as it were. If, in the evening, I eat anchovies, olives, or other strongly salted foods, I am thirsty at night, and therefore I wake. The waking, however, is preceded by a dream, which has always the same content, namely, that I am drinking. I am drinking long draughts of water; it tastes as delicious as only a cool drink can taste when one's throat is parched; and then I wake, and find that I have an actual desire to drink. The cause of this dream is thirst, which I perceive when I wake. From this sensation arises the wish to drink and the dream shows me this wish as fulfilled. It thereby serves a function, the nature of which I soon surmise. I sleep well, and am not accustomed to being waked by a bodily need. If I succeed in appeasing my thirst by means of the dream that I am drinking, I need not wake up in order to satisfy my thirst. It is thus a *dream of convenience*. The dream takes the place of action, as elsewhere in life. . . .

Distortion in Dreams

If I now declare that wish-fulfilment is the meaning of *every* dream, so that there cannot be any dreams other than wish-dreams, I know beforehand that I shall meet with the most emphatic contradiction. . . .

Nevertheless, it is not difficult to parry these apparently invincible objections. It is merely necessary to observe that our doctrine is not based upon the estimates of the obvious dream-content but relates to the thought-content, which, in the course of interpretation, is found to lie behind the dream. Let us compare and contrast the *manifest* and the *latent dream-content*. It is true that there are dreams the manifest content of which is of the most painful nature. But has anyone ever tried to interpret these dreams—to discover their latent thought-content? If not, the two objections to our doctrine are no longer valid; for there is always the possibility that even our painful and terrifying dreams may, upon interpretation, prove to be wish-fulfilment. . . .

DISCUSSION QUESTIONS

1. How did Freud's theory of dream interpretation reject contemporary views about dreams on the one hand and accept them on the other?
2. What does Freud mean when he describes dreams as "wish-fulfilments"?
3. According to Freud, what is the relationship between a person's dreams and his or her waking state?

2
Emmeline Pankhurst
Speech from the Dock
1908

By granting working-class men the vote in 1884, the British government hoped to make politics more unified and orderly. Yet the realization of such hopes proved elusive, in part because a new political foe had appeared on the scene: the women's suffrage movement. The founder of the Women's Social and Political Union, Emmeline Pankhurst (1858–1928), was among the most influential voices of the movement. Although women in Britain had long been fighting for rights, the expansion of the male electorate further accentuated their political exclusion. In the following speech before a police court judge, Pankhurst defends the WSPU's tactics, which had become increasingly militant since its inception in 1903. She had been arrested for distributing a leaflet encouraging her supporters "to rush the House of Commons" and, along with two colleagues, faced a prison sentence for refusing to "bind themselves over"—in other words, to promise to behave properly. Her speech reflects her belief that the WSPU's struggle was more than a quest for the vote; it was a war against a patriarchical society.

Ever since my girlhood, a period of about 30 years, I have belonged to organisations to secure for women that political power which I have felt was essential to bringing about those reforms which women need. I have tried constitutional methods. I have been womanly. When you spoke to some of my colleagues the day before yesterday about their being unwomanly, I felt that bitterness which I know every one of them felt in their hearts. We have tried to be womanly, we have tried to use feminine influence, and we have seen that it is of no use. Men who have been impatient have invariably got reforms for their impatience. And they have not our excuse for being impatient. . . .

Now, while I share in the feeling of indignation which has been expressed to you by my daughter, I have lived longer in the world than she has. Perhaps I can look round the whole question better than she can, but I want to say here, deliberately, to you, that we are here to-day because we are driven here. We have taken this action, because as women—and I want you to understand it is as women we have taken this action—it is because we realise that the condition of our sex is so deplorable that it is our duty even to break the law in order to call attention to the reasons why we do so.

I do not want to say anything which may seem disrespectful to you, or in any way give you offence, but I do want to say that I wish, sir, that you could put yourself into the place of women for a moment before you decide upon this case. My

Emmeline Pankhurst, "Speech from the Dock [Police Court]," in *Votes for Women*, Oct. 29, 1908, 1.

daughter referred to the way in which women are huddled into and out of these police-courts without a fair trial. I want you to realise what a poor hunted creature, without the advantages we have had, must feel.

I have been in prison. I was in Holloway Gaol for five weeks. I was in various parts of the prison. I was in the hospital, and in the ordinary part of the prison, and I tell you, sir, with as much sense of responsibility as if I had taken the oath, that there were women there who have broken no law, who are there because they have been able to make no adequate statement.

You know that women have tried to do something to come to the aid of their own sex. Women are brought up for certain crimes, crimes which men do not understand—I am thinking especially of infanticide—they are brought before a man judge, before a jury of men, who are called upon to decide whether some poor, hunted woman is guilty of murder or not. I put it to you, sir, when we see in the papers, as we often do, a case similar to that of Daisy Lord, for whom a great petition was got up in this country, I want you to realise how we women feel, because we are women, because we are not men, we need some legitimate influence to bear upon our law-makers.

Now, we have tried every way. We have presented larger petitions than were ever presented for any other reform; we have succeeded in holding greater public meetings than men have ever had for any reform, in spite of the difficulty which women have in throwing off their natural diffidence, that desire to escape publicity which we have inherited from generations of our foremothers; we have broken through that. We have faced hostile mobs at street corners, because we were told that we could not have that representation for our taxes which men have won unless we converted the whole of the country to our side. Because we have done this, we have been misrepresented, we have been ridiculed, we have had contempt poured upon us. The ignorant mob at the street corner has been incited to offer us violence, which we have faced unarmed and unprotected by the safeguards which Cabinet Ministers have. We know that we need the protection of the vote even more than men have needed it.

I am here to take upon myself now, sir, as I wish the prosecution had put upon me, the full responsibility for this agitation in its present phase. I want to address you as a woman who has performed the duties of a woman, and, in addition, has performed the duties which ordinary men have had to perform, by earning a living for her children, and educating them. In addition to that, I have been a public officer. I enjoyed for 10 years an official post under the Registrar, and I performed those duties to the satisfaction of the head of the department. After my duty of taking the census was over, I was one of the few Registrars who qualified for a special bonus, and was specially praised for the way in which the work was conducted. Well, sir, I stand before you, having resigned that office when I was told that I must either do that or give up working for this movement.

I want to make you realise that it is a point of honour that if you decide—as I hope you will not decide—to bind us over, that we shall not sign any undertaking, as the Member of Parliament did who was before you yesterday. Perhaps his reason for signing that undertaking may have been that the Prime Minister had given some assurance to the people he claimed to represent that something should be done for them. We have no such assurance. Mr. Birrell told the women who questioned him the other day that he could not say that anything would be done to give an assurance to the women that their claims should be conceded. So, sir, if you decide against us to-day, to prison we must go, because we feel that we should be going back to the hopeless condition this movement was in three years ago if we consented to be bound over to keep the peace which we have never broken, and so, sir, if you decide to bind us over, whether it is for three or six months, we shall submit to the treatment, the degrading treatment, that we have submitted to before.

Although the Government admitted that we are political offenders, and, therefore, ought to be treated as political offenders are invariably treated, we shall be treated as pickpockets and drunkards; we shall be searched. I want you, if you can, as a man, to realise what it means to women like us. We are driven to do this, we are determined to go on with agitation, because we feel in honour bound. Just as it was the duty of your forefathers, it is our duty to make this world a better place for women than it is to-day. . . .

This is the only way we can get that power which every citizen should have of deciding how the taxes she contributes to should be spent, and how the laws she has to obey should be made, and until we get that power we shall be here— we are here to-day, and we shall come here over and over again. You must realise how futile it is to settle this question by binding us over to keep the peace. You have tried it; it has failed. Others have tried to do it, and have failed. If you had power to send us to prison, not for six months, but for six years, for 16 years, or for the whole of our lives, the Government must not think that they can stop this agitation. It will go on.

I want to draw your attention to the self-restraint which was shown by our followers on the night of the 13th, after we had been arrested. It only shows that our influence over them is very great, because I think that if they had yielded to their natural impulses, there might have been a breach of the peace on the evening of the 13th. They were very indignant, but our words have always been, "be patient, exercise self-restraint, show our so-called superiors that the criticism of women being hysterical is not true; use no violence, offer yourselves to the violence of others." We are going to win. Our women have taken that advice; if we are in prison they will continue to take that advice.

Well, sir, that is all I have to say to you. We are here not because we are law-breakers; we are here in our efforts to become law-makers.

DISCUSSION QUESTIONS

1. In what ways did the WSPU's tactics challenge conventional notions of proper behavior for women at the time?
2. According to Pankhurst, why was the WSPU forced to adopt such tactics?
3. Why did she think that women had both a right to and a need for political enfranchisement?

3

The I-ho-ch'uan (Boxers)
The Boxers Demand Death
for All "Foreign Devils"
1900

Despite Europe's domination of the globe, the glow of imperial glory was starting to fade in the late nineteenth and early twentieth centuries. In many places, Europeans' hold on their colonial territories was increasingly tenuous as local resistance to foreign rule and interference mounted. The following placard exposes the beliefs driving one such uprising in China, where Western nations had recently made significant inroads. It was written and circulated by the Boxers at the height of their mass revolt against foreign powers in 1900, during which they burned churches, destroyed telegraph lines and railways, and murdered Chinese Christians and missionaries. As the document reveals, an amalgam of distinctive spiritual values and overt hostility to the trappings of modern "progress" fueled the Boxers' actions. Although brutally repressed, the Boxer rebellion strengthened Chinese nationalist sentiment, which ultimately undermined Western imperialism in China.

The Gods assist the Boxers,
The Patriotic Harmonious corps,
It is because the "Foreign Devils" disturb the "Middle Kingdom."
Urging the people to join their religion,
To turn their backs on Heaven,
Venerate not the Gods and forget the ancestors.

Men violate the human obligations,
Women commit adultery,
"Foreign Devils" are not produced by mankind,
If you do not believe,
Look at them carefully.

The eyes of all the "Foreign Devils" are bluish,
No rain falls,
The earth is getting dry,
This is because the churches stop Heaven,
The Gods are angry;
The Genii are vexed;
Both come down from the mountain to deliver the doctrine.

Louis L. Snyder, ed., *The Imperialism Reader: Documents and Readings on Modern Expansionism* (Princeton: Van Nostrand, 1962), 322–23.

This is no hearsay,
The practices of boxing will not be in vain;
Reciting incantations and pronouncing magic words,
Burn up yellow written prayers,
Light incense sticks
To invite the Gods and Genii of all the grottoes.

The Gods come out from grottoes,
The Genii come down from mountains,
Support the human bodies to practice the boxing.
When all the military accomplishments or tactics
Are fully learned,
It will not be difficult to exterminate the "Foreign Devils" then.

Push aside the railway tracks,
Pull out the telegraph poles,
Immediately after this destroy the steamers.

The great France
Will grow cold and downhearted.
The English and Russians will certainly disperse.
Let the various "Foreign Devils" all be killed.
May the whole Elegant Empire of the Great Ching Dynasty be ever prosperous!

DISCUSSION QUESTIONS

1. Why do the Boxers describe foreigners as "devils"?

2. What forces do the Boxers believe are on their side?

3. In addition to killing foreigners, why do you think the Boxers call for an attack on railways, telegraph lines, and steamers?

4. What type of society do the Boxers desire for China?

4

Léon Daudet
The Punishment
1895

At the close of the nineteenth century, more and more Europeans embraced militant nationalism and anti-Semitism as weapons against the struggles of modern society. The combination of these two forces fueled what became a defining event of the period, the Dreyfus Affair. A Jewish captain in the French Army, Alfred Dreyfus, was accused of spying for Germany in 1894. Despite his protestations of innocence (which in the end proved true), he was convicted and subjected to a public degradation in Paris, as the following document recounts. It was written by journalist Léon Daudet and published in the newspaper Le Figaro *with the headline "The Punishment." Thousands witnessed the degradation in person, but Daudet provided even more with a firsthand account of Dreyfus's symbolic execution, colored by his hatred of Jews and his desire to "preserve France for the French." Throughout the course of the affair, newspaper articles such as this one nurtured the public's prejudices and helped anti-Semitism enter mainstream politics.*

Behind the high iron gate, in the vast, square, and solemn Morland Courtyard, troops begin to assemble. Companies march past. I hear that singular step, formed of hundreds of steps, the rattling of rifles, leather belts and sabers. . . .

The hour strikes nine. The general pulls his sword. The drums roll, their dull rumble translating the shudders felt by the entire silent gathering. The fatal door opens on the hideous cortege: four artillerymen and, between them, the criminal; close by, the executioner, a sergeant major of the Republican Guard. That small and mournful group crosses the diagonal at a military step and stops a few meters in front of the general. Every heart trembles. A riotous silence reigns. Clouds give way to a ray of sunshine, brief and bloody, pouring a bit of life on this death worse than death.

The military clerk comes forward. He reads the verdict. But his voice, like that of the general, is lost in the vast space. Quickly, the executioner, a sort of helmeted giant, approaches the condemned man, a rigid and dark silhouette on which all attention is focused. Without an instant of hesitation, the executioner goes for the military cap; he tears off the insignia, the fine gold braids, the ornaments of the jacket and sleeves. The dump puppet prepares himself for the atrocious work; he even lifts his arms. He shouts a few words—"Innocent! . . . Innocent! . . . Long live France! . . ."—which hardly carry through the heavy, anguish-filled atmosphere.

In the public square beyond the courtyard . . . the crowd grows restless and clamorous. It howls. It hisses. It is a strident and intersecting storm of outrage. Anger prevails over dejection and stupor.

But nothing stirs among the soldiers who witness and judge. I take up my opera glass. It dances in my hands, and through a kind of steam, I find myself close to this symbolic act of stripping away, to the fall of buttons and epaulets. . . . I catch a glimpse of the condemned man's wan and weasel-like face, raised up in final defiance. But I am engrossed by his body, that run-down body of a liar, from which is skinned away, piece by piece, everything that gave it social value. . . .

The giant takes the sword of the man who had been a captain and, with a final, sharp, lightning blow, breaks it over his knee. The vestiges are on the ground, pitiful rags, punished for the wretch who wore them, dead in his place, and dishonored with him.

What more can one do with this little automaton, completely black and stripped of everything, with this hideous beast of treason who remains upright on his rigid limbs, survivor of his own catastrophe . . . ? He will be exposed to the contempt of those who were his comrades, and for whom he prepared defeat, all

---

Michael Burns, *France and the Dreyfus Affair: A Documentary History* (Boston: Bedford/ St. Martin's, 1999), 52–53.

those brave officers, all those humble soldiers, motionless and terrified. Within them rage struggles with disgust and the remains of pity that exist in noble souls, even in the presence of the worst crimes. He will march in front of these honorable men, in front of rectitude, discipline, duty, in front of that empire of heroism, all the sentiments that mean nothing to him, the traitor. . . .

He approaches, between his guards, a walking corpse, with the step of a zombie on parade, thin in appearance, but magnified by infamy. . . . Close to us he finds again the strength to shout "Innocent!" in a voice without tone. There is he before me, at the instant of passing, the cold eye, the look lost in the past, no doubt, since his future is dead with his honor. He no longer has age. He no longer has a name. He no longer has a complexion. He is the color of *treason*. His face is ashen . . . without appearance of remorse, surely foreign, a wreck of the ghetto. . . .

The shouts of the crowd have stopped. The ray of sunlight has disappeared. Our strength has been sapped. It is time for the drama to end. The degradation and parade have lasted only ten minutes, but our emotions have been stirred, it seems, for twenty-four hours. The sinister march ends down there, at the black carriage of the prison guard, on the back-street where the corpse, lifted up by gendarmes, is finally put in its oven (*s'enfourne*). We are relieved at its presence.

Life resumes. The troops disband. Beat the drums! Sound the fanfare! Cast your proud and sonorous mantle over this obscene burial. . . . The soldiers march ahead firmly, the spectacle fixed forever in their eyes. For the idea of the fatherland is so deep-seated and so proud that it can be strengthened by its antithesis, by the assaults directed against it. On the wreckage of so many beliefs, a single faith remains genuine and sincere: that which safeguards our race, our language, the blood of our blood, and which brings us together in solidarity. The closed ranks are our ranks. The wretch was not French. We knew it by his actions, his demeanor, his face. He plotted our disaster, but his crime has exalted us. And as I leave this cursed spectacle, in the midst of the tumult, the words of command, the martial processions, I see standing before me the proud and simple column raised "to the memory of the officers and soldiers of the land and sea forces who have fallen on the field of honor in defense of the fatherland."

DISCUSSION QUESTIONS

1. What does this account suggest about the basis of contemporary prejudices against Jews?
2. For many French people at this time, the army was a near sacred institution. In what ways does Daudet capitalize on these attitudes, and to what effect?
3. Why does Daudet consider Dreyfus's degradation to be so vital to France's general welfare?

COMPARATIVE QUESTIONS

1. How are Daudet's and the Boxers' views similar?
2. What do both Pankhurst and Daudet suggest about the role of the public in contemporary political affairs?
3. In what ways did all four of these authors challenge liberal beliefs and values?

CHAPTER

26

War, Revolution, and Reconstruction
1914–1929

SUMMARY   Contemporaries dubbed World War I the "Great War" with good reason. Over the course of four years, millions died in battle—victims of advanced military technologies, outdated tactics, wretched leadership, and a desire for total victory. The first document allows us to see these horrors through two soldiers' eyes. The second document reveals that civilians contributed to the staggering death toll, for it was they who manufactured the grenades, rifles, and other weapons used on the front with such devastating effects. Yet the war's legacy did not stop there, as the third and fourth documents attest. Civilian protests against the war unleashed the Russian Revolution, which transformed the world's political landscape. To the west, governments faced their own challenges as they struggled under the weight of postwar reconstruction and popular discontent. Among the people who capitalized on these troubled times was the founder of Italian fascism, Benito Mussolini, who ushered in a new age of violent dictatorship in Europe.

1
Fritz Franke and Siegfried Sassoon
Two Soldiers' Views of the Horrors of War
1914–1918

When the war broke out in August 1914, no one foresaw the years of massive destruction and bloodshed that lie ahead. By late autumn, the two sides were entrenched along a line that extended from France into Belgium, and so the Western Front was born. Here millions of soldiers like Fritz Franke and Siegfried Sassoon faced unspeakable horrors. In the following letter written in the war's first months, Franke, a medical student from Berlin, describes trench warfare as a living hell of

127

shells and corpses. His description also reveals what already had become and would remain the war's defining feature in the West: immobility and stalemate. Franke paid the ultimate price for both: he was killed in May 1915. By contrast, Sassoon, a British officer, survived and became famous for poems like the one following Franke's letter, "Counterattack," which describes the war's misery and futility.

Fritz Franke

Louve, November 5th, 1914

Yesterday we didn't feel sure that a single one of us would come through alive. You can't possibly picture to yourselves what such a battle-field looks like. It is impossible to describe it, and even now, when it is a day behind us, I myself can hardly believe that such bestial barbarity and unspeakable suffering are possible. Every foot of ground contested; every hundred yards another trench; and everywhere bodies—rows of them! All the trees shot to pieces; the whole ground churned up a yard deep by the heaviest shells; dead animals; houses and churches so utterly destroyed by shell-fire that they can never be of the least use again. And every troop that advances in support must pass through a mile of this chaos, through this gigantic burial-ground and the reek of corpses.

In this way we advanced on Tuesday, marching for three hours, a silent column, in the moonlight, towards the Front and into a trench as Reserve, two to three hundred yards from the English, close behind our own infantry.

There we lay the whole day, a yard and a half to two yards below the level of the ground, crouching in the narrow trench on a thin layer of straw, in an overpowering din which never ceased all day or the greater part of the night—the whole ground trembling and shaking! There is every variety of sound—whistling, whining, ringing, crashing, rolling . . . the beastly things pitch right above one and burst and the fragments buzz in all directions, and the only question one asks is: "Why doesn't one get me?" Often the things land within a hand's breadth and one just looks on. One gets so hardened to it that at the most one ducks one's head a little if a great, big naval-gun shell comes a bit too near and its grey-green stink is a bit too thick. Otherwise one soon just lies there and thinks of other things. And then one pulls out the Field Regulations or an old letter from home, and all at once one has fallen asleep in spite of the row.

Then suddenly comes the order: "Back to the horses. You are relieved!" And one runs for a mile or so, mounts, and is a gay trooper once more; hola, away, through night and mist, in gallop and in trot!

One just lives from one hour to the next. For instance, if one starts to prepare some food, one never knows if one mayn't have to leave it behind within an hour. If you lie down to sleep, you must always be "in Alarm Order." On the road, you have just to ride behind the man in front of you without knowing where you are going, or at the most only the direction for half a day.

A. F. Wedd, trans., *German Students' War Letters* (New York: E. P. Dutton, 1929), 123–25.

All the same, there is a lot that is pleasant in it all. We often go careering through lovely country in beautiful weather. And above all one acquires a knowledge of human nature! We all live so naturally and unconventionally here, every one according to his own instincts. That brings much that is good and much that is ugly to the surface, but in every one there is a large amount of truth, and above all strength—strength developed almost to a mania!

Siegfried Sassoon

Counter-Attack

We'd gained our first objective hours before
While dawn broke like a face with blinking eyes,
Pallid, unshaved and thirsty, blind with smoke.
Things seemed all right at first. We held their line,
With bombers posted, Lewis guns well placed,
And clink of shovels deepening the shallow trench.
    The place was rotten with dead; green clumsy legs
    High-booted, sprawled and grovelled along the saps
    And trunks, face downward, in the sucking mud,
    Wallowed like trodden sand-bags loosely filled;
    And naked sodden buttocks, mats of hair,
    Bulged, clotted heads slept in the plastering slime.
    And then the rain began—the jolly old rain!

A yawning soldier knelt against the bank,
Staring across the morning blear with fog;
He wondered when the Allemands would get busy;
And then, of course, they started with five-nines
Traversing, sure as fate, and never a dud.
Mute in the clamour of shells he watched them burst
Spouting dark earth and wire with gusts from hell,
While posturing giants dissolved in drifts of smoke.
He crouched and flinched, dizzy with galloping fear,
Sick for escape—loathing the strangled horror
And butchered, frantic gestures of the dead.

An officer came blundering down the trench:
"Stand-to and man the fire-step!" On he went . . .
Gasping and bawling, "Fire-step . . . counter-attack!"
    Then the haze lifted. Bombing on the right
    Down the old sap: machine-guns on the left;
    And stumbling figures looming out in front.
    "O Christ, they're coming at us!" Bullets spat,

Siegfried Sassoon, *Collected Poems* (New York: Viking Press, 1949), 68–69.

And he remembered his rifle . . . rapid fire . . .
And started blazing wildly . . . then a bang
Crumpled and spun him sideways, knocked him out
To grunt and wriggle: none heeded him; he choked
And fought the flapping veils of smothering gloom,
Lost in a blurred confusion of yells and groans . . .
Down, and down, and down, he sank and drowned,
Bleeding to death. The counter-attack had failed.

Discussion Questions

1. Although they fought on opposite sides, what attributes did Franke and Sassoon share?

2. Based on Franke's and Sassoon's descriptions of the battlefront, what physical and psychological effects did trench warfare have on soldiers?

3. How does Franke's letter challenge the Allies' propaganda in which German soldiers were depicted as being devoid of humanity?

2

L. Doriat
Women on the Home Front
1917

Trench warfare was not the only distinctive feature of World War I. The massive mo-
bilization of the homefront also made the war like no other fought to date. Across
Europe, thousands of civilians poured into factories to manufacture supplies for the
troops. With casualties mounting and more and more men leaving to replenish the
armed forces, women became particularly vital to sustaining the wartime labor force.
Consequently, new employment opportunities arose for them, especially in tradition-
ally masculine domains such as munitions. The following interview of a French fac-
tory worker in the city of Saint-Nazaire in Brittany by journalist L. Doriat puts a
human face on this aspect of the war's impact beyond the battlefield. In it, the worker,
whom Doriat never identifies, reveals her sense of patriotic duty mingled with her de-
termination not to lose her femininity amid the din and dirt of her job.

The dwelling I enter is tidy, sun lights up the main room and makes the household objects shine; everything speaks of an orderly woman who likes her home.
A few flowers in a vase on the table near which she is working prove to me that I
was right about the woman I've come to see. The factory has not destroyed her

Margaret R. Higonnet, ed., *Lines of Fire: Women Writers of World War I* (New York: Plume,
1999), 129–131.

feminine sense of delicacy. Without a hat she seems to me younger; she is surprised to see me, she confesses, because she doubted I would come. Convalescent, she hasn't worked for a whole month, which is why I am lucky enough to find her.

"The very day after my arrival, I found work, thanks to the foreman of a factory of shells who knew my husband," she hastens to tell me. "There is no comparison between this extremely hard and much more precise work and the little toy-like petards that I was making. Here it's not sheets of white metal but big 120 shells. You must also pay much more attention, a defect is serious. The factory never stops, day and night shifts of eight alternate. It's intensive production; no mawkishness here, we are not women by the arms of the machine. Scarcely any apprenticeship, one or two days and you're set.

"I am in a workshop for tempering the steel, or rather I was—will they give me back my place and my machine when I return to the workshop? At the moment of my accident, which I'll tell you about, I was doing the shop-trial of the steel for the shell, testing or inspecting the casing, of course. Right after the tempering bath, when the steel is still hot and black, the other workers and I had to tap it with a buffing wheel in order to polish the steel on a small surface of the bottom and the ogive of the shell. Doing this we handle at least a thousand shells a day, and as I told you, they are big, very heavy to manipulate. Other workers take these same pieces and make a light mark on the polished area, which must not etch the steel further than a certain depth, in a kind of test; they are equipped with a graduated sheet of metal that lets them evaluate the etched lines. If the mark is too deep, the steel is too soft; if it's too shallow, it is too hard; in either case it can't be used and goes back to be recast. The inspection requires great attentiveness. A final verification is made by a controller and as we are always required to put our number on the pieces that pass through our hands, the imperfections, the errors can be traced to their authors.

"There too you don't talk, you don't even think of it. The deafening noise of the machines, the enormous heat of the ovens near which you work, the swiftness of the movements make this precision work into painful labor. When we do it at night, the glare together with the temperature of the furnace exhausts your strength and burns your eyes. In the morning when you get home, you throw yourself on your bed without even the strength to eat a bite. There are also the lathe workshops, I've never been there; many workers learn quickly to turn a shell without needing to calibrate it; some turners do piece work; they are always the ones who hurt themselves. At the job you become very imprudent, as I told you.

"However, you see, I hurt myself too. Forgetting that my buffing machine does an incalculable number of turns a second, I brushed against it with my arm. Clothing and flesh were all taken off before I even noticed. They had to scrape the bone, bandage me every day, I was afraid of an amputation, which luckily was avoided. Only in the last few days have I been able to go without a sling and use my arm; next week I go back to the workshop. I don't want them to change my job, I'm used to my machine and a fresh apprenticeship would not please me at all. I assure you, the first day I was in this noise, near these enormous blast furnaces, opposite the huge machine at which I had to work for hours, I was afraid. We are all like that, all the more so that we are not given time to reflect. You have to understand and act quickly. Those who lose their heads don't accomplish anything, but they are rare. In general, one week suffices to turn a novice into a skilled worker.

"The foremen scold now and then, but they mustn't count it against us; doesn't everyone know that a man is an apprentice before he becomes a mechanic? But at present, however simplified, however divided up the tasks may be, you become a qualified mechanic right away.

"Yet among us there are women like myself who had never done anything; others who did not know how to sew or embroider; nothing discouraged us. As for me I don't complain, this strained activity pleases me. I can thus forget my loneliness—and not having any children, what else should I do with all my time?

"When the war is over, I will look for a job that corresponds better to my taste. I have enough education to become a cashier in a store. I will then be able to be neater than now, for you can't imagine what care it takes to stay more or less clean if you work in a metallurgy.

"A woman is always a woman; I suffered a lot from remaining for hours with my hands and face dirty with dust and smoke. Everything is a matter of habit; among us there are women who seem fragile and delicate—well! if you saw them at work, you would be stunned: it's a total transformation. As for me, I would never have thought I had so much stamina; when I remember that the least little errand wore me out before, I don't recognize myself. Certainly when the day or the night is over, you go home, the fatigue is great, but we are not more tired than the men are. True, we are more sober because we maintain better hygiene and as a result, our sources of energy are more rational and regular, we don't turn to alcohol for strength.

"Our sense of the present need, of the national peril, of hatred for the enemy, of the courage of our husbands and sons—all this pricks us on, we work with all our heart, with all our strength, with all our soul. It is not necessary to stimulate us, each one is conscious of the task assigned to her and in all simplicity she does it, convinced that she defends her country by forging the arms that will free it. We are very proud of being workers for the national defence."

On that proud phrase, I left this valiant woman, with a warm handshake to thank her and to express my admiration.

Discussion Questions

1. What does this account suggest about women's role in the war effort?

2. How do both the interviewer and interviewee cast light on people's fears about the war's effects on traditional gender roles?

3. In what ways does this interview reflect the national consensus supporting the war, as fostered by government-directed propaganda campaigns?

3

John Reed
Ten Days That Shook the World
1919

As the war dragged on, European governments faced a new foe: civilian protest. The Russian tsar was ill equipped for this challenge, owing to his poor leadership skills, which opened the door to revolution. John Reed (1887–1920), an American journalist and socialist supporter, was in Russia at the time as the correspondent for several newspapers. Arriving in Petrograd in September 1917, he witnessed and recorded the Russian Revolution as it unfolded. Upon his return home, he used his notes and papers as the basis for his book on Lenin's triumph, Ten Days That Shook the World. *In the following excerpt, Reed vividly recounts the events of November 8, the day after the Bolshevik takeover, when the new government issued two momentous decrees. The first reflects Lenin's immediate goal—peace—and the second his long-term plan to construct a proletarian socialist state.*

It was just 8.40 when a thundering wave of cheers announced the entrance of the presidium, with Lenin—great Lenin—among them. A short, stocky figure, with a big head set down in his shoulders, bald and bulging. Little eyes, a snubbish nose, wide, generous mouth, and heavy chin; clean-shaven now, but already beginning to bristle with the well-known beard of his past and future. Dressed in shabby clothes, his trousers much too long for him. Unimpressive, to be the idol of a mob, loved and revered as perhaps few leaders in history have been. A strange popular leader—a leader purely by virtue of intellect; colourless, humourless, uncompromising and detached, without picturesque idiosyncrasies—but with the power of explaining profound ideas in simple terms, of analysing a concrete situation. And combined with shrewdness, the greatest intellectual audacity. . . .

Now Lenin, gripping the edge of the reading stand, letting his little winking eyes travel over the crowd as he stood there waiting, apparently oblivious to the long-rolling ovation, which lasted several minutes. When it finished, he said simply, "We shall now proceed to construct the Socialist order!" Again that overwhelming human roar.

"The first thing is the adoption of practical measures to realise peace. . . . We shall offer peace to the peoples of all the belligerent countries upon the basis of the Soviet terms—no annexations, no indemnities, and the right of self-determination of peoples. At the same time, according to our promise, we shall publish and repudiate the secret treaties. . . . The question of War and Peace is so clear that I think that I may, without preamble, read the project of a Proclamation to the Peoples of All the Belligerent Countries. . . ."

John Reed, *Ten Days That Shook the World* (New York: International Publishers, 1967), 125–37.

His great mouth, seeming to smile, opened wide as he spoke; his voice was hoarse—not unpleasantly so, but as if it had hardened that way after years and years of speaking—and went on monotonously, with the effect of being able to go on forever. . . . For emphasis he bent forward slightly. No gestures. And before him, a thousand simple faces looking up in intent adoration.

Proclamation to the Peoples and Governments
of All the Belligerent Nations

The Workers' and Peasants' Government, created by the revolution of November 6th and 7th and based on the Soviets of Workers', Soldiers' and Peasants' Deputies, proposes to all the belligerent peoples and to their Governments to begin immediately negotiations for a just and democratic peace.

The Government means by a just and democratic peace, which is desired by the immense majority of the workers and the labouring classes, exhausted and depleted by the war—the peace which the Russian workers and peasants, after having struck down the Tsarist monarchy, have not ceased to demand categorically—immediate peace without annexations (that is to say, without conquest of foreign territory, without forcible annexation of other nationalities), and without indemnities.

The Government of Russia proposes to all the belligerent peoples immediately to conclude such a peace, by showing themselves willing to enter upon the decisive steps of negotiations aiming at such a peace, at once, without the slightest delay, before the definitive ratification of all the conditions of such a peace by the authorised assemblies of the people of all countries and of all nationalities. . . .

To continue this war in order to permit the strong and rich nations to divide among themselves the weak and conquered nationalities is considered by the Government the greatest possible crime against humanity; and the Government solemnly proclaims its decision to sign a treaty of peace which will put an end to this war upon the above conditions, equally fair for all nationalities without exception.

The Government abolishes secret diplomacy, expressing before the whole country its firm decision to conduct all the negotiations in the light of day before the people, and will proceed immediately to the full publication of all secret treaties confirmed or concluded by the Government of land-owners and capitalists, from March until November 7th, 1917. All the clauses of the secret treaties which, as occur in a majority of cases, have for their object to procure advantages and privileges for Russian capitalists, to maintain or augment the annexations of the Russian imperialists, are denounced by the Government immediately and without discussion.

In proposing to all Governments and all peoples to engage in public negotiations for peace, the Government declares itself ready to carry on these negotiations by telegraph, by post, or by pourparlers between the representatives of the different countries, or at a conference of these representatives. . . .

In addressing this offer of peace to the Governments and to the peoples of all the belligerent countries, the Provisional Workers' and Peasants' Government of Russia addresses equally and in particular the conscious workers of the three nations most devoted to humanity and the three most important nations among those taking part in the present war—England, France, and Germany. The workers of these countries have rendered the greatest services to the cause of progress and of Socialism. The splendid examples of the Chartist movement in England, the series of revolutions, of world-wide historical significance, accomplished by the French proletariat—and finally, in Germany, the historic struggle against the Laws of Exception, an example for the workers of the whole world of prolonged and stubborn action, and the creation of the formidable organisations of German proletarians—all these models of proletarian heroism, these monuments of history, are for us a sure guarantee that the workers of these countries will understand the duty imposed upon them to liberate humanity from the horrors and consequences of war; and that these workers, by decisive, energetic and continued action, will help us to bring to a successful conclusion the cause of peace—and at the same time, the cause of the liberation of the exploited working masses from all slavery and all exploitation.

When the grave thunder of applause had died away, Lenin spoke again:

"We propose to the Congress to ratify this declaration. We address ourselves to the Governments as well as to the peoples, for a declaration which would be addressed only to the peoples of the belligerent countries might delay the conclusion of peace. The conditions of peace, drawn up during the armistice, will be ratified by the Constituent Assembly. . . . This proposal of peace will meet with resistance on the part of the imperialist governments—we don't fool ourselves on that score. But we hope that revolution will soon break out in all the belligerent countries; that is why we address ourselves especially to the workers of France, England and Germany. . . .

"The revolution of November 6th and 7th," he ended, "has opened the era of the Social Revolution. . . . The labour movement, in the name of peace and Socialism, shall win, and fulfil its destiny. . . ."

There was something quiet and powerful in all this, which stirred the souls of men. It was understandable why people believed when Lenin spoke. . . .

It was exactly 10:35 when Kameniev asked all in favour of the proclamation to hold up their cards. One delegate dared to raise his hand against, but the sudden sharp outburst around him brought it swiftly down. . . . Unanimous.

Suddenly, by common impulse, we found ourselves on our feet, mumbling together into the smooth lifting unison of the *Internationale*. A grizzled old soldier was sobbing like a child. Alexandra Kollontai rapidly winked the tears back. The immense sound rolled through the hall, burst windows and doors and seared into the quite sky. "The war is ended! The war is ended!" said a young workman near me, his face shining. And when it was over, as we stood there in a kind of awkward hush, some one in the back of the room shouted, "Comrades! Let us remember those who have died for liberty!" So we began to sing the Funeral March, that slow, melancholy and yet triumphant chant, so Russian and so moving. The *Internationale* is an alien air, after all. The Funeral March seemed the very soul of those dark masses whose delegates sat in this hall, building from their obscure visions a new Russia—and perhaps more.

> You fell in the fatal fight
> For the liberty of the people, for the honour of the people . . .
> You gave up your lives and everything dear to you,
> You suffered in horrible prisons,
> You went to exile in chains. . . .
>
> Without a word you carried your chains because you could not ignore your
>   suffering brothers,
> Because you believed that justice is stronger than the sword. . . .
> The time will come when your surrendered life will count.
> That time is near; when tyranny falls the people will rise, great and free!
>
> Farewell, brothers, you chose a noble path,
> You are followed by the new and fresh army ready to die and to suffer. . . .
>
> Farewell, brothers, you chose a noble path,
> At your grave we swear to fight, to work for freedom and the people's happiness. . . .

For this did they lie there, the martyrs of March, in their cold Brotherhood Grave on Mars Field; for this thousands and tens of thousands had died in the prisons, in exile, in Siberian mines. It had not come as they expected it would come, nor as the *intelligentzia* desired it; but it had come—rough, strong, impatient of formulas, contemptuous of sentimentalism; *real.* . . .

Lenin was reading the Decree on Land:

> (1.) All private ownership of land is abolished immediately without compensation.
> (2.) All land-owners' estates, and all lands belonging to the Crown, to monasteries, church lands with all their live stock and inventoried property, buildings and all appurtenances, are transferred to the disposition of the township Land Committees and the district Soviets of Peasants' Deputies until the Constituent Assembly meets.
> (3.) Any damage whatever done to the confiscated property which from now on belongs to the whole People, is regarded as a serious crime, punishable by the revolutionary tribunals. The district Soviets of Peasants' Deputies shall take all necessary measures for the observance of the strictest order during the taking over of the land-owners' estates, for the determination of the dimensions of the plots of land and which of them are subject to confiscation, for the drawing up of an inventory of the entire confiscated property, and for the strictest revolutionary protection of all the farming property on the land, with all buildings, implements, cattle, supplies of products, etc., passing into the hands of the People.
> (4.) For guidance during the realisation of the great land reforms until their final resolution by the Constituent Assembly, shall serve the following peasant *nakaz* (instructions), drawn up on the basis of 242 local peasant *nakazi* by the

editorial board of the *"Izviestia* of the All-Russian Soviet of Peasants' Deputies," and published in No. 88 of said *"Izviestia"* (Petrograd, No. 88, August 19th, 1917).

　　The lands of peasants and of Cossacks serving in the Army shall not be confiscated. . . .

At two o'clock the Land Decree was put to vote, with only one against and the peasant delegates wild with joy. . . . So plunged the Bolsheviki ahead, irresistible, over-riding hesitation and opposition—the only people in Russia who had a definite programme of action while the others talked for eight long months.

DISCUSSION QUESTIONS

1. Lenin's call for peace stemmed in part from a desire to relieve Russia's wartime sufferings. How did it also reflect his political beliefs and goals?
2. In what ways did the Decree on Land embody Marxist principles?
3. How does this account reveal the author's own political views?

4

Benito Mussolini
The Doctrine of Fascism
1932

Like millions of his fellow Italians, Benito Mussolini (1883–1945) bitterly resented the outcome of War World I. The Allies had reneged on many of their territorial promises, and Italy's economy was in shambles. Mussolini tapped into these waves of discontent when he founded the Fascist movement in 1919, comprised of former socialists, war veterans, and others who embraced the radical right as the new symbol of authority and strength. Blaming the parliamentary government for the country's ills, the Fascists marched on Rome in 1922 to take matters into their own hands. Upon the king's request, Mussolini became prime minister. This marked the beginning of Mussolini's rise to political power. The following excerpt from an article by Mussolini, first published in the Enciclopedia Italiana *in 1932, illuminates the basic ideological contours of fascism as they had developed during the first decade of his authoritarian rule.*

Fundamental Ideas

　　7. Against individualism, the Fascist conception is for the State; and it is for the individual in so far as he coincides with the State, which is the conscience and universal will of man in his historical existence. It is opposed to classical Liberalism, which arose from the necessity of reacting against absolutism, and which

---

Michael Oakeshott, ed. and trans., *The Social and Political Doctrines of Contemporary Europe* (Cambridge: Cambridge University Press, 1947), 164–79.

brought its historical purpose to an end when the State was transformed into the conscience and will of the people. Liberalism denied the State in the interests of the particular individual; Fascism reaffirms the State as the true reality of the individual. And if liberty is to be the attribute of the real man, and not of that abstract puppet envisaged by individualistic Liberalism, Fascism is for liberty. And for the only liberty which can be a real thing, the liberty of the State and of the individual within the State. Therefore, for the Fascist, everything is in the State, and nothing human or spiritual exists, much less has value, outside the State. In this sense Fascism is totalitarian, and the Fascist State, the synthesis and unity of all values, interprets, develops and gives strength to the whole life of the people.

8. Outside the State there can be neither individuals nor groups (political parties, associations, syndicates, classes). Therefore Fascism is opposed to Socialism, which confines the movement of history within the class struggle and ignores the unity of classes established in one economic and moral reality in the State; and analogously it is opposed to class syndicalism. Fascism recognizes the real exigencies for which the socialist and syndicalist movement arose, but while recognizing them wishes to bring them under the control of the State and give them a purpose within the corporative system of interests reconciled within the unity of the State.

9. Individuals form classes according to the similarity of their interests, they form syndicates according to differentiated economic activities within these interests; but they form first, and above all, the State, which is not to be thought of numerically as the sum-total of individuals forming the majority of a nation. And consequently Fascism is opposed to Democracy, which equates the nation to the majority, lowering it to the level of that majority; nevertheless it is the purest form of democracy if the nation is conceived, as it should be, qualitatively and not quantitatively, as the most powerful idea (most powerful because most moral, most coherent, most true) which acts within the nation as the conscience and the will of a few, even of One, which ideal tends to become active within the conscience and the will of all—that is to say, of all those who rightly constitute a nation by reason of nature, history or race, and have set out upon the same line of development and spiritual formation as one conscience and one sole will. . . .

Political and Social Doctrine

Fascism is to-day clearly defined not only as a regime but as a doctrine. And I mean by this that Fascism to-day, self-critical as well as critical of other movements, has an unequivocal point of view of its own, a criterion, and hence an aim, in face of all the material and intellectual problems which oppress the people of the world.

3. Above all, Fascism, in so far as it considers and observes the future and the development of humanity quite apart from the political considerations of the moment, believes neither in the possibility nor in the utility of perpetual peace. It thus repudiates the doctrine of Pacifism—born of a renunciation of the struggle and an act of cowardice in the face of sacrifice. War alone brings up to their highest

tension all human energies and puts the stamp of nobility upon the peoples who have the courage to meet it. All other trials are substitutes, which never really put a man in front of himself in the alternative of life and death. A doctrine, therefore, which begins with a prejudice in favour of peace is foreign to Fascism; as are foreign to the spirit of Fascism. . . .

5. Such a conception of life makes Fascism the precise negation of that doctrine which formed the basis of the so-called Scientific or Marxian Socialism: the doctrine of historical Materialism, according to which the history of human civilizations can be explained only as the struggle of interest between the different social groups and as arising out of change in the means and instruments of production. That economic improvements—discoveries of raw materials, new methods of work, scientific inventions—should have an importance of their own, no one denies, but that they should suffice to explain human history to the exclusion of all other factors is absurd: Fascism believes, now and always, in holiness and in heroism, that is in acts in which no economic motive—remote or immediate—plays a part. With this negation of historical materialism, according to which men would be only by-products of history, who appear and disappear on the surface of the waves while in the depths the real directive forces are at work, there is also denied the immutable and irreparable "class struggle" which is the natural product of this economic conception of history, and above all it is denied that the class struggle can be the primary agent of social changes. . . .

6. After Socialism, Fascism attacks the whole complex of democratic ideologies and rejects them both in their theoretical premises and in their applications or practical manifestations. Fascism denies that the majority, through the mere fact of being a majority, can rule human societies; it denies that this majority can govern by means of a periodical consultation; it affirms the irremediable, fruitful and beneficent inequality of men, who cannot be levelled by such a mechanical and extrinsic fact as universal suffrage. By democratic regimes we mean those in which from time to time the people is given the illusion of being sovereign, while true effective sovereignty lies in other, perhaps irresponsible and secret, forces. Democracy is a regime without a king, but with very many kings, perhaps more exclusive, tyrannical and violent than one king even though a tyrant. . . .

8. In face of Liberal doctrines, Fascism takes up an attitude of absolute opposition both in the field of politics and in that of economics. It is not necessary to exaggerate—merely for the purpose of present controversies—the importance of Liberalism in the past century, and to make of that which was one of the numerous doctrines sketched in that century a religion of humanity for all times, present and future. . . . The "Liberal" century, after having accumulated an infinity of Gordian knots, tried to untie them by the hecatomb of the World War. Never before has any religion imposed such a cruel sacrifice. Were the gods of Liberalism thirsty for blood? Now Liberalism is about to close the doors of its deserted temples because the peoples feel that its agnosticism in economics, its indifferentism in politics and in morals, would lead, as they have led, the States to certain ruin. In this way one can understand why all the political experiences of the con-

temporary world are anti-Liberal, and it is supremely ridiculous to wish on that account to class them outside of history; as if history were a hunting ground reserved to Liberalism and its professors, as if Liberalism were the definitive and no longer surpassable message of civilization. . . .

If it is admitted that the nineteenth century has been the century of Socialism, Liberalism and Democracy, it does not follow that the twentieth must also be the century of Liberalism, Socialism and Democracy. Political doctrines pass; peoples remain. It is to be expected that this century may be that of authority, a century of the "Right," a Fascist century. If the nineteenth was the century of the individual (Liberalism means individualism) it may be expected that this one may be the century of "collectivism" and therefore the century of the State. . . .

10. The keystone of Fascist doctrine is the conception of the State, of its essence, of its tasks, of its ends. For Fascism the State is an absolute before which individuals and groups are relative. Individuals and groups are "thinkable" in so far as they are within the State. The Liberal State does not direct the interplay and the material and spiritual development of the groups, but limits itself to registering the results; the Fascist State has a consciousness of its own, a will of its own, on this account it is called an "ethical" State. In 1929, at the first quinquennial assembly of the regime, I said: "For Fascism, the State is not the night-watchman who is concerned only with the personal security of the citizens; nor is it an organization for purely material ends, such as that of guaranteeing a certain degree of prosperity and a relatively peaceful social order, to achieve which a council of administration would be sufficient, nor is it a creation of mere politics with no contact with the material and complex reality of the lives of individuals and the life of peoples. The State, as conceived by Fascism and as it acts, is a spiritual and moral fact because it makes concrete the political, juridical, economic organization of the nation and such an organization is, in its origin and in its development, a manifestation of the spirit. The State is the guarantor of internal and external security, but it is also the guardian and the transmitter of the spirit of the people as it has been elaborated through the centuries in language, custom, faith. The State is not only present, it is also past, and above all future. It is the State which, transcending the brief limit of individual lives, represents the immanent conscience of the nation. The forms in which States express themselves change, but the necessity of the State remains. It is the State which educates citizens for civic virtue, makes them conscious of their mission, calls them to unity; harmonizes their interests in justice; hands on the achievements of thought in the sciences, the arts, in law, in human solidarity; it carries men from the elementary life of the tribe to the highest human expression of power which is Empire; it entrusts to the ages the names of those who died for its integrity or in obedience to its laws; it puts forward as an example and recommends to the generations that are to come the leaders who increased its territory and the men of genius who gave it glory. When the sense of the State declines and the disintegrating and centrifugal tendencies of individuals and groups prevail, national societies move to their decline."

11. From 1929 up to the present day these doctrinal positions have been strengthened by the whole economico-political evolution of the world. It is the State alone that grows in size, in power. It is the State alone that can solve the dramatic contradictions of capitalism. What is called the crisis cannot be overcome except by the State, within the State. . . . Fascism desires the State to be strong, organic and at the same time founded on a wide popular basis. The Fascist State has also claimed for itself the field of economics and, through the corporative, social and educational institutions which it has created, the meaning of the State reaches out to and includes the farthest off-shoots; and within the State, framed in their respective organizations, there revolve all the political, economic and spiritual forces of the nation. A State founded on millions of individuals who recognize it, feel it, are ready to serve it, is not the tyrannical State of the medieval lord. It has nothing in common with the absolutist States that existed either before or after 1789. In the Fascist State the individual is not suppressed, but rather multiplied, just as in a regiment a soldier is not weakened but multiplied by the number of his comrades. The Fascist State organizes the nation, but it leaves sufficient scope to individuals; it has limited useless or harmful liberties and has preserved those that are essential. It cannot be the individual who decides in this matter, but only the State. . . .

13. The Fascist State is a will to power and to government. In it the tradition of Rome is an idea that has force. In the doctrine of Fascism Empire is not only a territorial, military or mercantile expression, but spiritual or moral. One can think of an empire, that is to say a nation that directly or indirectly leads other nations, without needing to conquer a single square kilometre of territory. For Fascism the tendency to Empire, that is to say, to the expansion of nations, is a manifestation of vitality; its opposite, staying at home, is a sign of decadence: peoples who rise or re-rise are imperialist, peoples who die are denunciatory. Fascism is the doctrine that is most fitted to represent the aims, the states of mind, of a people, like the Italian people, rising again after many centuries of abandonment or slavery to foreigners. But Empire calls for discipline, co-ordination of forces, duty and sacrifice; this explains many aspects of the practical working of the regime and the direction of many of the forces of the State and the necessary severity shown to those who would wish to oppose this spontaneous and destined impulse of the Italy of the twentieth century, to oppose it in the name of the superseded ideologies of the nineteenth, repudiated wherever great experiments of political and social transformation have been courageously attempted: especially where, as now, peoples thirst for authority, for leadership, for order. If every age has its own doctrine, it is apparent from a thousand signs that the doctrine of the present age is Fascism. That it is a doctrine of life is shown by the fact that it has resuscitated a faith. That this faith has conquered minds is proved by the fact that Fascism has had its dead and its martyrs.

Fascism henceforward has in the world the universality of all those doctrines which, by fulfilling themselves, have significance in the history of the human spirit.

DISCUSSION QUESTIONS

1. According to Mussolini, how is fascism opposed to liberalism, democracy, and socialism?
2. How is this opposition rooted in his concept of the individual's role in the Fascist state?
3. What does Mussolini mean when he describes fascism as "totalitarian"?
4. As elaborated here, in what ways were Mussolini's principles rooted in the legacy of World War I?

COMPARATIVE QUESTIONS

1. In what ways did communist and Fascist ideology offer radically different solutions to similar problems?
2. What do Franke, Sassoon, and the French factory worker reveal about the role of technology in World War I?
3. How do you think the French factory worker would have responded to Lenin's appeal for peace, and why?

An Age of Catastrophes
1929–1945

S U M M A R Y   The Great Depression of the 1930s ushered in an age of unprecedented violence and suffering around the globe. Millions were out of work, hungry, and disillusioned. Authoritarian leaders capitalized on the downhearted, gaining widespread support with their promises to revive the economy and restore national glory. The head of the Nazi party, Adolf Hitler, was among the most menacing of these political strongmen, as the first document vividly shows. Western democracies responded cautiously to the Nazi menace, hoping to contain Hitler's ambition through a policy of appeasement rather than military force. The second document illuminates this policy in action at a critical juncture in Hitler's march toward war. Once the war began, no one was truly prepared for its horrors. As the last two documents show, the combination of ideology and advanced technology fueling the war was especially cruel to the civilian population, setting a dangerous precedent for the future.

1
Joseph Goebbels
Nazi Propaganda Pamphlet
1930

Perhaps no one better personifies the power of authoritarian rulers to manipulate the minds of millions in the 1930s than Adolf Hitler. Among the secrets of Hitler's success was his propaganda chief, Joseph Goebbels (1895–1945). A member of the National Socialist party since 1922, Goebbels shared Hitler's belief that the masses were easily managed if the message directed to them was simple and repetitive. To this end, Goebbels wrote pamphlets such as the one that follows in support of the Nazi cause. In it, he reveals the virulent anti-Semitism that shaped the Nazis' political program and set them apart from other totalitarian regimes. Goebbels's tactics helped propel Hitler to national leadership in 1933.

WHY ARE WE NATIONALISTS?

We are NATIONALISTS because we see in the NATION the only possibility for the protection and the furtherance of our existence.

The NATION is the organic bond of a people for the protection and defense of their lives. He is nationally minded who understands this IN WORD AND IN DEED.

Today, in GERMANY, NATIONALISM has degenerated into BOURGEOIS PATRIOTISM, and its power exhausts itself in tilting at windmills. It says GERMANY and means MONARCHY. It proclaims FREEDOM and means BLACK-WHITE-RED.

Young nationalism has its unconditional demands. BELIEF IN THE NATION is a matter of all the people, not for individuals of rank, a class, or an industrial clique. The eternal must be separated from the contemporary. The maintenance of a rotten industrial system has nothing to do with nationalism. I can love Germany and hate capitalism; not only CAN I do it, I also MUST do it. The germ of the rebirth of our people LIES ONLY IN THE DESTRUCTION OF THE SYSTEM OF PLUNDERING THE HEALTHY POWER OF THE PEOPLE.

WE ARE NATIONALISTS BECAUSE WE, AS GERMANS, LOVE GERMANY. And because we love Germany, we demand the protection of its national spirit and we battle against its destroyers.

WHY ARE WE SOCIALISTS?

We are SOCIALISTS because we see in SOCIALISM the only possibility for maintaining our racial existence and through it the reconquest of our political freedom and the rebirth of the German state. SOCIALISM has its peculiar form first of all through its comradeship in arms with the forward-driving energy of a newly awakened nationalism. Without nationalism it is nothing, a phantom, a theory, a vision of air, a book. With it, it is everything, THE FUTURE, FREEDOM, FATHERLAND!

It was a sin of the liberal bourgeoisie to overlook THE STATE-BUILDING POWER OF SOCIALISM. It was the sin of MARXISM to degrade SOCIALISM to a system of MONEY AND STOMACH.

We are SOCIALISTS because for us THE SOCIAL QUESTION IS A MATTER OF NECESSITY AND JUSTICE, and even beyond that A MATTER FOR THE VERY EXISTENCE OF OUR PEOPLE.

SOCIALISM IS POSSIBLE ONLY IN A STATE WHICH IS FREE INSIDE AND OUTSIDE.

DOWN WITH POLITICAL BOURGEOIS SENTIMENT: FOR REAL NATIONALISM!

DOWN WITH MARXISM: FOR TRUE SOCIALISM!

Louis L. Snyder, ed., *Documents of German History* (New Brunswick, N.J.: Rutgers University Press, 1958), 414–16.

UP WITH THE STAMP OF THE FIRST GERMAN NATIONAL SOCIALIST STATE!

AT THE FRONT THE NATIONAL SOCIALIST GERMAN WORKERS PARTY! . . .

WHY DO WE OPPOSE THE JEWS?

We are ENEMIES OF THE JEWS, because we are fighters for the freedom of the German people. THE JEW IS THE CAUSE AND THE BENEFICIARY OF OUR MISERY. He has used the social difficulties of the broad masses of our people to deepen the unholy split between Right and Left among our people. He has made two halves of Germany. He is the real cause for our loss of the Great War.

The Jew has no interest in the solution of Germany's fateful problems. He CANNOT have any. FOR HE LIVES ON THE FACT THAT THERE HAS BEEN NO SOLUTION. If we would make the German people a unified community and give them freedom before the world, then the Jew can have no place among us. He has the best trumps in his hands when a people lives in inner and outer slavery. THE JEW IS RESPONSIBLE FOR OUR MISERY AND HE LIVES ON IT.

That is the reason why we, AS NATIONALISTS and AS SOCIALISTS, oppose the Jew. HE HAS CORRUPTED OUR RACE, FOULED OUR MORALS, UNDERMINED OUR CUSTOMS, AND BROKEN OUR POWER.

THE JEW IS THE PLASTIC DEMON OF THE DECLINE OF MANKIND.

THE JEW IS UNCREATIVE. He produces nothing. HE ONLY HANDLES PRODUCTS. As long as he struggles against the state, HE IS A REVOLUTIONARY; as soon as he has power, he preaches QUIET AND ORDER, so that he can consume his plunder at his convenience.

ANTI-SEMITISM IS UN-CHRISTIAN. That means, then, that he is a Christian who looks on while the Jew sews straps around our necks. TO BE A CHRISTIAN MEANS: LOVE THY NEIGHBOR AS THYSELF! MY NEIGHBOR IS ONE WHO IS TIED TO ME BY HIS BLOOD. IF I LOVE HIM, THEN I MUST HATE HIS ENEMIES. HE WHO THINKS GERMAN MUST DESPISE THE JEWS. The one thing makes the other necessary.

WE ARE ENEMIES OF THE JEWS BECAUSE WE BELONG TO THE GERMAN PEOPLE. THE JEW IS OUR GREATEST MISFORTUNE.

It is not true that we eat a Jew every morning at breakfast.

It is true, however, that he SLOWLY BUT SURELY ROBS US OF EVERYTHING WE OWN.

THAT WILL STOP, AS SURELY AS WE ARE GERMANS.

DISCUSSION QUESTIONS

1. According to this pamphlet, what do the terms *nationalist* and *socialist* mean within the context of the Nazi party?

2. Why does the pamphlet target Jews as enemies of the German people?

3. What does the pamphlet suggest about the link between the Nazis' racial views and their goals for Germany's future?

2

Neville Chamberlain
Speech on the Munich Crisis
1938

*During the troubled 1930s, many Europeans' deep longing for peace clouded their
ability to see the true nature of the Nazi threat. The British politician Neville Chamberlain (1869–1940) was no exception. He became prime minister in 1937 when
Hitler's preparations for war were well under way. Upon annexing Austria in March
1938, Hitler turned to his next target, Czechoslovakia. Chamberlain, Benito Mussolini (1883–1945), and French premier Edouard Daladier (1884–1970) met with
Hitler in Munich in September 1938 to defuse the situation; their meeting resulted
in an agreement that accepted Germany's territorial claims. In his closing speech,
delivered during a debate on the agreement in the House of Commons, Chamberlain
defended his policy of appeasement toward Hitler as the key to peace. Tragically, it
was instead a prelude to war.*

War today—this has been said before, and I say it again—is a different thing
not only in degree, but in kind from what it used to be. We no longer think of
war as it was in the days of Marlborough or the days of Napoleon or even in the
days of 1914. When war starts today, in the very first hour, before any profes-
sional soldier, sailor or airman has been touched, it will strike the workman, the
clerk, the man-in-the-street or in the 'bus, and his wife and children in their
homes. As I listened I could not help being moved, as I am sure everybody was
who heard the hon. Member for Bridgeton (Mr. Maxton) when he began to paint
the picture which he himself had seen and realised what it would mean in war—
people burrowing underground, trying to escape from poison gas, knowing that
at any hour of the day or night death or mutilation was ready to come upon
them. Remembering that the dread of what might happen to them or to those
dear to them might remain with fathers and mothers for year after year—when
you think of these things you cannot ask people to accept a prospect of that
kind; you cannot force them into a position that they have got to accept it; unless you feel yourself, and can make them feel, that the cause for which they are
going to fight is a vital cause—a cause that transcends all the human values, a
cause to which you can point, if some day you win the victory, and say, "That
cause is safe."

Since I first went to Berchtesgaden more than 20,000 letters and telegrams
have come to No. 10, Downing Street. Of course, I have only been able to look at
a tiny fraction of them, but I have seen enough to know that the people who
wrote did not feel that they had such a cause for which to fight, if they were asked
to go to war in order that the Sudeten Germans might not join the Reich. That is

---

Parliamentary Debates. Fifth Series. Volume 339. House of Commons Official Report (London,
1938), 544–52.

how they are feeling. That is my answer to those who say that we should have told Germany weeks ago that, if her army crossed the border of Czechoslovakia, we should be at war with her. We had no treaty obligations and no legal obligations to Czechoslovakia and if we had said that, we feel that we should have received no support from the people of this country. . . .

As regards future policy, it seems to me that there are really only two possible alternatives. One of them is to base yourself upon the view that any sort of friendly relations, or possible relations, shall I say, with totalitarian States are impossible, that the assurances which have been given to me personally are worthless, that they have sinister designs and that they are bent upon the domination of Europe and the gradual destruction of democracies. Of course, on that hypothesis, war has got to come, and that is the view—a perfectly intelligible view—of a certain number of hon. and right hon. Gentlemen in this House. I am not sure that it is not the view of some Members of the party opposite. [An HON. MEMBER: "Yes."] Not all of them. They certainly have never put it in so many words, but it is illustrated by the observations of the hon. Member for Derby (Mr. Noel-Baker), who spoke this afternoon, and who had examined the Agreement signed by the German Chancellor and myself, which he described as a pact designed by Herr Hitler to induce us to relinquish our present obligations. That shows how far prejudice can carry a man. The Agreement, as anyone can see, is not a pact at all. So far as the question of "never going to war again" is concerned, it is not even an expression of the opinion of the two who signed the paper, except that it is their opinion of the desire of their respective peoples. I do not know whether the hon. Member will believe me or attribute to me also sinister designs when I tell him that it was a document not drawn up by Herr Hitler but by the humble individual who now addresses this House.

If the view which I have been describing is the one to be taken, I think we must inevitably proceed to the next stage—that war is coming, broadly speaking the democracies against the totalitarian States—that certainly we must arm ourselves to the teeth, that clearly we must make military alliances with any other Powers whom we can get to work with us, and that we must hope that we shall be allowed to start the war at the moment that suits us and not at the moment that suits the other side. That is what some right hon. and hon. Gentlemen call collective security. Some hon. Members opposite will walk into any trap if it is only baited with a familiar catchword and they do it when this system is called collective security. But that is not the collective security we are thinking of or did think of when talking about the system of the League of Nations. That was a sort of universal collective security in which all nations were to take their part. This plan may give you security; it certainly is not collective in any sense. It appears to me to contain all the things which the party opposite used to denounce before the War—entangling alliances, balance of power and power politics. If I reject it, as I do, it is not because I give it a label; it is because, to my mind, it is a policy of utter despair.

If that is hon. Members' conviction, there is no future hope for civilisation or for any of the things that make life worth living. Does the experience of the Great War and of the years that followed it give us reasonable hope that if some new war started that would end war any more than the last one did? No. I do not believe that war is inevitable. . . . It seems to me that the strongest argument against the inevitability of war is to be found in something that everyone has recognised or that has been recognised in every part of the House. That is the universal aversion from war of the people, their hatred of the notion of starting to kill one another again. . . .

What is the alternative to this bleak and barren policy of the inevitability of war? In my view it is that we should seek by all means in our power to avoid war, by analysing possible causes, by trying to remove them, by discussion in a spirit of collaboration and good will. I cannot believe that such a programme would be rejected by the people of this country, even if it does mean the establishment of personal contact with dictators, and of talks man to man on the basis that each, while maintaining his own ideas of the internal government of his country, is willing to allow that other systems may suit better other peoples. The party opposite surely have the same idea in mind even if they put it in a different way. They want a world conference. Well, I have had some experience of conferences, and one thing I do feel certain of is that it is better to have no conference at all than a conference which is a failure. The corollary to that is that before you enter a conference you must have laid out very clearly the lines on which you are going to proceed, if you are at least to have in front of you a reasonable prospect that you may obtain success. I am not saying that a conference would not have its place in due course. But I say it is no use to call a conference of the world, including these totalitarian Powers, until you are sure that they are going to attend, and not only that they are going to attend, but that they are going to attend with the intention of aiding you in the policy on which you have set your heart.

I am told that the policy which I have tried to describe is inconsistent with the continuance, and much more inconsistent with the acceleration of our present programme of arms. I am asked how I can reconcile an appeal to the country to support the continuance of this programme with the words which I used when I came back from Munich the other day and spoke of my belief that we might have peace for our time. I hope hon. Members will not be disposed to read into words used in a moment of some emotion, after a long and exhausting day, after I had driven through miles of excited, enthusiastic, cheering people—I hope they will not read into those words more than they were intended to convey. I do indeed believe that we may yet secure peace for our time, but I never meant to suggest that we should do that by disarmament, until we can induce others to disarm too. Our past experience has shown us only too clearly that weakness in armed strength means weakness in diplomacy, and if we want to secure a lasting peace, I realise that diplomacy cannot be effective unless the consciousness exists, not here alone, but elsewhere, that behind the diplomacy is the strength to give effect to it.

One good thing, at any rate, has come out of this emergency through which we have passed. It has thrown a vivid light upon our preparations for defence, on their strength and on their weakness. I should not think we were doing our duty if we had not already ordered that a prompt and thorough inquiry should be made to cover the whole of our preparations, military and civil, in order to see, in the light of what has happened during these hectic days, what further steps may be necessary to make good our deficiencies in the shortest possible time. There have been references in the course of the Debate to other measures which hon. Members have suggested should be taken. I would not like to commit myself now, until I have had a little time for reflection, as to what further it may seem good to ask the nation to do, but I think nobody could fail to have been impressed by the fact that the emergency brought out that the whole of the people of this country, whatever their class, whatever their station, were ready to do their duty, however disagreeable, however hard, however dangerous it may have been.

I cannot help feeling that if, after all, war had come upon us, the people of this country would have lost their spiritual faith altogether. As it turned out the other way, I think we have all seen something like a new spiritual revival, and I know that everywhere there is a strong desire among the people to record their readiness to serve their country, wherever or however their services could be most useful. I would like to take advantage of that strong feeling if it is possible, and although I must frankly say that at this moment I do not myself clearly see my way to any particular scheme, yet I want also to say that I am ready to consider any suggestions that may be made to me, in a very sympathetic spirit.

Finally, I would like to repeat what my right hon. Friend the Chancellor of the Exchequer said yesterday in his great speech. Our policy of appeasement does not mean that we are going to seek new friends at the expense of old ones, or, indeed, at the expense of any other nations at all. I do not think that at any time there has been a more complete identity of views between the French Government and ourselves than there is at the present time. Their objective is the same as ours—to obtain the collaboration of all nations, not excluding the totalitarian States, in building up a lasting peace for Europe. . . .

DISCUSSION QUESTIONS
1. How did Chamberlain justify his policy of appeasement?
2. According to Chamberlain, why did some people oppose this policy?
3. What does Chamberlain's defense indicate about popular attitudes toward war and peace?

3

Sam Bankhalter and Hinda Kibort
Memories of the Holocaust
1938–1945

When Neville Chamberlain detailed the horrors that modern warfare would inflict on civilians, not even he knew how true his words would prove to be. Once the war erupted, one segment of the civilian population in particular was the target of Hitler's fury: Jews. The result was the Final Solution, a technologically and bureaucratically sophisticated system of camps for incarcerating or exterminating European Jews that the Germans put into place between 1941 and 1942. Either inmates were killed on their arrival or spared to endure a different kind of death: starvation, abuse, and overwork. The two interviews that follow allow us to see the Holocaust through the eyes of its victims. The first is that of Sam Bankhalter. At fourteen, he was captured by the Nazis in his native Poland and sent to Auschwitz. The second voice is that of Hinda Kibort, a Lithuanian who was nineteen when the Nazis began their assault on the local Jewish population. In 1944, she was deported to Stutthof, a labor camp in northern Poland.

Sam Bankhalter
Lodz, Poland

There was always anti-Semitism in Poland. The slogan even before Hitler was "Jew, get out of here and go to Palestine." As Hitler came to power, there was not a day at school I was not spit on or beaten up.

I was at camp when the Germans invaded Poland. The camp directors told us to find our own way home. We walked many miles with airplanes over our heads, dead people on the streets. At home there were blackouts. I was just a kid, tickled to death when I was issued a flashlight and gas mask. The Polish army was equipped with buggies and horses, the Germans were all on trucks and tanks. The war was over in ten days.

The Ghetto   The German occupation was humiliation from day 1. If Jewish people were wearing the beard and sidecurls, the Germans were cutting the beard, cutting the sidecurls, laughing at you, beating you up a little bit. Then the Germans took part of Lodz and put on barbed wire, and all the Jews had to assemble in this ghetto area. You had to leave in five or ten minutes or half an hour, so you couldn't take much stuff with you. . . .

Auschwitz   We were the first ones in Auschwitz. We built it. What you got for clothing was striped pants and the striped jacket, no underwear, no socks. In wintertime you put paper in your shoes, and we used to take empty cement sacks and put a string in the top, put two together, one in back and one in front, to keep warm.

If they told you to do something, you went to do it. There was no yes or no, no choices. I worked in the crematorium for about eleven months. I saw Dr. Mengele's experiments on children, I knew the kids that became vegetables. Later in Buchenwald I saw Ilse Koch with a hose and regulator, trying to get pressure to make a hole in a woman's stomach. I saw them cutting Greek people in pieces. I was in Flossenburg for two weeks, and they shot 25,000 Russian soldiers, and we put them down on wooden logs and burned them. Every day the killing, the hanging, the shooting, the crematorium smell, the ovens, and the smoke going out.

I knew everybody, knew every trick to survive. I was one of the youngest in Auschwitz, and I was like "adopted" by a lot of the older people, especially the fathers. Whole families came into Auschwitz together, and you got to Dr. Mengele, who was saying "right, left, left, right," and you knew, right there, who is going to

Rhoda G. Lewin, *Witnesses to the Holocaust: An Oral History* (Boston: Twayne Publishers, 1990), 5–8, 50–55.

the gas chamber and who is not. Most of the men broke down when they knew their wives and their kids—three-, five-, nine-year-olds—went into the gas chambers. In fact, one of my brothers committed suicide in Auschwitz because he couldn't live with knowing his wife and children are dead.

I was able to see my family when they came into Auschwitz in 1944. I had a sister, she had a little boy a year old. Everybody that carried a child went automatically to the gas chamber, so my mother took the child. My sister survived, but she still suffers, feels she was a part of killing my mother. . . .

Looking Back   Once you start fighting for your life, all the ethics are gone. You live by circumstances. There is no pity. You physically draw down to the point where you cannot think any more, where the only thing is survival, and maybe a little hope that if I survive, I'm gonna be with my grandchildren and tell them the story.

In the camps, death actually became a luxury. We used to say, "Look at how lucky he is. He doesn't have to suffer any more."

I was a lucky guy. I survived, and I felt pretty good about it. But then you feel guilty living! My children—our friends are their "aunts" and "uncles." They don't know what is a grandfather, a grandmother, a cousin, a holiday sitting as a family.

As you grow older, you think about it, certain faces come back to you. You remember your home, your brothers, children that went to the crematorium. You wonder, how did your mother and father feel when they were in the gas chamber? Many nights I hear voices screaming in those first few minutes in the gas chamber, and I don't sleep.

I talk to a lot of people, born Americans, and they don't relate. They can't understand, and I don't blame them. Sometimes it's hard even for me to understand the truth of this whole thing. Did it really happen? But I saw it.

The majority of the people here live fairly good. I don't think there's a country in the world that can offer as much freedom as this country can offer. But the Nazi party exists here, now. This country is supplying anti-Semitic material to the whole world, printing it here and shipping it all over, and our leaders are silent, just as the world was silent when the Jews were being taken to the camps. How quick we forget.

When I sit in a plane, I see 65 percent of the people will pick up the sports page of the newspaper. They don't care what is on the front page! And this is where the danger lies. All you need is the economy to turn a little sour and have one person give out the propaganda. With 65 percent of the population the propaganda works, and then the other 35 percent is powerless to do anything about it.

Hinda Kibort
Kovno, Lithuania

When the Germans marched in in July 1941, school had let out for the summer, so our whole family was together, including my brother who was in the university and my little sister who was in tenth grade. We tried to leave the city, but it was just like you see in the documentaries—people with their little suitcases walking along highways and jumping into ditches because German planes were strafing, coming down very low, and people killed, and all this terror. German tanks overtook us, and we returned home.

The Occupation We did not have time like the German Jews did, from '33 until the war broke out in '39, for step-by-step adjustments. For us, one day we were human, the next day we're subhuman. We had to wear yellow stars. Everybody could command us to do whatever they wanted. They would make you hop around in the middle of the street, or they made you lie down and stepped on you, or spit on you, or they tore at beards of devout Jews. And there was always an audience around to laugh. . . .

The Ghetto In September all the Jews were enclosed in a ghetto. We lived together in little huts, sometimes two families to a room. There were no schools, no newspapers, no concerts, no theater. Officially, we didn't have any radios or books, but people brought in many books and they circulated. We also had a couple of radios and we could hear the BBC, so we were very much aware of what was going on with the war.

As long as we were strong and useful, we would survive. Everybody had to go to work except children under twelve and the elderly. There were workshops in the ghetto where they made earmuffs for the army, for instance, but mostly people went out to work in groups, with guards. A few tried to escape, but were caught.

We did not know yet about concentration camps.

In 1943 the war turned, and we could feel a terrible tension from the guards and from Germans we worked with on the outside. We could exchange clothing or jewelry for food, but this was extremely dangerous because every time a column came back from work, we were all searched. A baker, they found some bread and a few cigarettes in his pocket. He was hanged publicly, on a Sunday. There was a little orchard in the ghetto, a public place, and we Jews had to build a gallows there and a Jew had to hang him. We were all driven out by the guards and had to stand and watch this man being hanged.

November 5, 1943, was the day all the children were taken away. They brought in Romanian and Ukrainian S.S. to do it. All five of us in our family were employed in a factory adjacent to the ghetto, so we could see through the window what was happening. They took everybody out who stayed in the ghetto—all the children, all the elderly. When we came back after work we were a totally childless society! You can imagine parents coming home to—nothing. Everybody was absolutely shattered.

People were looking for answers, for omens. They turned to seances or to heaven to look for signs. And this was the day when we heard for the first time the word *Auschwitz*. There was a rumor that the children were taken there, but we didn't know the name so we translated it as *Der Schweiz*—Switzerland. We hoped that the trains were going to Switzerland, that the children would be hostages there.

The Transport On July 16, 1944, the rest of the ghetto were put on cattle trains, with only what we could carry. We had no bathrooms. There was a pail on one side that very soon was full. We were very crowded. The stench and the lack of water and the fear, the whole experience, is just beyond explanation.

At one time, when we were in open country, a guard opened the door and we sat on the side and let our feet down and got some fresh air. We even tried to sing. But then they closed it up, and we were all inside again.

Labor Camp   When we arrived at Stutthof our family was separated—the men to one side of the camp, women to the other. My mother and sister and I had to undress. There were S.S. guards around, men and women. In the middle of the room was a table and an S.S. man in a white coat. We came in in batches, totally naked.

I cannot describe how you feel in a situation like this. We were searched, totally, for jewelry, gold, even family pictures. We had to stand spread-eagle and spread out our fingers. They looked through the hair, they looked into the mouth, they looked in the ears, and then we had to lie down. They looked into every orifice of the body, right in front of everybody. We were in total shock.

From this room we were rushed through a room that said above the door "shower room." There were little openings in the ceiling and water was trickling through. In the next room were piles of clothing, rags, on the floor. You had to grab a skirt, a blouse, a dress, and exchange among yourselves to find what fit. The same thing with shoes. Some women got big men's shoes. I ended up with brown suede pumps with high heels and used a rock to break off the heels, so I could march and stand in line on roll calls.

After this we went into registration and they took down your profession, scholastic background, everything. We got black numbers on a white piece of cloth that had to be sewn on the sleeve. My mother and sister and I had numbers in the 54,000s. People from all over Europe—Hungarian women and Germans, Czechoslovakia, Belgium, you name it—they were there. Children, of course, were not there. When families came with children, the children were taken right away.

As prisoners of Stutthof we were taken to outside work camps. A thousand of us women were taken to dig antitank ditches, a very deep V-shaped ditch that went for miles and miles. The Germans had the idea that Russian tanks would fall into those ditches and not be able to come up again!

When we were done, 400 of us were taken by train deeper into Germany. We ended up in tents, fifty women to a tent. We had no water for washing and not even a latrine. If at night you wanted to go, you had to call a guard who would escort you to this little field, stand there watching while you were crouching down, and then escort you back.

We were covered with lice, and we became very sick and weak. But Frau Schmidt taught us to survive. She was a chemist, and she taught us what roots or grasses we could eat that weren't poisonous. She also said that to survive we have to keep our minds occupied and not think about the hunger and cold. She made us study every day! . . .

By the middle of December we had to stop working because the snow was very deep and everything was frozen. January 20, 1945, they made a selection. The strong women that could still work would be marched out, and the sick, those who couldn't walk or who had bent backs, or who were just skeletons and too weak to work, would be left behind. My mother was selected and my sister and I decided to stay behind with her.

We were left without food, with two armed guards. We thought the guards will burn the tents, with us in them. Then we heard there was a factory where they boiled people's bodies to manufacture soap. But the next day the guards put us in formation and marched us down the highway until we came to a small town.

We were put in the jail there. There we were, ninety-six women standing in a small jail cell, with no bathroom, pressed so close together we couldn't sit down, couldn't bend down. Pretty soon everybody was hysterical, screaming. Then slowly we quieted down.

In the morning when they opened the doors, we really spilled outside! They had recruited a bunch of Polish guards and they surrounded us totally, as if in a box. So there we were, ninety-six weak, emaciated women, marching down the highway with all these guards with rifles.

Then the German guards told us to run into the woods. The snow was so deep, up to our knees, and most of us were barefoot, frozen, our feet were blistered. We couldn't really run, but we spread out in a long line, with my mother and sister and I at the very end. I was near one guard, and all of a sudden I heard the sound of his rifle going "click." I still remember the feeling in the back of my spine, very strange and very scary. Then the guards began to shoot.

There was a terrible panic, screams. People went really crazy. The three of us always hand-held with my mother in the middle, but now she let go of us and ran toward the guards, screaming not to shoot her children. They shot her, and my sister and I grabbed each other by the hand and ran into the woods.

We could hear screaming and shooting, and then it got very quiet. We were afraid to move. The guards wore those awesome-looking black uniforms with the skull and crossbones insignia, and every tree looked like another guard! A few women came out from behind the trees, and eventually, ten of us made it out to the highway.

With our last strength, we made it to a small Polish village about a mile away. We knocked on doors, but they didn't let us in, and they started to throw things at us. We went to the church, and the priest said he couldn't help us because the Germans were in charge.

We were so weak we just sat there on the church steps, and late in the evening the priest came with a man who told us to go hide in a barn that was empty. We did not get any other help, whatsoever, from that whole Polish village—not medical help, not a rag to cover ourselves, not even water. Nothing.

Liberation   The next morning there was a terrible battle right in front of the barn. We were so afraid. Then it got very quiet. We opened the door, and we saw Russian tanks. We were free!

The Russians put us into an empty farmhouse. They gave us Vaseline and some rags, all they had, to cover our wounds. Then they put us on trucks and took us to a town where we found a freight train and just jumped on it.

At the border Russian police took us off the train. They grilled us. "How did you survive? You must have cooperated with the Germans." It was terrible. But finally we got identity cards—in Russia, you are nobody without some kind of I.D.— and my sister and I decided to go to the small town where we had lived. We thought somebody might have survived. . . .

Looking Back I was a prisoner from age nineteen to twenty-three. I lost my mother and twenty-eight aunts, uncles and cousins—all killed. To be a survivor has meant to me to be a witness because being quiet would not be fair to the ones that did not survive.

There are people writing and saying the Holocaust never happened, it's a hoax, it's Jewish propaganda. We should keep talking about it, so the next generation won't grow up not knowing how a human being can turn into a beast, not knowing the danger in keeping quiet when you see something brewing. The onlooker, the bystander, is as much at fault as the perpetrator because he lets it happen. That is why I have this fear of what is called the "silent majority."

So when a non-Jewish friend or a student asks, "What can I do?" I say, when you see something anti-Semitic happen, get up and say, "This is wrong" or "I protest." Send a letter to the newspaper saying, "This should not happen in my community," and sign your name. Then maybe somebody else will be brave enough to come forward and say that he protests, too.

DISCUSSION QUESTIONS

1. What role did the ghettos play in the Final Solution?
2. What was the principal difference between camps like Auschwitz and those like Stutthof?
3. What do these accounts reveal about conditions in the camps and the inmates' strategies for survival?
4. According to these survivors, what lessons does the Holocaust hold for the future?

4

Harry S. Truman
Harry Truman Announces the Dropping of the Atom Bomb on Hiroshima
1945

Although World War II began in Europe, in 1941 the conflict engulfed the world as Japan and the United States entered the war on opposite camps. Despite initial successes, within a year the Japanese began to lose ground to the Allies' formidable forces. Even so, they fought on, unwilling to surrender no matter what the material and human costs. This strategy prompted the Allied leaders to make a fateful decision. On August 6, 1945, an American plane dropped an atomic bomb on the Japanese city of Hiroshima, adding tens of thousands to the war's civilian death toll. That same day, the president of the United States, Harry S. Truman (1884–1972), made the following public announcement regarding the event. Here he described the Allies' successful race to develop the bomb before the Germans. The result, he proclaimed, was a marvel of modern science that would bring the war to an end. Although right on both counts, Truman did not foresee that with the dawning of the atomic age a potentially more deadly conflict was about to begin: the Cold War.

Statement by the President of the United States
August 6, 1945
The White House, Washington, D. C.

Sixteen hours ago an American airplane dropped one bomb on Hiroshima, an important Japanese Army base. That bomb had more power than 20,000 tons of T.N.T. It had more than two thousand times the blast power of the British "Grand Slam" which is the largest bomb ever yet used in the history of warfare.

The Japanese began the war from the air at Pearl Harbor. They have been repaid many fold. And the end is not yet. With this bomb we have now added a new and revolutionary increase in destruction to supplement the growing power of our armed forces. In their present form these bombs are now in production and even more powerful forms are in development.

It is an atomic bomb. It is a harnessing of the basic power of the universe. The force from which the sun draws its power has been loosed against those who brought war to the Far East.

Before 1939, it was the accepted belief of scientists that it was theoretically possible to release atomic energy. But no one knew any practical method of doing it. By 1942, however, we knew that the Germans were working feverishly to find a way to add atomic energy to the other engines of war with which they hoped to enslave the world. But they failed. We may be grateful to Providence that the Germans got the V-1's and the V-2's late and in limited quantities and even more grateful that they did not get the atomic bomb at all.

The battle of the laboratories held fateful risks for us as well as the battles of the air, land, and sea, and we have now won the battle of the laboratories as we have won the other battles.

Beginning in 1940, before Pearl Harbor, scientific knowledge useful in war was pooled between the United States and Great Britain, and many priceless helps to our victories have come from that arrangement. Under that general policy the research on the atomic bomb was begun. With American and British scientists working together we entered the race of discovery against the Germans.

The United States had available the large number of scientists of distinction in the many needed areas of knowledge. It had the tremendous industrial and financial resources necessary for the project and they could be devoted to it without undue impairment of other vital war work. In the United States the laboratory work and the production plants, on which a substantial start had already been made, would be out of reach of enemy bombing, while at that time Britain was

Department of State, *The International Control of Atomic Energy: Growth of a Policy* (Washington, D. C.: The U.S. Government Printing Office, 1946), 95–97.

exposed to constant air attack and was still threatened with the possibility of invasion. For these reasons Prime Minister Churchill and President Roosevelt agreed that it was wise to carry on the project here. We now have two great plants and many lesser works devoted to the production of atomic power. Employment during peak construction numbered 125,000 and over 65,000 individuals are even now engaged in operating the plants. Many have worked there for two and a half years. Few know what they have been producing. They see great quantities of material going in and they see nothing coming out of these plants, for the physical size of the explosive charge is exceedingly small. We have spent two billion dollars on the greatest scientific gamble in history—and won.

But the greatest marvel is not the size of the enterprise, its secrecy, nor its cost, but the achievement of scientific brains in putting together infinitely complex pieces of knowledge held by many men in different fields of science into a workable plan. And hardly less marvellous has been the capacity of industry to design, and of labor to operate, the machines and methods to do things never done before so that the brain child of many minds came forth in physical shape and performed as it was supposed to do. Both science and industry worked under the direction of the United States Army, which achieved a unique success in managing so diverse a problem in the advancement of knowledge in an amazingly short time. It is doubtful if such another combination could be got together in the world. What has been done is the greatest achievement of organized science in history. It was done under high pressure and without failure.

We are now prepared to obliterate more rapidly and completely every productive enterprise the Japanese have above ground in any city. We shall destroy their docks, their factories, and their communications. Let there be no mistakes; we shall completely destroy Japan's power to make war.

It was to spare the Japanese people from utter destruction that the ultimatum of July 26 was issued at Potsdam. Their leaders promptly rejected that ultimatum. If they do not now accept our terms they may expect a rain of ruin from the air, the like of which has never been seen on this earth. Behind this air attack will follow sea and land forces in such numbers and power as they have not yet seen and with the fighting skill of which they are already well aware.

The Secretary of War, who has kept in personal touch with all phases of the project, will immediately make public a statement giving further details.

His statement will give facts concerning the sites at Oak Ridge near Knoxville, Tennessee, and at Richland near Pasco, Washington, and an installation near Santa Fe, New Mexico. Although the workers at the sites have been making materials to be used in producing the greatest destructive force in history they have not themselves been in danger beyond that of many other occupations, for the utmost care has been taken of their safety.

The fact that we can release atomic energy ushers in a new era in man's understanding of nature's forces. Atomic energy may in the future supplement the power that now comes from coal, oil, and falling water, but at present it cannot be produced on a basis to compete with them commercially. Before that comes there must be a long period of intensive research.

It has never been the habit of the scientists of this country or the policy of this Government to withhold from the world scientific knowledge. Normally, therefore, everything about the work with atomic energy would be made public.

But under present circumstances it is not intended to divulge the technical processes of production or all the military applications, pending further examination of possible methods of protecting us and the rest of the world from the danger of sudden destruction.

I shall recommend that the Congress of the United States consider promptly the establishment of an appropriate commission to control the production and use of atomic power within the United States. I shall give further consideration and make further recommendations to the Congress as to how atomic power can become a powerful and forceful influence towards the maintenance of world peace.

Discussion Questions

1. Why, according to Truman, was the development and use of the atomic bomb necessary?
2. How did the bomb's development reflect the general wartime trend of increasing government involvement in industrial production?
3. What future potential uses does Truman see for atomic power?

Comparative Questions

1. In what ways was the central message of Goebbels's pamphlet translated into reality in the lives of Burkhalter and Kibort?
2. What similarities and differences do you see between Chamberlain's and Truman's views on military power as an instrument of peace?
3. How did both the use of the atomic bomb and the implementation of the Final Solution set World War II apart from the Great War?

CHAPTER

28

The Atomic Age
c. 1945–1960

S U M M A R Y   Despite widespread feelings of relief and joy when World War II at last came to an end, an uncertain path lie ahead for the world. With Europe in shambles, two new superpowers emerged from the rubble: the United States and Soviet Union. Their rivalry, known as the Cold War, shaped international affairs for decades to come. The first two documents illuminate the ideological and political roots of U.S. and Soviet Cold War policies. The bipolarization of world politics was not the only sign of Europe's diminished international identity, as the third document shows. War-weary and bitter, colonial peoples from Asia to Africa successfully battled for independence from European rule. The fourth document points to another campaign for freedom waiting in the wings. As societal and governmental pressures reasserted traditional boundaries between men and women that had been blurred by the war, some women called for change, setting the stage for the women's liberation movement in the 1960s.

1
The Formation of the Communist
Information Bureau (Cominform)
1947

Despite his instrumental role in defeating fascism, the head of the Soviet Union, Joseph Stalin (1879–1953), deeply mistrusted his Western allies. Convinced that their ultimate goal was to destroy communism, Stalin moved rapidly to establish a buffer zone of satellite states in Eastern Europe. At a meeting in September 1947, Communist leaders consolidated the Soviets' hold in the East by establishing a centralized association of Communist parties, the Communist Information Bureau (Cominform). As the following document justifying their actions reveals, the Cominform embodied Stalin's belief that only by coordinating their efforts could the Soviet Union and its clients defeat the "imperialist" threat. His Western rivals worked to put their own counterstrategies in place, thus hardening the battle lines of the Cold War.

The representatives of the Communist Party of Yugoslavia, the Bulgarian Workers' Party (Communists), the Communist Party of Rumania, the Hungarian Communist Party, the Polish Workers' Party, the Communist Party of the Soviet Union (Bolsheviks), the Communist Party of France, the Communist Party of Czechoslovakia and the Communist Party of Italy, having exchanged views on the international situation, have agreed upon the following declaration.

Fundamental changes have taken place in the international situation as a result of the Second World War and in the post-war period.

These changes are characterized by a new disposition of the basic political forces operating in the world arena, by a change in the relations among the victor states in the Second World War, and their realignment.

While the war was on, the Allied States in the War against Germany and Japan went together and comprised one camp. However, already during the war there were differences in the Allied camp as regards the definition of both war aims and the tasks of the post-war peace settlement. The Soviet Union and the other democratic countries regarded as their basic war aims the restoration and consolidation of democratic order in Europe, the eradication of fascism and the prevention of the possibility of new aggression on the part of Germany, and the establishment of a lasting all-round cooperation among the nations of Europe. The United States of America, and Britain in agreement with them, set themselves another aim in the war: to rid themselves of competitors on the markets (Germany and Japan) and to establish their dominant position. This difference in the definition of war aims and the tasks of the post-war settlement grew more profound after the war. Two diametrically opposed political lines took shape: on the one side the policy of the USSR and the other democratic countries directed at undermining imperialism and consolidating democracy, and on the other side, the policy of the United States and Britain directed at strengthening imperialism and stifling democracy. Inasmuch as the USSR and the countries of the new democracy became obstacles to the realization of the imperialist plans of struggle for world domination and smashing of democratic movements, a crusade was proclaimed against the USSR and the countries of the new democracy, bolstered also by threats of a new war on the part of the most zealous imperialist politicians in the United States of America and Britain.

Thus two camps were formed—the imperialist and anti-democratic camp having as its basic aim the establishment of world domination of American imperialism and the smashing of democracy, and the anti-imperialist and democratic

United States Senate, 81st Congress, 1st Session, Document No. 48, *North Atlantic Treaty: Documents Relating to the North Atlantic Treaty* (Washington, D.C.: U.S. Government Printing Office, 1949), 117–20.

camp having as its basic aim the undermining of imperialism, the consolidation of democracy, and the eradication of the remnants of fascism.

The struggle between the two diametrically opposed camps—the imperialist camp and the anti-imperialist camp—is taking place in a situation marked by a further aggravation of the general crisis of capitalism, the weakening of the forces of capitalism and the strengthening of the forces of Socialism and democracy.

Hence the imperialist camp and its leading force, the United States, are displaying particularly aggressive activity. This activity is being developed simultaneously along all lines—the lines of strategic military measures, economic expansion and ideological struggle. The Truman-Marshall Plan is only a constituent part, the European sub-section, of the general plan for the policy of global expansion pursued by the United States in all parts of the World. The plan for the economic and political enslavement of Europe by American imperialism is being supplemented by plans for the economic and political enslavement of China, Indonesia, the South American countries. Yesterday's aggressors—the capitalist magnates of Germany and Japan—are being groomed by the United States of America for a new role, that of instruments of the imperialist policy of the United States in Europe and Asia.

The arsenal of tactical weapons used by the imperialist camp is highly diversified. It combines direct threats of violence, blackmail and extortion, every means of political and economic pressure, bribery, and utilization of internal contradictions and strife in order to strengthen its own positions, and all this is concealed behind a liberal-pacifist mask designed to deceive and trap the politically inexperienced....

Under these circumstances it is necessary that the anti-imperialist, democratic camp should close its ranks, draw up an agreed program of actions and work out its own tactics against the main forces of the imperialist camp, against American imperialism and its British and French allies, against the right-wing Socialists, primarily in Britain and France.

To frustrate the plan of imperialist aggression the efforts of all the democratic anti-imperialist forces of Europe are necessary. The right-wing Socialists are traitors to this cause. With the exception of those countries of the new democracy where the bloc of the Communists and the Socialists with other democratic, progressive parties forms the basis of the resistance of these countries to the imperialist plans, the Socialists in the majority of other countries, and primarily the French Socialists and the British Labourites ... by their servility and sycophancy are helping American capital to achieve its aims, provoking it to resort to extortion and impelling their own countries on to the path of vassal-like dependence on the United States of America.

This imposes a special task on the Communist Parties. They must take into their hands the banner of defense of the national independence and sovereignty of their countries. If the Communist Parties stick firmly to their positions, if they do not let themselves be intimidated and blackmailed, if they courageously safeguard democracy and the national sovereignty, liberty and independence of their countries, if in their struggle against attempts to enslave their countries economically and politically they be able to take the lead of all the forces that are ready to fight for honour and national independence, no plans for the enslavement of the countries of Europe and Asia can be carried into effect.

This is now one of the principal tasks of the Communist Parties.

It is essential to bear in mind that there is a vast difference between the desire of the imperialists to unleash a new war and the possibility of organizing such a war. The nations of the world do not want war. The forces standing for peace are so large and so strong that if these forces be staunch and firm in defending the peace, if they display stamina and resolution, the plans of the aggressors will meet with utter failure. It should not be forgotten that the war danger hullabaloo raised by the imperialist agents is intended to frighten the nervous and unstable elements and by blackmail to win concessions for the aggressor.

The principal danger for the working class today lies in underestimating their own strength and overestimating the strength of the imperialist camp. Just as the Munich policy untied the hands of Hitlerite aggression in the past, so yielding to the new line in the policy of the United States and that of the imperialist camp is bound to make its inspirers still more arrogant and aggressive. Therefore, the Communist Parties must take the lead in resisting the plans of imperialist expansion and aggression in all spheres—state, political, economic and ideological; they must close their ranks, unite their efforts on the basis of a common anti-imperialist and democratic platform and rally around themselves all the democratic and patriotic forces of the nation.

Resolution on Interchange of Experience and Coordination of Activities of the Parties Represented at the Conference

The Conference states that the absence of contacts among the Communist Parties participating at this Conference is a serious shortcoming in the present situation. Experience has shown that such lack of contacts among the Communist Parties is wrong and harmful. The need for interchange of experience and voluntary coordination of action of the various Parties is particularly keenly felt at the present time in view of the growing complication of the post-war international situation, a situation in which the lack of connections among the Communist Parties may prove detrimental to the working class.

In view of this, the participants in the Conference have agreed on the following:

1. To set up an Information Bureau consisting of representatives of the Communist Party of Yugoslavia, the Bulgarian Workers' Party (Communists), the Communist Party of Rumania, the Hungarian Communist Party, the Polish Workers' Party, the Communist Party of the Soviet Union (Bolsheviks), the Communist Party of France, the Communist Party of Czechoslovakia and the Communist Party of Italy.

2. To charge the Information Bureau with the organization of interchange of experience, and if need be, coordination of the activities of the Communist Parties on the basis of mutual agreement.

3. The Information Bureau is to consist of two representatives from each Central Committee, the delegations of the Central Committees to be appointed and replaced by the Central Committees.

4. The Information Bureau is to have a printed organ—a fortnightly and subsequently, a weekly. The organ is to be published in French and Russian, and when possible, in other languages as well.

5. The Information Bureau is to be located in the city of Belgrad [*sic*].

DISCUSSION QUESTIONS

1. According to this document's authors, how and why did the relationship between the Soviet Union and its Western allies change in the postwar period?

2. What does the document mean when it describes the United States as an "imperialist" power?

3. What course of action does the document set forth to undermine this power, and to what end?

4. How does this document distort the reality of the Soviets' actions in Eastern Europe?

2

National Security Council
Paper Number 68
1950

Although he had helped to end World War II, U.S. President Harry S. Truman (1945–1953) had little time to celebrate. Daunting challenges still lie ahead as the fragile wartime alliance between the United States and Soviet Union collapsed. By 1949, the Soviet bloc in Eastern Europe was firmly in place, and the threat of international communism loomed large with the triumph of Mao Zedong in China. In response, Truman set out to devise a coherent strategy for combating the expansion of Soviet power. To this end, he commissioned the State and Defense departments to compile a report on the subject, which they completed in 1950, on the eve of the outbreak of the Korean War. The classified report, excerpted here, elucidates not only the basis of U.S. Cold War tactics but also the fears and perceptions underlying them.

Within the past thirty-five years the world has experienced two global wars of tremendous violence. . . . During the span of one generation, the international distribution of power has been fundamentally altered. For several centuries it had proved impossible for any one nation to gain such preponderant strength that a coalition of other nations could not in time face it with greater strength. The international scene was marked by recurring periods of violence and war, but a system of sovereign and independent states was maintained, over which no state was able to achieve hegemony.

Two complex sets of factors have now basically altered this historical distribution of power. First, the defeat of Germany and Japan and the decline of the

---

National Security Council, Paper Number 68, *Foreign Relations of the United States* (Washington, D.C.: Government Printing Office, 1977), 235–92.

British and French Empires have interacted with the development of the United States and the Soviet Union in such a way that power has increasingly gravitated to these two centers. Second, the Soviet Union, unlike previous aspirants to hegemony, is animated by a new fanatic faith, antithetical to our own, and seeks to impose its absolute authority over the rest of the world. Conflict has, therefore, become endemic and is waged, on the part of the Soviet Union, by violent or non-violent methods in accordance with the dictates of expediency. . . .

On the one hand, the people of the world yearn for relief from the anxiety arising from the risk of atomic war. On the other hand, any substantial further extension of the area under the domination of the Kremlin would raise the possibility that no coalition adequate to confront the Kremlin with greater strength could be assembled. It is in this context that this Republic and its citizens in the ascendancy of their strength stand in their deepest peril.

The issues that face us are momentous, involving the fulfillment or destruction not only of this Republic but of civilization itself. They are issues which will not await our deliberations. With conscience and resolution this Government and the people it represents must now take new and fateful decisions. . . .

Our overall policy at the present time may be described as one designed to foster a world environment in which the American system can survive and flourish. It therefore rejects the concept of isolation and affirms the necessity of our positive participation in the world community.

This broad intention embraces two subsidiary policies. One is a policy which we would probably pursue even if there were no Soviet threat. It is a policy of attempting to develop a healthy international community. The other is the policy of "containing" the Soviet system. . . .

As for the policy of "containment," it is one which seeks by all means short of war to (1) block further expansion of Soviet power, (2) expose the falsities of Soviet pretensions, (3) induce a retraction of the Kremlin's control and influence and (4) in general, so foster the seeds of destruction within the Soviet system that the Kremlin is brought at least to the point of modifying its behavior to conform to generally accepted international standards.

It was and continues to be cardinal in this policy that we possess superior overall power in ourselves or in dependable combination with other like-minded nations. One of the most important ingredients of power is military strength. In the concept of "containment," the maintenance of a strong military posture is deemed to be essential for two reasons: (1) as an ultimate guarantee of our national security and (2) as an indispensable backdrop to the conduct of the policy of "containment." . . .

At the same time, it is essential to the successful conduct of a policy of "containment" that we always leave open the possibility of negotiation with the U.S.S.R. A diplomatic freeze—and we are in one now—tends to defeat the very purposes of "containment" because it raises tensions at the same time that it makes Soviet retractions and adjustments in the direction of moderated behavior more difficult. It also tends to inhibit our initiative and deprives us of opportunities for maintaining a moral ascendancy in our struggle with the Soviet system. . . .

It is quite clear from Soviet theory and practice that the Kremlin seeks to bring the free world under its dominion by the methods of the cold war. The preferred technique is to subvert by infiltration and intimidation. Every institution of our society is an instrument which it is sought to stultify and turn against our purposes. Those that touch most closely our material and moral strength are obviously the prime targets, labor unions, civil enterprises, schools, churches, and all media for influencing opinion. The effort is not so much to make them serve obvious Soviet ends as to prevent them from serving our ends, and thus to make them sources of confusion in our economy, our culture, and our body politic. The doubts and diversities that in terms of our values are part of the merit of a free system, the weaknesses and the problems that are peculiar to it, the rights and privileges that free men enjoy, and the disorganization and destruction left in the wake of the last attack in our freedoms, all are but opportunities for the Kremlin to do its evil work. Every advantage is taken of the fact that our means of prevention and retaliation are limited by those principles and scruples which are precisely the ones that give our freedom and democracy its meaning for us. None of our scruples deter those whose only code is, "morality is that which serves the revolution."

At the same time the Soviet Union is seeking to create overwhelming military force, in order to back up infiltration with intimidation. In the only terms in which it understands strength, it is seeking to demonstrate to the free world that force and the will to use it are on the side of the Kremlin, that those who lack it are decadent and doomed. In local incidents it threatens and encroaches both for the sake of local gains and to increase anxiety and defeatism in all the free world. . . .

Our position as the center of power in the free world places a heavy responsibility upon the United States for leadership. We must organize and enlist the energies and resources of the free world in a positive program for peace which will frustrate the Kremlin design for world domination by creating a situation in the free world to which the Kremlin will be compelled to adjust. Without such a cooperative effort, led by the United States, we will have to make gradual withdrawals under pressure until we discover one day that we have sacrificed positions of vital interest. . . .

In summary, we must, by means of a rapid and sustained build-up of the political, economic, and military strength of the free world, and by means of an affirmative program intended to wrest the initiative from the Soviet Union, confront it with convincing evidence of the determination and ability of the free world to frustrate the Kremlin to the new situation. Failing that, the unwillingness of the determination and ability of the free world to the Kremlin design of a world dominated by its will [sic]. Such evidence is the only means short of war which eventually may force the Kremlin to abandon its present course of action and to negotiate acceptable agreements on issues of major importance.

The whole success of the proposed program hangs ultimately on recognition by this Government, the American people, and all free peoples, that the cold war is in fact a real war in which the survival of the free world is at stake. Essential prerequisites to success are consultations with Congressional leaders designed to make the program the object of nonpartisan legislative support, and a presentation to the public of a full explanation of the facts and implications of the present international situation. The prosecution of the program will require of us all the ingenuity, sacrifice, and unity demanded by the vital importance of the issue and the tenacity to persevere until our national objectives have been attained.

DISCUSSION QUESTIONS

1. As described here, how did World War II transform the international distribution of power?
2. According to the report, in what ways did the Soviet Union pose a danger to Americans and all "free peoples"?
3. What solutions does the document set forth to counter this danger?
4. Why does the report describe the Cold War as a "real" war?

3
Ho Chi Minh
Declaration of Independence of the Republic of Vietnam
1945

The devastation wrought by World War II encompassed more than the countless bombed buildings and millions of dead. The war had also fatally weakened the European powers' grip on their empires, as colonial peoples around the globe rose up against imperialist rule. French Indochina was no exception. In 1939, a small nationalist organization, Viet Minh, had formed, which achieved new prominence in the wake of World War II when the French sought to reassert their control in the region. Less than a month after Japan's surrender, the Viet Minh declared Vietnam's independence from France, reprinted in the following document. It was signed by "President Ho Chi Minh," one of the organization's original leaders who had lived in Paris, Moscow, and China. The document explicitly draws on the language of the French Enlightenment to further the Viet Minh's cause and condemn that of France.

"All men are created equal. They are endowed by their Creator with certain unalienable rights, among these are Life, Liberty and the pursuit of happiness."

This immortal statement was made in the Declaration of Independence of the United States of America in 1776. Now if we enlarge the sphere of our thoughts, this statement conveys another meaning: All the peoples on the earth are equal from birth, all the peoples have a right to live, be happy and free.

The Declaration of the Rights of Man and of the Citizen of the French Revolution in 1791 also states: "All men are born free and with equal rights, and must always be free and have equal rights."

Allan B. Cole, ed., *Conflict in Indo-China and International Repercussions: A Documentary History, 1945–1955* (Ithaca, N.Y.: Cornell University Press, 1956), 20–21.

Before the Outbreak of War

Those are undeniable truths.

Nevertheless, for more than 80 years, the French imperialists deceitfully raising the standard of Liberty, Equality and Fraternity, have violated our Fatherland and oppressed our fellow-citizens. They have acted contrarily to the ideals of humanity and justice.

In the province of politics, they have deprived our people of every liberty.

They have enforced inhuman laws; to ruin our unity and national consciousness, they have carried out three different policies in the North, the Center and the South of Viet-nam.

They have founded more prisons than schools. They have mercilessly slain our patriots; they have deluged our revolutionary areas with innocent blood. They have fettered public opinion; they have promoted illiteracy.

To weaken our race they have forced us to use their manufactured opium and alcohol.

In the province of economics, they have stripped our fellow-citizens of everything they possessed, impoverishing the individual and devastating the land.

They have robbed us of our rice fields, our mines, our forests, our raw materials. They have monopolized the printing of bank-notes, the import and export trade; they have invented numbers of unlawful taxes, reducing our people, especially our countryfolk, to a state of extreme poverty.

They have stood in the way of our businessmen and stifled all their undertakings; they have extorted our working classes in a most savage way.

In the Autumn of the year 1940, when the Japanese fascists violated Indochina's territory to get one more foothold in their fight against the Allies, the French imperialists fell on their knees and surrendered, handing over our country to the Japanese, adding Japanese fetters to the French ones. From that day on the Vietnamese people suffered hardships yet unknown in the history of mankind. The result of this double oppression was terrific: from Quangtri to the Northern border two million people were starved to death in the early months of 1945.

On the 9th of March 1945 the French troops were disarmed by the Japanese. Once more the French either fled, or surrendered unconditionally, showing thus that not only they were incapable of "protecting" us, but that they twice sold us to the Japanese.

Yet, many times before the month of March, the Vietminh had urged the French to ally with them against the Japanese. The French colonists never answered. On the contrary they intensified their terrorizing policy. Before taking their flight they even killed a great number of our patriots who had been imprisoned at Yenbay and Caobang.

Democratic Republic of Vietnam

Nevertheless, towards the French people our fellow-citizens have always manifested an attitude pervaded with toleration and humanity. Even after the Japanese putsch of March 1945 the Vietminh have helped many Frenchmen to reach the frontier, have delivered some of them from the Japanese jails, and never failed to protect their lives and properties.

The truth is that since the Autumn of 1940 our country had ceased to be a French colony and had become a Japanese outpost. After the Japanese had surrendered to the Allies our whole people rose to conquer political power and institute the Republic of Vietnam.

The truth is that we have wrested our independence from the Japanese and not from the French. The French have fled, the Japanese have capitulated, Emperor Bao Dai has abdicated, our people has broken the fetters which for over a century have tied us down; our people has at the same time overthrown the monarchic constitution that had reigned supreme for so many centuries and instead has established the present Republican Government.

For these reasons, we, members of the provisional Government, representing the whole population of Vietnam, have declared and renew here our declaration that we break off all relations with the French people and abolish all the special rights the French have unlawfully acquired on our Fatherland.

The whole population of Vietnam is united in a common allegiance to the Republican Government and is linked by a common will which is to annihilate the dark aims of the French imperialists.

We are convinced that the Allied nations which have acknowledged at Teheran and San Francisco the principles of self determination and equality of status will not refuse to acknowledge the independence of Viet-nam.

A people that has courageously opposed French domination for more than 80 years, a people that has fought by the Allies' side these last years against the fascists, such a people must be free, such a people must be independent.

For these reasons we, members of the Provisional Government of Vietnam, declare to the world that Vietnam has the right to be free and independent, and has in fact become a free and independent country. We also declare that the Vietnamese people is determined to make the heaviest sacrifices to maintain its independence and its Liberty.

Discussion Questions

1. How does the document characterize the actions of the French in Vietnam? Why does it describe them as deceitful?
2. In what ways did World War II further the cause of the Viet Minh?
3. Why did the Viet Minh believe that the Vietnamese people had an undeniable right to independence?

4

Simone de Beauvoir
The Second Sex
1949

Like Ho Chi Minh, Simone de Beauvoir (1908–1986) challenged traditional power structures in the postwar era. However, although she watched the growing independence movement in French Indochina with interest, her battle did not center on the plight of colonized peoples. Rather, she dedicated herself to examining the condition of modern women, which, she argued, was similarly marked by injustice and dis-crimination. She presented her views to the world in her book The Second Sex, *pub-lished in 1949. In the following excerpt, Beauvoir outlines the fundamental premise of her work: throughout history, women's identities have been defined by men and thus subjugated to them. Only by taking charge of their own lives could women break free from their subservience. Her views would help galvanize the women's liberation movement in the United States and Europe in the 1960s.*

A man would never get the notion of writing a book on the peculiar situation of the human male. But if I wish to define myself, I must first of all say: "I am a woman"; on this truth must be based all further discussion. A man never begins by presenting himself as an individual of a certain sex; it goes without saying that he is a man. The terms *masculine* and *feminine* are used symmetrically only as a matter of form, as on legal papers. In actuality the relation of the two sexes is not quite like that of two electrical poles, for man represents both the positive and the neutral, as is indicated by the common use of *man* to designate human be-ings in general; whereas woman represents only the negative, defined by limiting criteria, without reciprocity. In the midst of an abstract discussion it is vexing to hear a man say: "You think thus and so because you are a woman"; but I know that my only defense is to reply: "I think thus and so because it is true," thereby removing my subjective self from the argument. It would be out of the question to reply: "And you think the contrary because you are a man," for it is understood that the fact of being a man is no peculiarity. A man is in the right in being a man; it is the woman who is in the wrong. It amounts to this: just as for the an-cients there was an absolute vertical with reference to which the oblique was de-fined, so there is an absolute human type, the masculine. Woman has ovaries, a uterus; these peculiarities imprison her in her subjectivity, circumscribe her within the limits of her own nature. It is often said that she thinks with her glands. Man superbly ignores the fact that his anatomy also includes glands, such as the testicles, and that they secrete hormones. He thinks of his body as a direct and normal connection with the world, which he believes he apprehends objectively, whereas he regards the body of woman as a hindrance, a prison, weighed down by everything peculiar to it. . . . And she is simply what man decrees; thus she is called "the sex," by which is meant that she appears essentially to the male as a sexual being. For him she is sex—absolute sex, no less. She is defined and differ-entiated with reference to man and not he with reference to her; she is the inci-dental, the inessential as opposed to the essential. He is the Subject, he is the Absolute—she is the Other. . . .

Thus it is that no group ever sets itself up as the One without at once setting up the Other over against itself. If three travelers chance to occupy the same com-partment, that is enough to make vaguely hostile "others" out of all the rest of

Simone de Beauvoir, *The Second Sex*, trans. and ed. H. M. Parshley (New York: Knopf, 1953), xvi–xx.

the passengers on the train. In small-town eyes all persons not belonging to the village are "strangers" and suspect; to the native of a country all who inhabit other countries are "foreigners"; Jews are "different" for the anti-Semite, Negroes are "inferior" for American racists, aborigines are "natives" for colonists, proletarians are the "lower class" for the privileged. . . .

No subject will readily volunteer to become the object, the inessential; it is not the Other who, in defining himself as the Other, establishes the One. The Other is posed as such by the One in defining himself as the One. But if the Other is not to regain the status of being the One, he must be submissive enough to accept this alien point of view. Whence comes this submission in the case of woman?

There are, to be sure, other cases in which a certain category has been able to dominate another completely for a time. Very often this privilege depends upon inequality of numbers—the majority imposes its rule upon the minority or persecutes it. But women are not a minority, like the American Negroes or the Jews; there are as many women as men on earth. Again, the two groups concerned have often been originally independent; they may have been formerly unaware of each other's existence, or perhaps they recognized each other's autonomy. But a historical event has resulted in the subjugation of the weaker by the stronger. The scattering of the Jews, the introduction of slavery into America, the conquests of imperialism are examples in point. In these cases the oppressed retained at least the memory of former days; they possessed in common a past, a tradition, sometimes a religion or a culture.

The parallel drawn . . . between women and the proletariat is valid in that neither ever formed a minority or a separate collective unit of mankind. And instead of a single historical event it is in both cases a historical development that explains their status as a class and accounts for the membership of *particular individuals* in that class. But proletarians have not always existed, whereas there have always been women. They are women in virtue of their anatomy and physiology. Throughout history they have always been subordinated to men, and hence their dependency is not the result of a historical event or a social change—it was not something that *occurred*. The reason why otherness in this case seems to be an absolute is in part that it lacks the contingent or incidental nature of historical facts. A condition brought about at a certain time can be abolished at some other time, as the Negroes of Haiti and others have proved; but it might seem that a natural condition is beyond the possibility of change. In truth, however, the nature of things is no more immutably given, once for all, than is historical reality. If woman seems to be the inessential which never becomes the essential, it is because she herself fails to bring about this change. Proletarians say "We"; Negroes also. Regarding themselves as subjects, they transform the bourgeois, the whites, into "others." But women do not say "We," except at some congress of feminists or similar formal demonstration; men say "women," and women use the same word in referring to themselves. They do not authentically assume a subjective attitude. The proletarians have accomplished the revolution in Russia, the Negroes in Haiti, the Indo-Chinese are battling for it in Indo-China; but the women's effort has never been anything more than a symbolic agitation. They have gained only what men have been willing to grant; they have taken nothing, they have only received.

The reason for this is that women lack concrete means for organizing themselves into a unit which can stand face to face with the correlative unit. They have no past, no history, no religion of their own; and they have no such solidarity of work and interest as that of the proletariat. They are not even promiscuously herded together in the way that creates community feeling among the American Negroes, the ghetto Jews, the workers of Saint-Denis, or the factory hands of Rennault. They live dispersed among the males, attached through residence, housework, economic condition, and social standing to certain men—fathers or husbands—more firmly than they are to other women. If they belong to the bourgeoisie, they feel solidarity with men of that class, not with proletarian women; if they are white, their allegiance is to white men, not to Negro women. The proletariat can propose to massacre the ruling class, and a sufficiently fanatical Jew or Negro might dream of getting sole possession of the atomic bomb and making humanity wholly Jewish or black; but woman cannot even dream of exterminating the males. The bond that unites her to her oppressors is not comparable to any other. The division of the sexes is a biological fact, not an event in human history. . . . The couple is a fundamental unity with its two halves riveted together, and the cleavage of society along the line of sex is impossible. Here is to be found the basic trait of woman: she is the Other in a totality of which the two components are necessary to one another.

DISCUSSION QUESTIONS
1. What does Beauvoir mean when she describes women as the "Other"?
2. According to Beauvoir, how does women's status both resemble and differ from that of other oppressed groups, such as colonized peoples?
3. Why, unlike some of these groups, have women been unable to change their status?

COMPARATIVE QUESTIONS
1. Based on the Cominform declaration and National Security Council paper, how did the Communists' and the Americans' Cold War attitudes and corresponding policies mirror each other?
2. In what ways did the legacy of World War II explicitly shape the message of the first three documents?
3. How were Ho Chi Minh and Beauvoir waging similar battles? How were they also fundamentally different?

CHAPTER

29

Challenges to the Postindustrial West
1960–1990

S UMMARY   The 1960s was a decade of momentous turmoil fueled by feelings of both optimism and despair. In these years, millions of people across Europe and the United States took to the streets to challenge Cold War politics and society. At the same time, technological changes transformed everyday life. The following documents allow us to see the events and trends of the 1960s through the eyes of contemporaries. For many, nothing was sacred, whether in politics, as the student protesters of 1968 revealed, or in culture, as the popularity of rock music demonstrated. The last two documents illuminate the effects of the increasing importance of technology in the postindustrial world. On the one hand, technological advances improved people's lives and enhanced their knowledge of the world and the universe. On the other, technology offered new opportunities for mass destruction.

1

Student Voices of Protest
1968

College campuses were hotbeds of social activism in the 1960s, and they exploded into action with unprecedented force in the spring of 1968. The year was beset with tragedies, from the mounting number of casualties in the Vietnam War to the assassination of American civil rights leader Martin Luther King, Jr. Students from New York to Paris to Berlin rose up in protest, particularly over racial and antiwar issues. They demonstrated, occupied buildings, shut down classes, and went on strike. The following excerpts bring these students to life in their own words, which convey not only frustration and despair but also a desire to bring about lasting change.

My most vivid memory of May '68? The new-found ability for everyone to *speak*—to speak of anything with anyone. In that month of talking during May you learnt more than in the whole of your five years of studying. It was really another world—a dream world perhaps—but that's what I'll always remember: the need and the right for everyone to speak.—René Bourrigaud, student at the École Supérieure d'Agriculture, Angers, France

People were learning through doing things themselves, learning self-confidence. It was magic, there were all these kids from nice middle-class homes who'd never done or said anything and were now suddenly speaking. It was democracy of the public space in the market place, a discourse where nobody was privileged. If anything encapsulated what we were trying to do and why, it was that. . . .—Pete Latarche, leader of the university occupation at Hull, England, 1968

It's a moment I shall never forget. Suddenly, spontaneously, barricades were being thrown up in the streets. People were building up the cobblestones because they wanted—many of them for the first time—to throw themselves into a collective, spontaneous activity. People were releasing all their repressed feelings, expressing them in a festive spirit. Thousands felt the need to communicate with each other, to love one another. That night has forever made me optimistic about history. Having lived through it, I can't ever say, "It will never happen. . . ."—Dany Cohn-Bendit, student leader at Nanterre University, on the night of the Paris barricades, 10/11 May 1968

The unthinkable happened! Everything I had ever dreamt of since childhood, knowing that it would never happen, now began to become real. People were saying, fuck hierarchy, authority, this society with its cold rational elitist logic! Fuck all the petty bosses and the mandarins at the top! Fuck this immutable society that refuses to consider the misery, poverty, inequality and injustice it creates, that divides people according to their origins and skills! Suddenly, the French were showing they understood that they had to refuse the state's authority because it was malevolent, evil, just as I'd always thought as a child. Suddenly they realized that they had to find a new sort of solidarity. And it was happening in front of my eyes. That was what May '68 meant to me!—Nelly Finkielsztejn, student at Nanterre University, Paris . . . .

My world had been very staid, very traditional, very frightened, very middle-class and respectable. And here I was doing these things that six months before I would have thought were just horrible. But I was in the midst of an enormous tide of people. There was so much constant collective reaffirmation of it. The ecstasy was stepping out of time, out of traditional personal time. The usual rules of the game in capitalist society had been set aside. It was phenomenally liberating. . . . At the same time it was a political struggle. It wasn't just Columbia. There *was* a fucking

Ronald Fraser et al., *1968: A Student Generation in Revolt* (New York: Pantheon Books, 1988), 9–12.

war on in Vietnam, and the civil rights movement. These were profound forces that transcend that moment. 1968 just cracked the universe open for me. And the fact of getting involved meant that never again was I going to look at something outside with the kind of reflex condemnation or fear. Yes, it was the making of me— or the unmaking.—Mike Wallace, occupation of Columbia University, New York, April 1968 . . . .

We'd been brought up to believe in our hearts that America fought on the side of justice. The Second World War was very much ingrained in us, my father had volunteered. So, along with the absolute horror of the war in Vietnam, there was also a feeling of personal betrayal. I remember crying by myself late at night in my room listening to the reports of the war, the first reports of the bombing. Vietnam was the catalyst. . . .—John Levin, student leader at San Francisco State College

I was outraged, what shocked me most was that a highly developed country, the super-modern American army, should fall on these Vietnamese peasants—fall on them like the conquistadores on South America, or the white settlers on the North American Indians. In my mind's eye, I always saw those bull-necked fat pigs— like in Georg Grosz's pictures—attacking the small, child-like Vietnamese.— Michael von Engelhardt, German student

The resistance of the Vietnamese people showed that it could be done—a fight back was possible. If poor peasants could do it well why not people in Western Europe? That was the importance of Vietnam, it destroyed the myth that we just had to hold on to what we had because the whole world could be blown up if the Americans were "provoked." The Vietnamese showed that if you were attacked you fought back, and then it depended on the internal balance of power whether you won or not.—Tariq Ali, a British Vietnam Solidarity Campaign leader. . . .

So we started to be political in a totally new way, making the connection between our student condition and the larger international issues. A low mark in mathematics could become the focal point of an occupation by students who linked the professor's arbitrary and authoritarian behaviour to the wider issues, like Vietnam. Acting on your immediate problems made you understand better the bigger issues. If it hadn't been for that, perhaps the latter would have remained alien, you'd have said "OK, but what can *I* do?"—Agnese Gatti, student at Trento Institute of Social Sciences, Italy

Creating a confrontation with the university administration you could significantly expose the interlocking network of imperialism as it was played out on the campuses. You could prove that they were working hand-in-hand with the military and the CIA, and that ultimately, when you pushed them, they would call upon all the oppressive apparatus to defend their position from their own students.—Jeff Jones, Students for a Democratic Society (SDS), New York regional organizer. . . .

Everybody was terribly young and didn't know what was going on. One had a sort of megalomaniac attitude that by sheer protest and revolt things would be changed. It was true of the music, of the hallucinogenics, of politics, it was true across the board—people threw themselves into activity without experience. The desire to do something became tremendously intense and the capacity to do it diminished by the very way one was rejecting the procedures by which things could be done. It led to all sorts of crazy ideas.—Anthony Barnett, sociology student, Leicester University, England

DISCUSSION QUESTIONS

1. What were some of the students' principal targets for criticism, and why?
2. In what ways did the events of 1968 personally transform many of these students?
3. Some historians argue that the student protests of 1968 made governments less inviolable and sacred. What evidence can you find here to support this assertion?

2
Beatlemania in America
1966

The growth of youth culture also contributed to the spirit of protest galvanizing the West in the 1960s. Rock musicians were the heroes of this culture as objects of adoration and models of rebellion against established authority. Few musical groups were as popular or influential as the Beatles in this period, especially in the United States. Since their first American appearance in 1964, they attracted legions of fans and sold millions of records. The group also generated controversy, as the two following newspaper articles on the Beatles' performance in Memphis, Tennessee, in 1966 reveal. The Memphis City Council had tried to ban the show in reaction to a comment made earlier in the year by one of the group's four members, John Lennon, that the Beatles were more popular than Jesus. The council failed in their efforts, but local conservative groups stepped in to oppose the Beatles' concert and collided head on with forces of cultural change.

"Show by the Beatles Is a Scream"

Emily Strider, hands folded, face emotionless and sweet 16, yawned as The Remains bounced their music, with the help of seven amplifiers, off the walls and ceiling of the Coliseum.

And then it happened. The Beatles pranced on stage in their gray, Mod suits with red vertical stripes and abbreviated jackets. Emily, who drove to Memphis early yesterday afternoon from her home in Charleston, Miss., started to cry. Then she started to scream. Then she started shaking her head wildly and pounding her knees with her fists.

Thomas BeVier, "Show by the Beatles Is a Scream," and Dale Enoch, "Rally Provides 8,000 Answers to Beatle Cries," *Memphis Commercial Appeal*, August 20, 1966, pp. 1, 17.

It was a commentary on uninhibitedness, just the sort of thing Jerry Leighton had been talking about earlier when he was trying to figure out the difference between a nickel and a quarter.

Leighton is a disk jockey from England who is traveling with the Beatles on their tour of the United States. His is a "pirate station," one of several that operate on ships off the English coast because commercial stations aren't allowed in England.

"The Beatles are a phenomenon," he said in the studied accent of a true Englishman. "I asked them once how it felt to be a phenomenon and they said they didn't feel anything."

With help from the Yankee press, Leighton was able to figure out how to operate the cigaret machine and just then Brian Epstein, the Beatles' manager, walked by.

"Give me two seconds," he was asked.

"Two seconds—my life is spent giving people two seconds," he said.

His quick comment was that, "Yes, the Memphis performance is very important to us" because of the John Lennon comment that the group is more popular than Christ.

The Ku Klux Klan made its opinion known by picketing at the Southern Avenue entrance to Coliseum grounds. The sheets and hoods lent an incongruous touch to the stream of bell-bottomed trousers, paisley shirts and high heeled boots worn by the Beatles' faithful who filed by.

There were 7,589—mostly girls and almost all teenagers—at the first performance, and another 12,539 at the second. You couldn't hear the Beatles for the screaming.

Before they came on stage there were threats that anybody leaving his seat would be thrown out. It worked and Early Maxwell, Memphis promoter of the show, was glad.

"This was a real test," he said. "I've never had so much security (80 policemen) at an event, even Bob Hope."

Security started at 1:45 p.m. when the chartered American Airlines Electra with the Beatles and their entourage touched down on the military side of the airport. Only 10 Beatle bugs managed to slip by guards.

One, Charles Hardy, 19, of 4931 Montgomery, even infiltrated the press corps and got a hurried, almost legible autograph from Paul McCartney for his persistence.

One of those meeting the plane was a harried man of about 45 from Washington. He was Cabell Bowles, the group's advance man.

"No, you can't ride in on the bus with them," he said.

"No, we don't allow exclusive interviews."

"Yes, I'm tired."

Someone asked him his opinion of the Beatles and their music.

"No comment," he said sharply.

"Rally Provides 8,000 Answers to Beatle Cries"

About 8,000 persons, at least half of them adults, crammed The Auditorium Amphitheatre and overflowed into the Music Hall last night to "stand up and be counted" for Christ.

The program, which approached three hours in length, was without mention of the Mid-South Coliseum concert by the Beatles, a rock-and-roll group which had provoked the organization of the "Memphis Christian Youth Rally" by a statement by one that the singers were more popular than Christ.

Jimmy Stroud, director of Memphis Union Mission and an organizer of the rally, told the crowd that the rally was "to show Memphis and the whole world that Christianity will not vanish and that young people will stand up and be counted on the Lord's side. This is not anti-anything."

The crowd was devoid of string-haired girls or mop-topped boys and showed no signs of beatlemania, but they applauded lustily through the tight schedule of singing, testimonies by young people and two 30-minute speeches.

Gregory Walcott, Hollywood television and film star and leading Baptist layman, made no mention of the Beatles or of their remarks on religion.

He and a featured co-speaker, Dave Wilkerson, director of Teen Challenge in New York City, were presented keys to the city mid-way in the program by Mayor William B. Ingram.

But all were not in accord at the rally.

One angry father, who said he had been in on the planning session, walked out with about 30 others as a vocal group, Sing-Out Memphis, swept into another religious song with a beat early in the program.

"Many young people were decoyed into going down there for a Christian testimonial service. We might as well have gone to the Coliseum," he said as the vocal group continued singing to a modified "twist" and the accompanying combo maintained a throbbing beat.

DISCUSSION QUESTIONS

1. Based on the first article, how would you define "Beatlemania"?
2. Why did some people find the Beatles in particular and rock music in general so threatening?
3. Why is the issue of the concertgoers' appearance important in both articles?

3

The *New York Times* and
Neil Armstrong and Edwin Aldrin
The First Men Walk on the Moon
1969

Along with the rise of civic activism and youth culture, the expanding role of technology in postindustrial society changed people's worldview. Perhaps nothing captures technology's growing importance more dramatically than U.S. astronauts Neil Armstrong and Edwin ("Buzz") Aldrin's walk on the moon in July 1969. Spurred by the United States' desire to demonstrate its technological superiority over the Soviet Union, their moon walk was an unprecedented technological feat. So, too, was the fact that the event was broadcast on television to millions of viewers around the world. The two following documents capture the mood at the time of both the astronauts and their audience. The first is an editorial published in the New York Times on July 20, the same day that Armstrong and Aldrin took their momentous steps. In the second document, we hear Armstrong's and Aldrin's own recollections of their historic lunar landing.

To Walk to the Moon

In a world long given to marking off its historical progress in periods—the Age of Faith, the Renaissance, the Age of Reason, the Industrial Revolution—language seems too impoverished to encompass so neatly the era that begins with man's first walk on the moon. As a term, the Space Age is grossly inadequate, failing completely to convey the nature of the change that this event portends. For the lunar landing of the astronauts is more than a step in history; it is a step in evolution.

The journey of Neil Armstrong and his companions cannot be viewed in the same perspective as the voyage of Columbus or of any other traveler in recorded time—and the difference is not at all in degrees of courage or individual skill. In truth, Columbus's feat may well have taken more courage than Armstrong's because it was preceded by no unmanned probes and took him to regions unknown to the science of his day, in contrast to the photographed, spectographed and charted terrain of the moon.

What gives the astronauts' expedition a different dimension entirely, what removes it indeed from any venture in the whole history of the human race are two circumstances that stagger the mind: it is man's first step in adapting to an environment beyond this planet's and it is a *willed* step in the evolutionary process, one made deliberately and in the full consciousness of its import.

For the adaptation itself there are comparable precedents in nature, though for one as full of meaning for the future one might have to go back to the first fishy creature that emerged from the Devonian sea to make a feeble try at life on dry land.

For the conscious willing of an evolutionary act there is no precedent. Man has of course taught himself to ride over and under the waves and to fly through space, but what is contemplated now is no such passing accommodation but in time the transfer of human life to other sites in the universe—with ultimate consequences that almost surely must be evolutionary in nature.

It will take years, decades, perhaps centuries, for man to colonize even the moon, but that is the end inherent in Armstrong's first step on extraterrestrial soil. Serious and hard-headed scientists envision, even in the not remote future, lunar communities capable of growing into domed cities subsisting on hydroponically grown food, of developing the moon's resources, and eventually of acquiring a breathable atmosphere and a soil capable of being farmed. What with the dire threats of population explosion at best and nuclear explosion at worst, the human race, as Sir Bernard Lovell warns, may find itself sometime in the 21st century "having to consider how best to insure the survival of the species."

It is not possible to imagine that any such cosmic movement would leave the transported segment of mankind unchanged. Over the centuries and through countless transitions it would adapt biologically and psychologically, following Darwinian law, to existence in an environment differing as much from its earthly ancestors as that of the early mammals differed from the environment in the primeval seas.

Reflections on man's social shortcomings, speculation on what else he might have done instead of sending men to the moon—all this melts away in the moment of awe and wonder.

First on the Moon

Neil Armstrong said. . . . "The most dramatic recollections I had were the sights themselves. Of all the spectacular views we had, the most impressive to me was on the way to the moon, when we flew through its shadow. We were still thousands of miles away, but close enough so that the moon almost filled our circular window. It was eclipsing the sun, from our position, and the corona of the sun was visible around the limb of the moon as a gigantic lens-shaped or saucer-shaped light, stretching out to several lunar diameters. It was magnificent, but the moon was even more so. We were in its shadow, so there was no part of it illuminated by the sun. It was illuminated only by earthshine. It made the moon appear blue-gray, and the entire scene looked decidedly three-dimensional.

"I was really aware, visually aware, that the moon was in fact a sphere, not a disc. It seemed almost as if it were showing us its roundness, its similarity in shape to our earth, in a sort of welcome. I was sure that it would be a hospitable host. It had been awaiting its first visitors for a long time." . . .

[Buzz Aldren:] "The moon was a very natural and very pleasant environment in which to work. It had many of the advantages of zero-gravity, but it was in a sense less *lonesome* than zero G, where you always have to pay attention to securing attachment points to give you some means of leverage. In one-sixth gravity, on the moon, you had a distinct feeling of being *somewhere,* and you had a constant, though at many times ill defined, sense of direction and force.

"One interesting thing was that the horizontal reference on the moon is not at all well defined. That is, it's difficult to know when you are leaning forward or backward and to what degree. This fact, coupled with the rather limited field of vision from our helmets, made local features of the moon appear to change slope, depending on which way you were looking and how you were standing. The weight of the backpack tends to pull you backward, and you must consciously lean forward just a little to compensate. I believe someone has described the posture as 'tired ape'—almost erect but slumped forward a little. It was difficult sometimes to know when you were standing erect. It felt as if you could lean farther in any direction, without losing your balance, than on earth. By far the easiest and most natural way to move on the surface of the moon is to put one foot in front of the other. The kangaroo hop did work, but it led to some instability; there was not so much control when you were moving around.

"As we deployed our experiments on the surface we had to jettison things like lanyards, retaining fasteners, etc., and some of these we tossed away. The objects would go away with a slow, lazy motion. If anyone tried to throw a baseball back and forth in that atmosphere he would have difficulty, at first, acclimatizing himself to that slow, lazy trajectory; but I believe he could adapt to it quite readily. . . .

"Odor is very subjective, but to me there was a distinct smell to the lunar material—pungent, like gunpowder or spent cap-pistol caps. We carted a fair amount of lunar dust back inside the vehicle with us, either on our suits and boots or on the conveyor system we used to get boxes and equipment back inside. We did notice the odor right away.

"It was a unique, almost mystical environment up there."

DISCUSSION QUESTIONS

1. What does the editorial mean when it describes Armstrong and Aldrin's lunar landing as a step in human evolution?
2. How does the editorial link this event to contemporary concerns regarding the future of mankind?

4

Pope John XXIII
Vatican II
1961

As protesters took to the streets and scientists raced to put a man on the moon, the Catholic church devised its own response to the changes of the day. In 1961, Pope John XXIII (1958–1963) announced his plans in the following document to convene an ecumenical council to promote spiritual renewal and reevaluate the place of the church in the modern world. Almost one hundred years had passed since the last council of this type had met. A new council was urgently needed, the pope proclaimed, because the technological and economic advances of the twentieth century posed unprecedented challenges to the church and its faithful. The result was the largest Catholic council ever assembled, known as Vatican II, which met between 1962 and 1965. The decrees, constitutions, and declarations issued by the council established the blueprint for Catholic worship in the postindustrial world.

Painful Considerations

Today the Church is witnessing a crisis under way within society. While humanity is on the edge of a new era, tasks of immense gravity and amplitude await the Church, as in the most tragic periods of its history. It is a question in fact of bringing the modern world into contact with the vivifying and perennial energies of the gospel, a world which exalts itself with its conquests in the technical and scientific fields, but which brings also the consequences of a temporal order which some have wished to reorganize excluding God. This is why modern society is earmarked by a great material progress to which there is not a corresponding advance in the moral field.

Hence there is a weakening in the aspiration toward the values of the spirit. Hence an urge for the almost exclusive search for earthly pleasures, which progressive technology places with such ease within the reach of all. And hence there is a completely new and disconcerting fact: the existence of a militant atheism which is active on a world level.

Reasons for Confidence

These painful considerations are a reminder of the duty to be vigilant and to keep the sense of responsibility awake. Distrustful souls see only darkness burdening the face of the earth. We, instead, like to reaffirm all our confidence in our Savior, who has not left the world which He redeemed.

Indeed, we make ours the recommendation of Jesus that one should know how to distinguish the "signs of the times" (Mt. 16:4), and we seem to see now, in the midst of so much darkness, a few indications which auger well for the fate of the Church and of humanity.

The bloody wars that have followed one on the other in our times, the spiritual ruins caused by many ideologies, and the fruits of so many bitter experiences have not been without useful teachings. Scientific progress itself, which gave man the possibility of creating catastrophic instruments for his destruction, has raised questions. It has obliged human beings to become thoughtful, more conscious of their own limitations, desirous of peace, and attentive to the importance of spiritual values. And it has accelerated that progress of closer collaboration and of mutual integration toward which, even though in the midst of a thousand uncertainties, the human family seems to be moving. And this facilitates, no doubt, the apostolate of the Church, since many people who did not realize the importance of its mission in the past are, taught by experience, today more disposed to welcome its warnings.

Present Vitality of the Church

Then, if we turn our attention to the Church, we see that it has not remained a lifeless spectator in the face of these events but has followed step by step the evolution of peoples, scientific progress, and social revolution. It has opposed deci-

Walter M. Abbott, trans. and ed., *The Documents of Vatican II: All Sixteen Official Texts Promulgated by the Ecumenical Council* (New York: Herder and Herder, 1966), 703–07.

sively the materialistic ideologies which deny faith. Lastly, it has witnessed the rise and growth of the immense energies of an apostolate of prayer, of action in all fields. It has seen the emergence of a clergy constantly better equipped in learning and virtue for its mission; and of a laity which has become ever more conscious of its responsibilities within the bosom of the Church, and, in a special way, of its duty to collaborate with the Church hierarchy.

To this should be added the immense suffering of entire Christian communities, through which a multitude of admirable bishops, priests, and laymen seal their adherence to the faith, bearing persecutions of all kinds and revealing forms of heroism which certainly equal those of the most glorious periods of the Church.

Thus, though the world may appear profoundly changed, the Christian community is also in great part transformed and renewed. It has therefore strengthened itself socially in unity; it has been reinvigorated intellectually; it has been interiorly purified and is thus ready for trial.

The Second Vatican Ecumenical Council

In the face of this twofold spectacle—a world which reveals a grave state of spiritual poverty and the Church of Christ, which is still so vibrant with vitality—we, from the time we ascended to the supreme pontificate, despite our unworthiness and by means of an impulse of Divine Providence, have felt immediately the urgency of the duty to call our sons together, to give the Church the possibility to contribute more efficaciously to the solution of the problems of the modern age.

For this reason, welcoming as from above the intimate voice of our spirit, we considered that the times now were right to offer to the Catholic Church and to the world the gift of a new Ecumenical Council, as an addition to, and continuation of, the series of the twenty great councils, which have been through the centuries a truly heavenly providence for the increase of grace and Christian progress. . . .

The forthcoming Council will meet therefore and at a moment in which the Church finds very alive the desire to fortify its faith, and to contemplate itself in its own awe-inspiring unity. In the same way, it feels more urgent the duty to give greater efficiency to its sound vitality and to promote the sanctification of its members, the diffusion of revealed truth, the consolidation of its agencies. . . .

And, finally, to a world, which is lost, confused, and anxious under the constant threat of new frightful conflicts, the forthcoming Council must offer a possibility for all men of good will to turn their thoughts and their intentions toward peace, a peace which can and must, above all, come from spiritual and supernatural realities, from human intelligence and conscience, enlightened and guided by God the Creator and Redeemer of humanity.

DISCUSSION QUESTIONS
1. Why did Pope John XXIII think that modern society was in a state of crisis?
2. How did he link this crisis specifically to the effects of scientific and technological progress on everyday life?
3. How did the pope hope that Vatican II would counter these effects?

COMPARATIVE QUESTIONS

1. In the 1950s, many social critics condemned Western society as too uniform and complaisant. Based on the first and second documents, how did the events and cultural trends of the 1960s turn this society upside down, and why?

2. What do both the *New York Times* editorial and the Vatican II document suggest about the role of technology in modern life? Do you see any similarities and differences in their views?

3. As described in the documents, what set the 1960s apart from all other periods in human history?

30

The New Globalism: Opportunities and Dilemmas
1980 to the Present

S U M M A R Y   After decades of conflict, the Cold War virtually came to a halt in 1989 when the Soviet empire disintegrated. The end of superpower rivalries ushered in a new age of global challenges and opportunities. The first two documents that follow pull back the curtain on the first act of this drama, revealing that an explosive combination of government-sponsored reforms and grassroots political activism fueled communism's demise. The third document illuminates the collaborative efforts of European leaders to redefine Europe's place on the post–Cold War stage, just as they had done after World War II. Yet, as the fourth document vividly reveals, the world was now a far different place, where peoples, cultures, and economies were increasingly bound together, as were the problems they faced.

1
Glasnost *and the Soviet Press*
1988

When Mikhail Gorbachev (b. 1931) became the general secretary of the Soviet Communist party in 1985, the nation's economy was in ruins, and people struggled to meet even their most basic needs. Gorbachev implemented revolutionary policies of economic restructuring (perestroika) and "openness" (glasnost) to confront the crisis. The two articles excerpted here illuminate the crucial role of the Soviet press in this process as a forum for public debate. Never before had Soviet citizens experienced such freedom of speech and expression. Written by Nina Andreyeva, the first article appeared as a letter to the editor on the front page of the prestigious newspaper Sovetskaya Rossiya *in March 1988. Politically conservative, Andreyeva attacked Gorbachev's reforms as a violation of socialist ideology. Gorbachev and his supporters countered her assault in an article of their own, published three weeks later in* Pravda, *defending* glasnost *and* perestroika *as the path to a better future.*

Polemics: I Cannot Waive Principles

Nina Andreyeva

I decided to write this letter after lengthy deliberation. I am a chemist, and I lecture at Leningrad's Lensovet Technology Institute. Like many others, I also look after a student group. Students nowadays, following the period of social apathy and intellectual dependence, are gradually becoming charged with the energy of revolutionary changes. Naturally, discussions develop about the ways of restructuring and its economic and ideological aspects. *Glasnost*, openness, the disappearance of zones where criticism is taboo, and the emotional heat of mass consciousness (especially among young people) often result in the raising of problems that are, to a greater or lesser extent, "prompted" either by Western radio voices or by those of our compatriots who are shaky in their conceptions of the essence of socialism. And what a variety of topics that are being discussed! A multiparty system, freedom of religious propaganda, emigration to live abroad, the right to broad discussion of sexual problems in the press, the need to decentralize the leadership of culture, abolition of compulsory military service. There are particularly numerous arguments among students about the country's past. . . .

In the numerous discussions now taking place on literally all questions of the social sciences, as a college lecturer I am primarily interested in the questions that have a direct effect on young people's ideological and political education, their moral health, and their social optimism. Conversing with students and deliberating with them on controversial problems, I cannot help concluding that our country has accumulated quite a few anomalies and one-sided interpretations that clearly need to be corrected. I would like to dwell on some of them in particular.

Take, for example the question of Joseph Stalin's place in our country's history. The whole obsession with critical attacks is linked with his name, and in my opinion this obsession centers not so much on the historical individual himself as on the entire highly complex epoch of transition, an epoch linked with unprecedented feats by a whole generation of Soviet people who are today gradually withdrawing from active participation in political and social work. The industrialization, collectivization, and cultural revolution which brought our country to the ranks of the great world powers are being forcibly squeezed into the "personality cult" formula. All of this is being questioned. Matters have gone so far that persistent demands for "repentance" are being made of "Stalinists" (and this category can be taken to include anyone you like). There is rapturous praise for novels and movies that lynch the epoch of "storms and onslaught," which is presented as a "tragedy of the peoples." . . .

I support the party's call to uphold the honor and dignity of the trailblazers of socialism. I think that these are the party-class positions from which we must

Isaac J. Tarasulo, ed., *Gorbachev and Glasnost: Viewpoints from the Soviet Press* (Wilmington, Del.: SR Books, 1989), 277–78, 281–85, 290–95, 299–302.

assess the historical role of all leaders of the party and the country, including Stalin. In this case, matters cannot be reduced to their "court" aspect or to abstract moralizing by persons far removed both from those stormy times and from the people who had to live and work in those times, and to work in such a fashion as to still be an inspiring example for us today. . . .

I think that, no matter how controversial and complex a figure in Soviet history Stalin may be, his genuine role in the building and defense of socialism will sooner or later be given an objective and unambiguous assessment. Of course, unambiguous does not mean an assessment that is one-sided, that whitewashes, or that eclectically sums up contradictory phenomena making it possible subjectively (albeit with slight reservations) "to forgive or not forgive," "to reject or retain." Unambiguous means primarily a specific historical assessment detached from short-term considerations which would demonstrate—according to historical results!—the dialectics of the correlation between the individual's actions and the basic laws governing society's development. In our country these laws were also linked with the answer to the question "Who will defeat whom?" in its domestic as well as international aspects. If we are to adhere to the Marxist-Leninist methodology of historical analysis then, in Mikhail Gorbachev's words, we must primarily and vividly show how the millions of people lived, how they worked, and what they believed in, as well as the coupling of victories and failures, discoveries and errors, the bright and the tragic, the revolutionary enthusiasm of the masses and the violations of socialist legality and even crimes at times. . . .

It seems to me that the question of the role and position of socialist ideology is extremely acute today. The authors of timeserving articles circulating under the guise of moral and spiritual "cleansing" erode the dividing lines and criteria of scientific ideology, manipulate *glasnost*, and foster nonsocialist pluralism, which applies the brakes on *perestroika* in the public conscience. This has a particularly painful effect on young people which, I repeat, is clearly sensed by us, the college lecturers, schoolteachers, and all who have to deal with young people's problems. As Mikhail Gorbachev said at the CPSU Central Committee February *plenum*, "our actions in the spiritual sphere—and maybe primarily and precisely there—must be guided by our Marxist-Leninist principles. Principles comrades, must not be compromised on any pretext whatever."

This is what we stand for now, and this is what we will continue to stand for. Principles were not given to us as a gift, we have fought for them at crucial turning points in the fatherland's history.

Principles of Perestroika: *The Revolutionary Nature of Thinking and Acting*
Pravda Editorial

The CPSU Central Committee February *plenum* solidified the party's new tasks in restructuring all spheres of life at the present stage. The *plenum* speech of Mikahil Gorbachev, general secretary of the CPSU Central Committee ("Revolutionary *Perestroika* Requires Ideology of Renewal") made a clear analysis of today's problems and set forth a program of ideological support for *perestroika*.

People want to be better aware of the nature of the changes that have begun in society, to see the essence and significance of the proposed solutions, and to know what is meant by the new quality of society we want to achieve. The struggle for *perestroika* is being waged both in production and in the spiritual sphere. And even though this struggle does not take the form of class antagonisms, it is proceeding sharply. The emergence of something new always excites attitudes toward and judgments about the new thing.

The debate itself and its nature and thrust attest to the democratization of our society. The diversity of judgments, assessments, and positions is one of the most important signs of the times and attests to the socialist pluralism of opinions which really exists now.

But it is impossible not to notice one very specific dimension of this debate. It occasionally declares itself not in a desire to interpret what is happening and to investigate it nor in a wish to advance the cause but, on the contrary, in attempts to slow it down by shouting the usual incantations: "They are betraying ideals!" "Abandoning principles!" "Undermining foundations!" . . .

The long article "I Cannot Waive Principles" [Document #28] that appeared in the newspaper *Sovetskaya Rossiya* on March 13 was a reflection of such feelings. . . .

Whether the author wanted it or not, primarily the article artificially sets off certain categories of Soviet people against one another. And this at precisely the moment when the unity of creative forces, despite all the shades of opinion, is more necessary than ever and when such unity is the prime requirement of *perestroika* and an absolute necessity simply for normal life, work, and the constructive renewal of society. Herein resides the fundamental feature of *perestroika*, which is designed to unite the maximum number of like-minded people in the struggle against phenomena impeding our life. Precisely and principally against all of these phenomena, not only or simply against certain incorrigible proponents of bureaucracy, corruption, abuse, and so forth.

In addition, the article is unconstructive. In an extensive, pretentiously titled article essentially no space was found to work out a single problem of *perestroika*. Whatever it discussed—*glasnost*, openness, the disappearance of areas free from criticism, youth—these processes and *perestroika* itself were linked only with difficulties and adverse consequences. . . .

There are, in point of fact, two basic theses running throughout the article: Why all of this *perestroika*, and haven't we gone too far with democratization and *glasnost*? The article urges us to amend and adjust *perestroika*; otherwise, it is alleged, "people in authority" will have to rescue socialism.

It is evident that not everyone has realized clearly yet the dramatic nature of the situation the country found itself in by April 1985, a situation which today we rightfully describe as precrisis. It is evident that not everyone is fully aware yet that administrative edict methods are totally obsolete. It is time that anyone who still places hopes in these methods or in their modification understands that all of this has already been tried, tried repeatedly, and it has failed to produce the desired results. Any ideas about the simplicity and effectiveness of these methods are nothing but illusions without any historical justification.

So, how is socialism to be "saved" today?

Should authoritarian methods, the practice of blind obedience, and the stifling of initiative be retained? Should we retain the system in which bureaucratism, lack of control, corruption, bribery, and petty bourgeois degeneration flourished lavishly?

Or should we revert to Leninist principles, whose essence is democratism, social justice, economic accountability, and respect for the individual's honor, life, and dignity? Do we have the right, in the face of the real difficulties and unsatisfied needs of the people, to adhere to the same old approaches that prevailed in the 1930s and 1940s? Has not the time come to clearly differentiate between the essence of socialism and the historically restricted forms of its implementation? Has not the time come for a scientifically critical investigation of our history, primarily in order to change the world in which we live and to learn harsh lessons for the future?

Almost half of the article is devoted to an assessment of our distant and recent history. The last few years have provided graphic proof of the growing interest in the past shown by the broadest strata of the population. The principles of scientific historicism and truth are increasingly the basis on which the people's historical awareness is taking shape. At the same time, there are instances of people playing on the idea of patriotism. Those who loudly scream about alleged "internal threats" to socialism, those who join certain political extremists and look everywhere for internal enemies, "counterrevolutionary nations," and so on, those are not patriots. The patriots are those who act in the country's interests and for the people's benefit, without fearing any difficulties. We do not need contemplative or verbal patriotism, we need creative patriotism. Not nostalgic and backward-looking patriotism, but the patriotism of socialist transformations. Patriotism based not only on love for the area of your birth, but also imbued with pride in the accomplishments of the great motherland of socialism.

Past experience is vitally necessary for the present, for solving the tasks of *perestroika*. Life's demand—"More socialism!"—makes it incumbent upon us to investigate what we did yesterday and how we did it, what has to be rejected and what has to be retained. Which principles and values ought to be considered really socialist? And if today we are taking a critical look at our history, we are doing so only because we want a better and more complete idea of our path into the future. . . .

The best teacher of *perestroika*—the one to whom we should constantly listen—is life, and life is dialectical. We should constantly remember the words of [Friedrich] Engels to the effect that nothing has been unconditionally established once and for all as sacrosanct. It is this continual motion and the constant renewal of nature, society, and our thinking that is the point of departure for and the initial, most cardinal principle in our thinking.

Let us return to the question: What has been done already? How are the party's course and the decisions of the 27th Party Congress and Central Committee *plenums* being implemented? What positive changes are taking place in people's lives?

We have really got down to tackling the most pressing, highest priority problems: housing, food, and the supply of goods and services to the population. A turn toward accelerated development of the social sphere has begun. Concrete decisions about restructuring education and health care have been adopted. Radical economic reform, our main lever for implementing large-scale transformations, is being put into practice. "That is the main political result of the last three years," M. Gorbachev said at the 4th All-Union Congress of *kolkhoz* members.

The voice of the intelligentsia and of all the working people has begun to make itself heard powerfully and strongly in society's spiritual life. This is one of the first gains accomplished by *perestroika*. Democratism is impossible without freedom of thought and speech, without the open, broad clash of opinions, without keeping a critical eye on our life. . . .

There are no prohibited topics today. Journals, publishing houses, and studios decide for themselves what to publish. But the appearance of the article "I Cannot Waive Principles" is part of an attempt little by little to revise party decisions. It has been said repeatedly at meetings in the party Central Committee that the Soviet press is not a private concern, that Communists writing for the press and editors should have a sense of responsibility for articles and publications. In this case the newspaper *Sovetskaya Rossiya*, which, let us be frank, has done much for *perestroika*, departed from this principle.

Debates, discussions, and polemics are, of course, necessary. They lie in store for us in our future, too. There are also many pitfalls in store for us, traps laid by the past. We must all work together to clear these traps from our path. We need disputes that help to advance *perestroika* and lead to the consolidation of forces, to cohesion around *perestroika*, and not to disunity. . . .

More light. More initiative. More responsibility. A more rapid mastery of the full profundity of the Marxist-Leninist concept of *perestroika*, of the new political thinking. We can and must revive the Leninist practice of the socialist society— the most humane, the most just. We will firmly and steadily follow the revolutionary principles of *perestroika*: more *glasnost*, more democracy, more socialism.

DISCUSSION QUESTIONS

1. Why is Andreyeva so critical of Gorbachev's reforms?

2. What arguments do Gorbachev's supporters use to counter her criticisms?

3. According to the *Pravda* article, what are the fundamental features of *glasnost* and *perestroika*?

4. In what ways do these two articles reflect different understandings of Soviet history and its role in shaping the country's future?

2
Cornelia Matzke
Revolution in East Germany: An Activist's Perspective
1989

Gorbachev's reforms had a ripple effect throughout the Soviet bloc, sparking an explosion of political debate and civic activism. In the following interview, conducted in 1990, we hear the voice of a young East German activist, Cornelia Matzke, who was caught up in these currents of change. On the one hand, she was an ordinary citizen, leading her life as a physician-in-training in Leipzig, far removed from the activities of well-known dissenters. On the other, people like her were the backbone of the "year of miracles," 1989, which toppled Soviet communism. As she recounts, they were the ones who organized meetings, passed out pamphlets, and successfully urged others to challenge the status quo. Their efforts culminated on November 9, when the Berlin Wall came down.

So much has happened lately that I haven't thought about me and my development for a long time. . . .

I am a woman who has been interested in political issues as far back as I can remember. I always had a desire to have influence. Of course, one would have to reflect on the question as to what it means to "have influence," but it represented a basic motivation to become active politically; otherwise, I could have continued to live a normal life, like most others. . . .

During my training at the university I began to seek contact with grassroots groups here in Leipzig and with the ESG [Evangelical Student Community]. In November of 1985 I organized a presentation on the fortieth anniversary of the victory over fascism within the context of the Protestant Peace Decade that was held in Leipzig at the time. Before that, I had only had sporadic contacts with the church. . . .

My problem had always been to find a way to express myself politically, to find a context or people with whom I could work. . . .

Actually, I was trying to find the women's movement, except that I had not yet quite realized that at the time. . . .

You see, the church was the only possible alternative for any kind of political activism. There was absolutely nothing else. For a while I had considered joining one of the satellite parties, such as the LDPD [Liberal Democratic Party of Germany], but all of them were really the same as the SED; they were completely controlled by the SED and followed in every respect the party line. Just the language these people were using was appalling to me. One cannot express oneself in these abstract party-line categories.

So trying to change something from within the party, perhaps with friends who thought along the same lines as you, was never an option for you?

Well, maybe if I had fallen in love with a party member or something like that, but short of that, no. I don't think this would have been possible at all. You see, I always perceived myself as someone from the left, and I had always been very angry about how this party was ruining and corrupting left-wing ideas. I just felt betrayed by this party which claimed to be the bearer of an ideology which they themselves did not live up to at all. But this never resulted in my giving up on left-wing ideas, on the idea of socialism, on a more democratic and egalitarian alternative to capitalism. And I still think that way. . . .

My experiences with working in environmental groups was, on the other hand, that men were always in charge of everything, and they knew they were. . . .

Dirk Philipsen, *We Were the People: Voices from East Germany's Revolutionary Autumn of 1989* (Durham, N.C.: Duke University Press, 1993), 69–75, 248.

Were women's issues ever debated in any of those groups?

No, not really. It was simply not an issue, mostly because the women's movement was not an issue in the GDR. Women had no support for their grievances or their issues anywhere in the country. Which is, by the way, the main reason why I think women should organize their own groups: so that they can have a support network, a place where their issues and problems are taken seriously, and a forum through which to form some kind of political lobby. Because if women simply join male-dominated groups and parties—and I am not saying they should not do that as well—they will never get this kind of support; they will not be able to identify themselves as women. Women can only achieve some kind of identity by organizing as women, by having a network which allows them to realize that their problems are not individual problems, but rather that many other women have the same problems. . . .

How or when did you realize that you wanted to focus your political activities on women's issues?

The discussions with the men in the environmental group were just dreadful to me. In fact, that was true in all the groups I participated in. One of those was a so-called "discussion group." We met about once a month and talked about certain issues that had been decided upon earlier. Of course, we particularly focused on issues that one could not talk about in public anywhere else. What always bothered me a great deal was that if women came with their partners or husbands, they always ended up not saying anything. I was always drawn to these women in an emotional sense. I just wanted to find out how it would be to have such discussions only with women. . . .

There was an incredible atmosphere in the country during most of 1989, a sort of depression, a feeling of being severely oppressed, a sense that all the things we had put up with and we had suffered could not go on much longer. Everyone felt like that in one way or another.

We had organized a street music festival in June 1989, where I was arrested. I was totally depressed afterward. We simply could not believe that they could be that stupid, that they actually dared to arrest people at a street music festival. They simply went beyond their limits, or at least they did not seem to know anymore where those limits were. If they ever had, they certainly no longer understood where they had to allow some space in order then to be able to crack down on people when it *really* got dangerous for them. They were not even clever as holders of power. They certainly did not belong in the category of "intelligent dictators." In retrospect, it is amazing to see how many blatant mistakes they made from their point of view—in fact, it is astonishing how long they managed to hold on to power.

It was my understanding that this street music festival in 1989 was conceptualized not merely as a cultural event, but rather as a political statement as well. Is that correct?

Well, yes and no. It was not a political rally of any sort. But it was supposed to be a test as to whether the party would in fact react as if it were a political event. We had even tried to get an official permit for this festival, which we did not receive. But we decided to go ahead and invite bands and people anyway.

Prior to this, the musicians were put under a lot of pressure from the officials who said that if the musicians participated in the festival, they would lose their licenses. Most of the musicians buckled under this pressure and did not show up. So we mostly had amateur musicians and bands from other cities.

At first, the festival did not really get started, because the Stasi had a lot of agents there who were talking to the musicians, trying to convince them not to play, putting pressure on them and such. A few friends and I walked up to one of those conversations between Stasi officials and musicians and just began to sing— which was difficult, because we didn't really have any songs everyone readily knew.

Well, in the end we found one, and this idea of just beginning to sing and play spread rapidly. So this is how the festival started. Everything was OK until about noon, when the police drove up with trucks and began to arrest people. First, they arrested the musicians, and then others who had played any active role in putting together this festival.

Later on, I got to know quite a few very interesting people in the detention cell, people who had organized the monitoring of the elections in May and who had made public the large-scale election fraud that had been revealed by those members of the grass-roots groups who had organized this. It was a very interesting experience.

Why exactly did they arrest you?

Well, at the end they pretty much picked up people at random in front of the Thomas Church. Of course, they were particularly looking for people who they already knew were engaged in "subversive activities" and those who somehow looked conspicuously "alternative." I did not particularly look "alternative," and I could probably have avoided arrest. But first of all I thought that it was time for me to go through this experience as well, and second of all I figured it would be important for them also to arrest people once who did not fit into their preconceptions of who was and who was not opposed to the regime they were serving.

How long did they keep you in detention?

Until about 2:30 at night.

How did they treat you?

Not too badly. The guy who interrogated me was talking about "enemies of the state" and things like that, but that was normal. Surprisingly, I was also not scared at all. We knew, for example, that they were eavesdropping on us, but that did not matter to us at all; we talked to one another completely freely. There was a mood among us—the kind of mood that prevailed until October and, I think, that goes a long way in explaining the mass demonstrations of October—that it did not matter anymore. Things were so bad, it really no longer mattered. Something just *had* to happen, and people were increasingly willing to take risks in order to bring about change. . . .

Many things happened after, . . . the wave of emigration through Hungary and such. What also seemed important to me at the time was the fact that Honecker was sick, and that the entire party leadership simply came across as desolate. They seemed no longer capable of any real decisions. All of this, of course, left the impression that this "power"—this party and state leadership that we had come to know simply as "the power"—that this power had disintegrated so much primarily because Honecker was sick. It was somehow encouraging, because if that was true, it could not be all that great a "power" after all. I at least experienced it that way, and I believe many others did as well. It just signified that such power cannot be infinite.

I well remember a meeting we had in September among opposition activists and church members, and one person said "the whole system is so well organized, so stable, that it will certainly defend itself to the last man." Particularly older citizens, due to all their experiences, thought that this entire party apparatus could never be broken.

Many thought that inertia, or a kind of self-perpetuating dynamic would keep the apparatus in place indefinitely. How wrong everybody was. . . .

How did you experience the period between August and November of 1989?

I was kind of vacillating between doing more within the country and leaving it for good. All of my friends were in this position. We were simply not sure whether it could ever be more than hopeless martyrdom to get involved more openly and actively. It was a very difficult time. . . .

I think many of us would have left as well if nothing had happened until the end of the year. And, don't misunderstand me, not because we ever wanted to leave. Somehow we all felt responsible for this absolutely desolate country.

Let me ask you as someone who perceives herself to be "on the left": did you ever think that socialism in the GDR could be reformed, perhaps along the lines of what was happening in the Soviet Union, or at least that the opposition could be more decisive in determining the future political course, as perhaps it was the case in Czechoslovakia?

Yes, absolutely, that was our goal.

I am asking because you said earlier that you were thinking about emigrating because of how little, if anything, was possible in the GDR. So why did you think that it was more difficult to achieve reforms in the GDR than, for example, in the Soviet Union?

There were many reasons for that. But before I say something more, it is important to point out that what was going on in the Soviet Union was decisive for the entire movement; otherwise nothing would have ever happened here. So this was the basic event. And it was simply terrible how the GDR leadership responded to these openings and changes in the Soviet Union, high-ranking party functionaries like Kurt Hager saying, for example, "just because our neighbor changes his tapestry does not mean we have to do so as well."

DISCUSSION QUESTIONS

1. What general factors fueled Matzke's political activism?
2. What does her description of the street festival and its aftermath reveal about the political atmosphere in East Germany in 1989?
3. How did Matzke's gender shape her political identity?

3
François Mitterand
Speech to the European Parliament
1995

Although the collapse of the Soviet empire brought the Cold War to an end, another enemy loomed on the horizon: the economic clout of Asia. European leaders responded by campaigning for the further social, economic, and political integration of Europe. Their campaign bore fruit in 1994 with the creation of the European Union. The following extracts from a speech given by French president François Mitterand (president 1981–1995) to the European parliament in 1995 capture the mood at the time that a truly unified Europe could be achieved. His words reveal that the goals of the EU extended far beyond the concerns of the marketplace; they struck at the heart of Europe's ongoing quest to reshape its identity in the post–Cold War age.

Besides the essential coordination of our policies, . . . we must also, in the longer term, build the foundations of a Europe in which renewed—and, I hope, strong, sound and lasting—economic growth can take place. This will be possible, if we prove capable of using three of our major assets to the full. What is the first of those assets? It is the size of our internal market. So far, we have essentially succeeded in removing the administrative, customs and regulatory barriers which partitioned this vast economic area. That is the task that was accomplished by means of the Single European Act. We now have to eliminate or reduce the remaining barriers—which are far from insignificant—including the physical barriers which still restrict the free movement of people, goods and ideas. . . .

Our second major asset is, of course, economic and monetary union, which is the natural and essential complement, in my view, to the single market, and without which the single market—which I and, of course, others were so anxious to achieve, and which was the object of so much hard work—would be a recipe for anarchy and the worst forms of unfair competition.

The monetary tensions which we have witnessed in the past—and which, at least as far as the last few weeks are concerned, we are witnessing today—make clear the need to advance as quickly as possible towards the introduction of a single currency. I know that this is still the subject of discussion, that not everyone has been convinced. In any event, I wish to convey to you my personal conviction—which, I believe, is shared by the majority of people in authority in France; the introduction of a single currency is the only means of ensuring that Europe remains a great economic and monetary power, and it is the best means of ensuring the sustained growth of our economies. . . .

Our third major asset is the European Union's technological excellence. Our research scientists have been responsible for countless innovations. Such capital

Debates of the European Parliament, 1994–95, no. 4–456/45–51.

cannot fail to yield a profit if we prove capable of utilising it properly, and on a European scale. I shall not dwell on this point, but I am sure that the extraordinary number of technological, scientific, inventive and innovative successes which Europe has achieved since the second half of the nineteenth century will come to mind—whilst not forgetting, of course, those elsewhere in the world who have contributed to the general progress. . . .

Let us make no mistake: markets are no more than instruments, no more than mechanisms which are all too often governed by the law of the strongest, mechanisms which can lead to injustice, exclusion and dependence, unless the necessary counterweight is provided by those who can assert their democratic legitimacy. Alongside the markets, there is room for economic and social activities based on the concepts of solidarity, cooperation, partnership, reciprocity and the common interest—in short, public services. So far, we have drawn the outline of a social Europe, but it has no content. And will it not be an exciting, exhilarating venture to provide that content? Will it not be the task of the coming months and years? At that point, I shall be observing the social progress made from the outside and I shall rejoice whenever I see all Europe's leaders coming together—leaving behind their natural divisions and differences of opinion—to ensure that the Europe which is being built does not simply resemble a mechanical or Meccano toy, but is the potent work of men and women who are capable of shaping their own destiny. At present, there are some difficulties, but I hope that in collaboration with the social partners, we shall succeed in taking initiatives in the areas of training, education, the organisation of labour, and the campaign against all forms of exclusion. Indeed, nothing will be possible unless the social partners take their rightful place in the process of European integration.

. . . Such a Europe, our Europe, must be embodied in something more than simply balance sheets and freight tonnages. I would go as far as to say, while not wishing to become too rhetorical, that it needs a soul, so that it can give expression—and let us use more modest language here—to its culture, its ways of thinking, the intellectual make-up of its peoples, the fruits of the centuries of civilisation of which we are the heirs. The expressions of Europe's many forms of genius are rich and diverse; and, as in the past, we must share with the whole world—while not seeking to impose them, somewhat differently from in the past—our ideas, our dreams and, to the extent that they are of the right kind, our passions. . . .

To strengthen our approach, let us rediscover those places and objects which represent our common past. I should like to see the devising and implementation of a vast project to develop the sites of our European heritage. At the same time, let us teach about Europe. Let us educate our children on the subject. Let our schools prepare them for citizenship. Let them develop the teaching of history, geography and culture. Let us encourage the twinning of schools and universities, exchanges of schoolchildren and students. Let us stress the importance of multilingualism. To this end, France will be submitting a draft intergovernmental convention on the teaching of at least two foreign languages. At the same time, let us step up our efforts to promote the translation of written works. I have long observed that the French, my fellow countrymen, frequently complain that their great authors are seldom translated in, for example, some of the countries of Central and Eastern Europe. And I have also observed that in fact, we, the French, do not translate their works either; we complain of a fault of which we ourselves are guilty—because the Europe of cultures is the whole of Europe. . . .

. . . I thank you for the patience and attention with which you have been kind enough to listen to me, and I should like to finish with a few remarks of a more personal nature. Fate would have it that I was born during the First World War and fought in the Second. I therefore spent my childhood in the surroundings of families torn apart, all of them mourning loved ones and feeling great bitterness, if not hatred towards the recent enemy, the traditional enemy. However, ladies and gentlemen, such enemies have changed from century to century, as traditions have always changed. I have had occasion to say to this House before that France has engaged in wars with every European country, with the exception, I believe, of Denmark. We have to wonder why . . .

But my generation has almost completed its work; it is carrying out its last public acts, and this will be one of my last. It is therefore vital for us to pass on our experience. Many of you will remember the teaching of your parents, will have felt the suffering of your countries, will have experienced the grief, the pain of separation, the presence of death—all as a result of the mutual enmity of the peoples of Europe. It is vital to pass on not this hatred but, on the contrary, the opportunity which we have for reconciliation, thanks—it must be said—to those who, after 1944–1945, themselves blood-stained and with their personal lives destroyed, had the courage to envisage a more radiant future which would be based on peace and reconciliation. That is what we have done.

However, I did not acquire my own convictions in this way by chance. I did not acquire them in the German prisoner-of-war camps in which I was a captive, or in a country which itself was occupied—a situation which many of you will have experienced. I remember that even families who practiced the virtues of humanity, of kindness, spoke with animosity when they talked about the Germans. When I was an escaped prisoner of war—or rather, when I was in the process of escaping—I met some Germans, then I spent some time in a prison in Baden-Württemberg, and I used to talk to the people, Germans, there and I came to realise that the Germans liked the French more than the French liked the Germans.

I say this without wishing to denigrate my country, which is no more nationalistic than any other, far from it. I say this to make it clear that, at that time, everyone saw the world from his or her own viewpoint, and that those viewpoints were generally distorting. We must overcome such prejudices. What I am asking you to do is almost impossible, because it means overcoming our past. And yet, if we fail to overcome our past, let there be no mistake about what will follow: ladies and gentlemen, nationalism means war!

War is not only our past, it could also be our future! And it is us, it is you, ladies and gentlemen, the Members of the European Parliament, who will henceforth be the guardians of our peace, our security and our future!

DISCUSSION QUESTIONS
1. According to Mitterand, which assets must Europe use to ensure its economic growth?
2. What other factors does he consider to be important to European unity?
3. How did Mitterand's understanding of Europe's past shape his vision for its future?

4
Beijing International Conference on Women
Platform for Action
1995

In September 1995, representatives from 189 countries attending the Fourth International Conference on Women in Beijing, China, adopted the Platform for Action excerpted here. Sponsored by the United Nations, the conference embodied a new international commitment to promoting equality, development, and peace for all women. It also revealed that in the global age, not only were peoples and cultures interconnected, but their problems were as well. And just as these problems are worldwide, so, too, should their solutions be. Thus the platform calls for unprecedented cooperation among governments, international organizations, and institutions at all levels to translate the Western tradition of human rights into a reality around the world.

The Fourth World Conference on Women is taking place as the world stands poised on the threshold of a new millennium. . . .

The objective of the Platform for Action, which is in full conformity with the purposes and principles of the Charter of the United Nations and international law, is the empowerment of all women. The full realization of all human rights and fundamental freedoms of all women is essential for the empowerment of women. While the significance of national and regional particularities and various historical, cultural and religious backgrounds must be borne in mind, it is the duty of States, regardless of their political, economic and cultural systems, to promote and protect all human rights and fundamental freedoms. The implementation of this Platform, including through national laws and the formulation of strategies, policies, programmes and development priorities, is the sovereign responsibility of each State, in conformity with all human rights and fundamental freedoms, and the significance of and full respect for various religious and ethical values, cultural backgrounds and philosophical convictions of individuals and their communities should contribute to the full enjoyment by women of their human rights in order to achieve equality, development and peace. . . .

United Nations, *Report of the Fourth World Conference on Women*, Beijing, September 4–15, 1995 (New York: UN, 1995).

The end of the cold war has resulted in international changes and diminished competition between the super-Powers. The threat of a global armed conflict has diminished, while international relations have improved and prospects for peace among nations have increased. Although the threat of global conflict has been reduced, wars of aggression, armed conflicts, colonial or other forms of alien domination and foreign occupation, civil wars, and terrorism continue to plague many parts of the world. Grave violations of the human rights of women occur, particularly in times of armed conflict, and include murder, torture, systematic rape, forced pregnancy and forced abortion, in particular under policies of ethnic cleansing.

The maintenance of peace and security at the global, regional and local levels, together with the prevention of policies of aggression and ethnic cleansing and the resolution of armed conflict, is crucial for the protection of the human rights of women and girl children, as well as for the elimination of all forms of violence against them and of their use as a weapon of war.

Excessive military expenditures, including global military expenditures and arms trade or trafficking, and investments for arms production and acquisition have reduced the resources available for social development. As a result of the debt burden and other economic difficulties, many developing countries have undertaken structural adjustment policies. Moreover, there are structural adjustment programmes that have been poorly designed and implemented, with resulting detrimental effects on social development. The number of people living in poverty has increased disproportionately in most developing countries, particularly the heavily indebted countries, during the past decade.

In this context, the social dimension of development should be emphasized. Accelerated economic growth, although necessary for social development, does not by itself improve the quality of life of the population. In some cases, conditions can arise which can aggravate social inequality and marginalization. Hence, it is indispensable to search for new alternatives that ensure that all members of society benefit from economic growth based on a holistic approach to all aspects of development: growth, equality between women and men, social justice, conservation and protection of the environment, sustainability, solidarity, participation, peace and respect for human rights.

A world-wide movement towards democratization has opened up the political process in many nations, but the popular participation of women in key decision-making as full and equal partners with men, particularly in politics, has not yet been achieved. South Africa's policy of institutionalized racism—apartheid—has been dismantled and a peaceful and democratic transfer of power has occurred. In Central and Eastern Europe the transition to parliamentary democracy has been rapid and has given rise to a variety of experiences, depending on the specific circumstances of each country. While the transition has been mostly peaceful, in some countries this process has been hindered by armed conflict that has resulted in grave violations of human rights.

Widespread economic recession, as well as political instability in some regions, has been responsible for setting back development goals in many countries. This has led to the expansion of unspeakable poverty. Of the more than 1 billion people living in abject poverty, women are an overwhelming majority. The rapid process of change and adjustment in all sectors has also led to increased unemployment and underemployment, with particular impact on women. In many cases, structural adjustment programmes have not been designed to minimize their negative effects on vulnerable and disadvantaged groups or on women, nor have they been designed to assure positive effects on those groups by preventing their marginalization in economic and social activities. . . .

Absolute poverty and the feminization of poverty, unemployment, the increasing fragility of the environment, continued violence against women and the widespread exclusion of half of humanity from institutions of power and governance underscore the need to continue the search for development, peace and security and for ways of assuring people-centred sustainable development. The participation and leadership of the half of humanity that is female is essential to the success of that search. Therefore, only a new era of international cooperation among Governments and peoples based on a spirit of partnership, an equitable, international social and economic environment, and a radical transformation of the relationship between women and men to one of full and equal partnership will enable the world to meet the challenges of the twenty-first century.

DISCUSSION QUESTIONS
1. What are the goals of the Platform for Action?
2. How were these goals formulated explicitly in response to the particular problems faced by women in the new global age?
3. According to the platform, where do the solutions to these problems lie?

COMPARATIVE QUESTIONS
1. What evidence does Matzke provide on the impact of Gorbachev's reforms in East Germany?
2. How do you think Andreyeva would have reacted to Matzke's criticisms of the East German leadership, and why?
3. Do you see any common ground between Mitterand's and Gorbachev's efforts to reshape Europe and the Soviet Union, respectively?
4. According to the Beijing Platform for Action, what were the global repercussions of the end of the Cold War?

Acknowledgments

Chapter 16 Henry IV. "Edict of Nantes, 1598" (pp. 1–16) from "The Great Pressures and Grievances Of the Protestants in France," Edmund Everand.

Galileo. Excerpt from "Letter to the Grand Duchess Christina (1615)," from *Discoveries And Opinions of Galileo*, translated by Stillman Drake. Copyright © 1957 by Stillman Drake. Reprinted with the permission of Doubleday, a division of Random House, Inc.

David Pieterzen DeVries. Excerpt (pp. 167–71) from *Voyages from Holland to America* (1655), translated from the Dutch by Henry C. Murphy and privately printed by James Lenox, 1853, pp. 167–71.

Trial Record of Johannes Junius. "The Witch-Persecution at Bamberg, 1628" (pp. 23–28) from *Translations and Reprints from the Original Sources of European History*. Translated and edited by George L. Burr, vol. III, no. 4, (University of Pennsylvania 1912)

Chapter 17 Louis de Rouvroy. Duke of Saint-Simon, *Memoirs* (1648–1690), from *The Memoirs of The Duke of Saint-Simon*, translated by Bayle St. John, vol. II, and pp. 363–65.

British Parliament. "The English Bill of Rights (1689)," from *The Statutes: Revised Edition* (1871), vol. II, pp. 10–12.

Ludwig Fabritius. "Account of the Stenka Razin Revolt, 1670" (pp. 120–23) from *Russia under Western Eyes 1517–1825*, edited by Anthony Glenn Cross. Copyright © 1971 by Anthony Glenn Cross. Reprinted with permission.

Marie-Madeleine de Lafayette. "Madame de Lafayette to Joseph Marie de Lescheraine (13 April 1678)" and "Roger de Bussy-Rabutin to Marie de Sevigne (26 June 1678)" pp. 121–22 from *The Princess of Cleves*, edited and translated by John D. Lyons. Copyright © 1994 by John D. Lyons. Reprinted with the permission of the publishers.

Chapter 18 Olaudah Equiano. Excerpt from "The Slave Ship (1789)", from *Equiano's Travels: His Autobiography*, edited by Paul Edwards (Frederick A. Praeger 1966), pp. 25–32.

Tsar Peter I, "Letter to His Son, Alexei (October 11, 1715)" and "Alexei's Response (October 31, 1715)" from "Correspondence between Peter and Alexis, 1715–1717" in *A Source Book for Russian History from Early Times to 1917*, edited by George Vernadsky, vol. II, pp. 338–39. Copyright © 1972 by Yale University. Reprinted with the permission of Yale University Press.

Montesquieu. Excerpt from "Letter XXXVII, Usbek to Ibben at Smyrna," from *Persian Letters* translated by John Davidson, vol. I, pp. 85–86.

Mary Astell. Excerpt from *The First English Feminist: Reflections Upon Marriage* and *Other Writings*, (pp. 69–76), edited by Bridget Hill. Copyright © 1986 by Bridget Hill. Reprinted with the permission of St. Martin's Press.

Chapter 19 Marie-Therese Geoffrin and M. d'Alembert. "The Salon of Madame Geoffrin" (1765) "Mme. Geoffrin Writes to the King of Poland" as reprinted in *Historical & Literary Memoirs and Anecdotes Selected from the Correspondence of Baron de Grimm and Diderot with the Duke of saxe-Gotha, and Many Other Distinguished Persons between the years of 1753 and 1790*, 2nd edition, 1815, vol. III, pp. 400–05 and "Madame Geoffrin" as described by M. D'Alembert in his *Memoir of d'Alembert* and reprinted in *Connection with the Past: The D.C. Heath Document Sets for Western Civilization*, (D.C. Heath 1995), vol. II, p. 486.

Frederick II of Prussia. "Political Testament 1752" excerpt from "The Rise of Prussia" in *Europe in Review* (pp. 110–12) edited by George Lachmann Mosse, Rondo E. Cameron, Henry Bertram Hill, and Michael B. Petrovich. Published by Rand McNally & Company, 1957. Reprinted with permission.

Jacques-Louis Ménétra. Excerpt from *Journal of My Life* (1764–1802) pp. 129–130, Translated by Arthur Goldhammer. Copyright © 1986 by Arthur Goldhammer. Reprinted with the permission of the publisher.

Thomas Jefferson. "Letter to Colonel Edward Carrington" (1787). From *The Writings of Thomas Jefferson*, edited by Andrew A. Lipscomb, vol. I, pp. 55–59. Courtesy of The Thomas Jefferson Memorial Association.

Chapter 20 Abbé Sieyès. "What is the Third Estate?" (January 1789) from *The French Revolution and Human Rights: A Brief Documentary History*, edited and translated by Lynn Hunt, pp. 65–70. Copyright © 1996 by Lynn Hunt. Reprinted with the permission of Bedford/St. Martin's.

National Assembly, "The Declaration of the Rights of Man and of the Citizen (1789)" from *Readings in European History: A Collection of Extracts from the Sources* by James Harvey Robinson (Ginn and Company 1906), vol. II, pp. 409–11.

"The Trial of A Feminist Revolutionary, Olympe de Gouges" from *Women in Revolutionary Paris 1789–1795* translated by Darline Gay Levy, Harriet Branson Applewhite, and Mary Durham Johnson, pp. 254–59. Copyright © 1979 by the Board of Trustees of the University of Illinois. Reprinted with permission of the University of Illinois Press.

"Revolution in the Colonies (1794–1795)," translated by Katharine J. Lualdi, from *Toussaint L'Ouverture a travers sa correspondence* by Gerard M. Lauent, 1953, pp. 169–72. Reprinted with permission.

Chapter 21 "Napoleon in Egypt (1798)." Excerpt from *Napoleon in Egypt: Al-Jabartî's Chronicle of the French Occupation, 1798* translated by Shmuel Moreh, pp. 24–33. Copyright © 1993 by Shumel Moreh. Reprinted with the permission of E. J. Brill Publishers, Leiden, The Netherlands.

T.B. Macaulay. "Speeches on Parliamentary Reform (1831)" excerpt from *Miscellanies* by Lord Macaulay, (Houghton, Mifflin and Company 1901) vol. I, pp. 1–19.

Robert Owen. "Constitution of the Preliminary Society of New Harmony (1825)" excerpts from *The New Harmony Communities* by George Browning Lockwood, (The Chronicle Company 1902), pp. 105–09.

Joseph Mazzini. Excerpt from *Life and Writings of Joseph Mazzini 1805–1872*, vol. 1, (Smith, Elder & Company 1890), pp. 1–4.

Chapter 22 "Factory Rules in Berlin (1844)" excerpt from *Documents of European Economic History: The Process of Industrialization 1750–1870* by Sidney Pollard and C. Holmes, vol. I, pp. 534–36. Copyright © 1968 St. Martin's Press. Reprinted with permission of the publisher.

Isabella Beeton. "The Household General: Duties of the Mistress of the House" excerpt from *Beeton's Book of Household Management*. (Samuel O. Beeton, Publisher 1861).

Frederich Engels, "Draft of a Communist Confession of Faith, June 9, 1847" from *Collected Works* by Karl Marx and Frederich Engels. International Publishers, Vol. 6, pp. 103. Reprinted with the permission of International Publishers.

Victor Hugo. "Preface to *Cromwell (1827)*" excerpt from *The Dramatic Works of Victor Hugo*, (The Athenaeum Society 1909), vol. III, pp. 3–54.

Chapter 23 Rudolf von Ihering. "To J. Glaser, Giessen, 1 May," and "To B. Windscheid, Giessen 19 August" from *Germany in the Age of Bismark* by Walter Michael Simon, (George Allen and Unwin Ltd. 1968), pp. 110–13. Reprinted with the permission of Routledge.

Alexander II. "Address in the State Council, January 28, 1861" from *A Source Book for Russian History* by George Vernadsy, general editor, vol. II, pp. 599–600. Copyright © 1972 by Yale University. Reprinted with the permission of Yale University Press.

Krupa Sattianadan. "Saguna: A Story of Native Christian Life (1887–1888)" excerpt from *Women Were Writing in India 600 B.C. to the Present,* edited by Susie Tharu and K. Lalita, vol. 1, pp. 277–81. Copyright © 1991 The Feminist Press at the City University of New York. Reprinted with the permission of the publisher.

Charles Darwin. Excerpt from "General Summary and Conclusion (1871)" in *The Descent of Man and Selection in Relation to Sex* (D. Appleton and Company 1896), pp. 606–19.

Chapter 24   Jules Ferry. "Speech Before the French National Assembly (1883)," pp. 70–73, from *Modern Imperialism, Western Overseas Expansion and It's Aftermath 1776–1965,* edited by Ralph Austen (D.C. Heath and Company 1969).

Ernest Edwin Williams. Excerpt from *Made in Germany* (William Heinemann 1896), pp. 1–18.

Margaret Bondfield. Excerpts from "The Shop Girl" in *A Life's Work* (Hutchinson & Company Ltd. 1948), pp. 27–37. Reprinted with the permission of Hutchinson/The Random House Archive & Library.

Emile Zola. "On Impressionism" from *Movements, Currents, Trends: Aspects of European Thought in the Nineteenth and Twentieth Centuries,* translated by Eugen Weber. Copyright © 1992 by D.C. Heath and Company. Reprinted with the permission of Eugen Weber.

Chapter 25   Sigmund Freud. "The Interpretation of Dreams" excerpt from *The Basic Writings of Sigmund Freud,* translated and edited by D. A. A. Brill. (The Modern Library 1938).

Emmeline Pankhurst. "Speech from the Dock," excerpt from *Votes for Women,* October 29, 1908, pp. 183–18.

The I-ho-ch'uan (Boxers). "The Boxers Demand Death for All 'Foreign Devils' 1900" from *The Imperialism Reader: Documents and Readings on Modern Expansionism,* edited by Louis L. Snyder (D. Van Nostrand Company, Inc. 1962), pp. 322–23.

Léon Daudet. "The Punishment (1895)" from *France and the Dreyfus Affair: A Documentary History* by Michael Burns. Copyright © 1999 by Bedford/St. Martin's. Reprinted with the permission of the translator.

Chapter 26   "Two Solidiers' Views of the Horrors of War" (1914–1918): Fritz Franke. "Louve, November 5, 1914" pp. 123–25, from *A German Student's War Letters,* translated by A. F. Wedd. Reprinted with the permission of Routledge. Siegfried Sassoon. "Counter-Attack" from *Collected Poems.* Copyright 1918, 1920 by E. P. Dutton. Copyright 1936, 1946, 1947, 1948 by Siegfried Sassoon. Reprinted with the permission of Viking Penguin, a division of Penguin Putnam Inc. and the Barbara Levy Literary Agency.

L. Doriat. "At the Factory" (pp. 129–31) excerpt from *Lines of Fire: Women Writers of World War I,* edited by Margaret R. Higonnet. Copyright © 1999 by Margaret R. Higonnet. Reprinted with the permission of Plume/Dutton, a division of Penguin Putnam Inc.

John Reed. "Plunging Ahead" (pp. 125–37) excerpt from *Ten Days That Shook the World.* Copyright © 1919 by Boni & Liveright, Inc. Copyright © 1934, 1967 by International Publishers Company, Inc. Reprinted with the permission of the publisher.

Benito Mussolini. "The Doctrine of Facism" (pp. 164–79) excerpts from *The Social and Political Doctrines of Contemporary Europe,* edited and translated by Michael Oakeshott. Reprinted with the permission of Cambridge University Press.

Chapter 27   Joseph Goebbels. "A Goebbels Propaganda Pamphlet, 1930" (pp. 414–16) from *Documents of German History,* edited and translated by Louis L. Snyder. Copyright © 1958 by Rutgers, The State University. Reprinted with the permission of Rutgers University Press.

Neville Chamberlain Replies to His Critics: "Speech on the Munich Crisis, London 1938" from *Parliamentary Debates, Fifth Series,* Volume 339, House of CommonsOfficial Report, pp. 544–52.

Sam Bankhalter and Hinda Kibort. "Memories of the Holocaust" (pp. 5–8, 50–55) excerpts from *Witnesses to the Holocaust: An Oral History* edited by Rhoda G. Lewin. Copyright © 1980 by the Jewish Community Relations Council and Anit-Defamation League of Minnesota and the Dakotas. Reprinted with the permission of The Gale Group.

"Harry S. Truman Announces the Dropping of the Atomic Bomb on Hiroshima, 1945" (pp. 95–97) from *The International Control of Atomic Energy: Growth of a Policy.* The Department of State, Washington, D.C.

Chapter 28 Excerpts from "One World—Or Two: The Formation of the Communist Information Bureau" (pp. 117–20) in *Documents Relating to the North Atlantic Treaty.* U.S. Senate, 81st Congress, 1st Session. Document #48. Washington, D.C. (1949).

Excerpts from "Paper Number 68" (pp. 235–92) in *Foreign Relations of the United States.* National Security Council reports, Washington, D.C. (1977).

Ho Chi Minh. "Declaration of Independence of the Republic of Vietnam, September 2, 1945" (pp. 19–21) from *Conflict in Indo-China and International Repercussions: A Documentary History, 1945–1955,* edited by Allen B. Cole. Copyright © 1956 Cornell University Press. Reprinted with the permission of Cornell University Press.

Simone de Beauvoir. Excerpt from "The Second Sex" (pp. xv-xx). Translated and edited by H. M. Parshley. Copyright 1952 and renewed 1980 by Alfred A. Knopf, Inc. Reprinted with the permission of Alfred A. Knopf, a division of Random House, Inc.

Chapter 29 Student Voices of Protest, 1968. "The Whole World is Watching: 1968 . . . and After" excerpts from *Takin' it to the streets: A Sixties Reader,* edited by Alexander Bloom and Wini Brienes. Copyright © 1995 by Alexander Bloom and Wini Breines. Reprinted with the permission of Oxford University Press, Inc.

Ronald Fraser. Excerpts from *1968: A Student Generation in Revolt.* Copyright © 1988 by Ronald Fraser. Reprinted with the permisison of Pantheon Books, a division of Random House, Inc.

Beatlemania in America, 1968: Thomas BeVier, "Show by the Beatles is a Scream" and Dale Enoch, "Rally Provides 8,000 answers to Beatle Cries." From *Memphis Commercial Appeal,* August 20, 1966, pp. 1, 17. Reprinted with the permission of the *Memphis Commercial Appeal.*

The New York Times Editorial. "To Walk on the Moon," July 20, 1969. Copyright © 1969 The New York Times Company. Reprinted with permission.

Neil Armstrong, Michael Collins and Edwin E. Aldrin, Jr., with Gene Farmer and Dora Jane Hamblin. Excerpt (pp. 324, 350–51) from *First Man On the Moon: A Voyage with Neil Armstrong, Michael Collins and Edwin E. Aldrin, Jr..* Copyright © 1970 by Neil Armstrong, Michael Collins, Edwin E. Aldrin, Jr., Gene Farmer and Dora Jane Hamblin. Reprinted with the permission of Little, Brown and Company, subsidiary of Time Warner Trade Publishing.

Pope John XXIII. Convokes Vatican II, 1961. Excerpts (pp. 703–7) from *The Documents of Vatican II: All Sixteen Official texts Promulgated by the Ecumenical Council* published by Herder & Herder, 1966.

Chapter 30 Nina Andreyeva. Excerpts, including *Pravda* editorial, "Principles of Perestroika: The Revolutionary Nature of Thinking and Acting" (pp. 277–302) from *Gorbachev and Glasnost: Viewpoints from the Soviet Press* edited by Isaac Tarasulo. Originally published in *Pravda,* April 5, 1988. Copyright © 1988 by Pravda. Reprinted with permission.

Cornelia Matzke. Excerpts from *We Were the People: Voices from East Germany's Revolutionary Autumn of 1989*, edited by Dirk Philipsen. Copyright © 1993 by Duke University Press. Reprinted with the permission of the publisher. All rights reserved.

François Mitterand. Excerpt from speech to the European Parliament in Strasbourg, January 17,1995. From *Debates of the European Parliament 1994/95*, no. 4–456/45–51.

Report of the Fourth World Conference on Women, Beijing, 4–15 September 1995. From www.undp.org. /fwcw/dawoff.htm